FRAMEWORK

Of Related Interest

American History/American Film, John E. O'Connor and Martin A. Jackson, eds.

American History/American Television, John E. O'Connor, ed.

And the Winner Is . . . The History and Politics of the Oscar Awards, Emanuel Levy

The Cinema of Stanley Kubrick, Norman Kagan

The Dead That Walk: Dracula, Frankenstein, the Mummy, and Other Favorite Movie Monsters, Leslie Halliwell

Fellini the Artist, Edward Murray

The French Through Their Films, Robin Buss

Italian Cinema: From Neorealism to the Present, Peter Bonadella

Midnight Matinees: Movies and Their Makers, 1978–1985, Jay Scott

Modern European Filmmakers and the Art of Adaptation, Andrew S. Horton and Joan Magretta, eds.

A Project for the Theatre, Ingmar Bergman

Silent Magic: Rediscovering the Silent Film Era, Ivan Butler

Toms, Coons, Mulattoes, Mammies, & Bucks: An Interpretive History of Blacks in American Films, Donald Bogle

World Cinema Since 1945, William Luhr, ed.

FRAMEWORK

*A History of Screenwriting
in the American Film*

Tom Stempel

Foreword by Philip Dunne

A Frederick Ungar Book
CONTINUUM · NEW YORK

812.09
S82f

1988

The Continuum Publishing Company
370 Lexington Avenue
New York, NY 10017

Printed in the United States of America

Library of Congress Cataloging-in-Publication Data

Stempel, Tom, 1941–
    Framework: a history of screenwriting in the American film / Tom
Stempel; foreword by Philip Dunne.
        p.   cm.
    "A Frederick Ungar book."
    Includes index.
    ISBN 0-8264-0411-1
    1.   Motion picture authorship—History.   I. Title.
PN1996.S76   1988   88-11100
812'.03'09—dc19   CIP

Contents

Foreword

You can tell a great deal about a teacher by the behavior of his students. Over the past twenty years I have lectured to many university classes on my own craft, writing for the screen. The most intelligent students I have met, the quietest listeners, the sharpest questioners, have been Tom Stempel's at Los Angeles City College. This will come as no surprise to those who have known him as the foremost authority in his rather arcane field of screen literature, or have been privileged to be present when he talks to his classes.

In *Framework* he has produced the definitive work on the history of screenwriting. I do him an injustice, perhaps, in describing his book as mere history. There is much more to it: theory, analysis, character, conflict, anecdote, and more than a few wry shafts of humor. But *Framework's* framework is historical, tracing the sometimes-stormy and often-frustrating career of the screenwriter, from his or her beginnings in the days of custard pies, pratfalls and the heavy-breathing dramas of silent days, through the so-called Golden Age when sound movies were the chosen entertainment of the planet, to the superrealistic, superfrank, superexpensive extravaganzas of today. (I use "his and her" not to be in fashion, but to emphasize that a large percentage of screenwriters have been women.)

For me, the early chapters were an education, both liberal and fascinating. I had worked for pioneer producer Jesse Lasky, been a frequent guest in William de Mille's beach house, and batted against pitcher Buster Keaton in a Twentieth Century-Fox vs. Metro-Goldwyn-Mayer softball game, but it had never occurred to me to find out how—and even if—silent movies were written. Who was Salmi Morse? Roy McCardell? The Abraham and Isaac of our craft, *Framework* informed me, and I am richer for having met them in Tom Stempel's book.

The body of the book deals with the heyday of the writer; from the advent of sound to the importation from France of the pernicious auteur theory, which holds that the director is the author of something he didn't write. This was the time when playwrights, novelists, and newspapermen from the East dominated writers' tables in the West, with many winning fame and fortune, and a few retreating to New York to lick their wounds and heap abuse on Hollywood as the stultifying destroyer of everything that is artistic, good, and true. As Stempel remarks, it was only the failures who sang such songs.

There are chapters on the leading writers in each of the great film factories of the time, and a chapter on those who free-lanced from studio to studio.

Included are character sketches of the studio bosses, Zanuck, Thalberg, Mayer, Cohn, the Warners, etc., and keen analysis of their differing approaches to writers and their work. The writer-director relationship, the source of much controversy, is handled with fairness and tact. Stempel points out that writers were much more likely to be appointed chiefs of production in the studios than were directors.

In the same unbiased way, Stempel details the struggle of the writers to organize in a guild for collective bargaining, the long and bloody battle for recognition by production companies that feared that what the writers were really after was control of what went onto the screen, along with the accompanying radicalization of a few writers, and the ensuing witch-hunts and Blacklists that destroyed several promising careers, and created enmities among writers that persist to this day.

The final chapters provide a history of the craft in the modern era, dating from the dissolution of the great film factories with the advent of television, which swallowed the movies and in effect was swallowed by them in turn, as those of us can attest who watch the eerie parade of our half-forgotten brain children across the television screen.

This is not a book to be read through at one sitting, but one to be preserved, cherished, and used. It will always have a place of honor on my shelf.

—Philip Dunne

Acknowledgments

Several people have helped my general, and sometimes specific, thinking about the history of screenwriting and have thus contributed to this book: Howard Suber, Kevin Brownlow, Edward Azlant, Joe Adamson, Julie Mishkin, Don Knox, Tracy O'Kates, Charles Musser, Steven Higgins, Russell Merritt, George Pratt, Al Milgrom, Ron Shelton, Tovah Hollander (who also suggested the title) and my students at Los Angeles City College.

There are many people at many research facilities that were particularly helpful:

At the Margaret Herrick Library of the Motion Picture Academy of Arts and Sciences: Head Librarian Linda H. Mehr and her staff, especially Archivist Sam Gill and Anthony Slide. This book simply could not have been done without the resources of the Academy Library.

At the Louis B. Mayer Library at the American Film Institute's Center for Advanced Studies: Head Librarian Anne G. Schlosser and her staff, especially Howard Prouty and Don Lee.

At UCLA: Audree Malkin and her staff at the Theatre Arts Reading Room; Mrs. Stevenson at the UCLA Special Collections.

At the Library of Congress: John C. Broderick, James H. Huston, Emily Sieger, Charles Kelly, and Katharine Loughney.

At the Film Study Center of the Department of Film at the Museum of Modern Art: Eileen Bowser and Charles Silver.

At the Institute of the American Musical: president Miles Kreuger.

Kevin Brownlow, Edward Azlant and Anthony Slide read and made very useful comments on the silent film portion of the manuscript. Douglas Gomery and Philip Dunne read the entire first draft, and Mr. Dunne was also generous enough to provide the Foreword.

The photographs in the book came from the Academy of Motion Picture Arts and Sciences, the Larry Edmunds Bookshop, and Cinema Collectors.

At Continuum Michael Leach, Evander Lomke, Bruce Cassiday, and Kyle Miller have been both encouraging and helpful.

Support at home and on the road for the research and the writing has been provided by my brother John and his wife Nancy, my sister-in-law Ann Harris, and of course my wife Kerstin, who also helped in the editing and proofreading of the manuscript.

Needless to say, I owe a particular debt to the scholars, historians, journalists, and of course the screenwriters whose research and writing is listed in the notes for this book. Twenty years ago it probably would have been impossible to do a book like this because so little had been written or collected about screenwriting. I, along with many writers, both for the screen and about screenwriting, are delighted to see how much that has changed.

Tom Stempel
Los Angeles
April 1988

Introduction

S ome of what I told you before was wrong.

For the introduction to my 1980 biography of Nunnally Johnson, I wrote a brief history of screenwriting to put Johnson's career in perspective. My sources for that introduction were the standard sources for film historians. It occurred to me at the time that one could write an entire book that was a history of screenwriting. Easily. Eight years later. . . .

The problem I found was that much of the standard information tends to be wrong. Much film history about screenwriting is inaccurate because the sources are those who have reasons for downplaying the role of the screenwriter: actors, producers, directors, and their publicity machines, both in the industry and in film studies.

This is not to say accurate information is not available. I started out thinking I would have to dig out information like hidden veins of gold. Instead I found it lying around on the ground like nuggets waiting to be picked up. So I picked some up.

This is a book about screenwriting, about how screenwriting is a part of the process of making films. Too often screenwriting is seen as isolated from the "real" making of the film. As you will learn, I hope, the screenwriting process involves everything from the selection of material through to the editing, rewriting, and reshooting in post-production.

American films have always been noted as narrative films, and in view of that, it is surprising that more attention has not been paid to the screenwriting process in filmmaking. Often essays and books on directors talk more about the screenwriting process than about the directors' actual contributions to the film.

Since this book is about the history of the process of screenwriting, it is not only about screenwriters, although many writers are written about at some length (and many that I would have liked to have written about are not done justice; my apologies to them). The book also deals with producers, to a degree that surprised even me. One reason the films of the thirties and forties are so memorable is that they were made by producers who respected good writing, like Zanuck, Thalberg, and Wallis. Filmmaking in the studio days was set up so that the producer was in control and from good producers came good films made from good scripts. The shift to control by directors is part of the reason for the general decline in the quality of films, as part 3 makes clear.

Since this is a book about the process of screenwriting, there is not much about the social life of screenwriters (if you are looking for yet-another collection of anecdotes about the drinking habits of writers, look elsewhere). There is also not as much as you might expect about the political life of screenwriters. There is not the usual moral scorekeeping about the Blacklist that appears in books about screenwriting, but there is more about the black market that came out of the Blacklist, since its impact on the process was ultimately more important to the industry.

I have always been a believer in the idea that a book should be liftable, i.e., not give its readers medical problems when they pick it up, and that means that much has had to have been left out. On the other hand, many interesting details about the history of screenwriting are not in this book because neither I nor any other researcher has dug them up. Doing this book made me acutely aware of how much more research needs to be done on the history of screenwriting. I appreciate enormously Philip Dunne saying in his most gracious foreword this is the definitive history of screenwriting, but I would also hope this book will encourage others to get into the semi-virgin field of the historiography of screenwriting. If you think that might not be very interesting, read on and let me try to persuade you otherwise.

Part 1
Silent Beginnings
1894–1920

1

Starting Up

It was, we are told, about the size of "a large dog house."[1] And it was heavy. It was the Kinetograph, the machine Thomas Edison and his assistant, William Kennedy Laurie Dickson, invented to photograph a series of pictures. When the pictures were shown in a peep-show device called a Kinetoscope, they created the illusion of motion. Because the earliest Kinetograph was not particularly portable, the people who made the movement came to it.

In France the camera developed by the Lumière brothers—Louis Jean and Auguste—was more portable and was taken out to photograph the motions of everyday life. What moved in front of Edison's Kinetograph were movements staged for the camera. In late 1894 a film of a band drill was taken in Edison's Black Maria studio. That film was a scene from a play entitled A *Milk White Flag*, which had opened at Hoyt's Theatre in New York on October 8, 1894. In the first year after the Kinetoscope Company was founded in 1894, other acts in the company's films were a strongman, a contortionist, Annie Oakley, Buffalo Bill, Mae Lucas (a solo dancer from a then-current New York stage hit, A *Gaiety Girl*), Professor Batty's troupe of trained bears, monkey acts, and trained cats and dogs.[2] Each of these "acts" was just that: an act that had been created and sometimes actually written (even if not specifically for filming) before it appeared in front of the camera. From the very beginning, American films were structured, or written, before filming.

The two earliest known intentional uses of written "plans" for films both occurred in 1897. The length of films had increased beyond the original fifty feet allowed by the earliest cameras. One of the subjects that helped increase the length of films was the filmed prizefight. When the rights to the Corbett-Fitzsimmons fight were sold to the Enoch Rector/Veriscope Company, the enterprising Sigmund ("Pop") Lubin arranged a staged reenactment of the fight for his own company, using two freight handlers from the Pennsylvania Railroad terminal to "portray" the fighters. The director of the film used a round-by-round, blow-by-blow newspaper account of the fight as the script from which he directed the "boxers."[3]

In the same year W. B. Hurd, the American representative of the Lumière company approached Rich G. Hollaman with an idea for a film. Hollaman was the owner of the Eden Musée, which not only showed films, but also exhibited "death masks of Napoleon, executions of wax criminals by wax elephants, an automaton chess player and a program of song and sometimes dance."[4] Hurd had obtained the rights to do a film of a production in the Bohemian village of Horitz of the Oberammergau version of the passion play. When Hollaman hesitated, Hurd sold the rights to the famous theatrical producers Klaw and Erlanger. Hollaman saw the film and was not impressed, so he decided to make his own film.

Hollaman remembered an attempt some seventeen years before to present a passion play in New York. The author was Salmi Morse, "a great patriarchal figure of a man, with haughty carriage and a long white beard."[5] His play had been directed in San Francisco by impresario David Belasco in 1879. The play was lavishly mounted for a New York production in 1880, but was banned before it opened by the mayor of New York on the grounds it offended religious interests. The costumes were returned to one of the backers, costumer Albert G. Eaves, along with a copy of the manuscript of the play. Hollaman got Eaves to join in the production of the film, and as early film historian Terry Ramsaye recounts, "Salmi Morse's ill-fated script was brought to light, to become the first motion picture scenario."[6]

Hollaman's production was shot on the roof of the Grand Central Palace, and he engaged L. J. Vincent, a venerable theatrical director from Niblo's Garden Theatre, to stage the action. Vincent, however, thought the scenes were for a series of stereopticon slides, since it was beyond his comprehension that pictures would actually move. After he staged a scene, he would yell for the actors to stop at the height of the action. Vincent could not be fired, so William Paley, the cameraman, would announce the light was going as soon as Vincent had staged the scene, then Frank Russell, the leading actor, would direct the continuous action after Vincent left.[7]

Hollaman's production was an enormous success and was considered by viewers of the time as better than the "real" Passion Play film put out by Klaw and Erlanger. It was, however, too late for Salmi Morse. He had grown despondent earlier because of the problems with the production of the play, and had committed suicide. As the principal historian of silent screenwriting Edward Azlant notes, "The current Writers Guild could do worse than mark the spot where Salmi Morse threw himself into New York's North River."[8]

Roy McCardell

Roy McCardell was the first person to be hired for the specific job of writing for motion pictures, and had he wanted to prepare himself for that job he could not have planned his life better. Like many screenwriters to follow,

McCardell began his professional life as a journalist, working for newspapers in Birmingham and New York. He was on the editorial staff of a humor magazine, supervising the early comic strips of Frederick Burr Opper and M. M. Howarth, and when he joined the staff of Joseph Pulitzer's *New York World*, he developed the first color comic page supplement. At one point when he was holding out for more money from the *World*, he worked for the *Standard*, an entertainment weekly. The *Standard* featured photo illustrations, usually of actresses and other theatrical types, and by the mid-1890s the photos began to appear together, illustrating scenes from current theatrical productions. By the time McCardell worked for the *Standard*, these collections had turned into photo stories, complete with captions. McCardell would write ten captions to tell a complete story, then he and his boss would hire models and shoot pictures to fit the captions.[9] It is likely that McCardell's work combining pictures and stories made him consider the possibilities of writing for films. And perhaps his work made Biograph aware of his potential.

In 1898 McCardell went down to the Biograph office and asked if they needed someone to write stories. It was most likely Henry Marvin, the vice president of the company, who told him, "Indeed we do! Now we are depending for our stories on the momentary inspiration of directors, cameramen, players, or members of our office staff, and it's a great nuisance. If you can write ten scenarios a week for us I'll pay you ten dollars apiece, and if they are good, I'll make the price fifteen."

McCardell replied, "Let me have a typewriter and I'll do this week's ten right now." He was hired at the higher rate, and his weekly salary was soon increased to two hundred dollars a week.[10] Word of his salary quickly got out to other newspapermen (the average reporter's salary was then twenty-five dollars a week) and the flood of newspapermen turning screenwriters had begun.

We don't know the specific stories McCardell wrote for Biograph on that first day, or even in the following weeks, but we can say that they must have been relatively simple, since the films of the period were not much longer than a minute or so. At their least structured, the films of 1898 were still just photographs of interesting movement of some kind. At their more complex, they consisted of a single action, photographed in one take, from one angle. (The more elaborate productions of prizefights and passion plays were the exception rather than the rule.) As simple as those films were, note that Henry Marvin still found it a "nuisance" to have to wait for "inspiration" to strike the nonwriters they semidepended on for stories.

McCardell left Biograph less than a year later, but he continued to sell stories to the movies, and one of his contemporaries suggested McCardell sold over a thousand stories to films. He continued as a well-known screenwriter into the teens, but he also wrote successful novels and plays. The best writers for films, in McCardell's time and after, have his kinds of connections and experiences with the popular media, as opposed to the more highbrow media.

The Great Train Robbery

Edwin S. Porter went to work for Edison in 1896, and began to make more elaborate films. He was influenced by the exuberant spectacles of the French filmmaker Georges Méliès, and in 1902 Porter produced a film version of *Jack and the Beanstalk* that owes much to Méliès not only in its production values, but in the technique of using several shots, extending over a full reel (one thousand feet) to tell the story.[11] It is obvious from the lavish production of *Jack and the Beanstalk* that considerable pre-production preparation was done, which suggests the use of a scenario of some kind for planning purposes.

In 1903, the year after *Jack and the Beanstalk*, Porter created the film that has generally been considered the first American story film, although *Jack and the Beanstalk* might more legitimately claim the title. Billy Martinelli, an acrobat, scene painter, and handyman, told Porter, "I know a fellow that used to be in *The Great Train Robbery* on the road."[12] The play by Scott Marble had been produced in New York in 1896 and was noted for its special effects.[13] According to Terry Ramsaye, "Porter went to work on the idea, writing a memorandum of scenes of a simple story of a train hold-up, a pursuit, a dance hall episode and an escape."[14] From the third act of the play, Porter borrowed at least three scenes: a train stopping at a station, the express-car strongbox being blown up with dynamite, and a shoot-out with the bandits in a canyon.

When the company bosses saw the film, they were not convinced it would go over, but it was given a "sneak preview" at the Eden Musée. The audience demanded that it be shown over and over again, and by the time the first audience could be persuaded to leave the theater, another audience had formed outside. *The Great Train Robbery* was an enormous success, and the emphasis on narrative in American film (as well as word-of-mouth publicity) was established.

2

Early Writing

The success of story films led naturally to an increase in the use of scenarios and scenario writers, as they were then called. Story films, even "one-reelers" that ran between nine and fifteen minutes (depending on the speed at which they were shown), needed stories. The demand for scenarios also led to the development of story departments for each of the motion-picture companies. The people in these departments not only wrote stories, but read and evaluated story material that came in from outside sources.

Gene Gauntier

A writer who represents this transitional period was Gene Gauntier, who did more than just write. Gauntier acted in films; directed, helped with costumes, sets, and props; did stunts; served as story editor for two companies; edited and titled films; and adapted the story of Christ into Kalem's spectacular 1912 film *From the Manger to the Cross*. In that film she also played the Virgin Mary.

She was born Genevieve G. Liggett in Texas sometime in the 1880s. A graduate of the Kansas City Academy of Elocution and Oratory, she had a "loving, gloriously ambitious"[1] mother who made her clothes while Gauntier toured as an actress in stage melodramas. Gauntier acted for Biograph in 1906. In 1907 former Biograph business manager Frank Marion, George Kleine, and Samuel Long formed Kalem, and that February Gauntier did her first film for the new company. In the summer, actor Sidney Olcott took over as director, beginning a long creative partnership with Gauntier. Gauntier remembers that at this time "There was never a scenario on hand, and Sid, after finishing up the previous week's work, would hang around the lean-to office waiting for something to turn up."[2] Eventually Marion would tell Olcott a story to shoot:

> And he would hand Sid a business envelope (used) on the back of which, in his minute handwriting was sketched the outline of six scenes, supposed to run one hundred fifty feet to the scene—as much as our little Moy camera would hold. A bald dozen words or so described each scene; I believe that, to this day, Mr. Marion holds the championship for the shortest working scenario.[3]

Gauntier was asked by Frank Marion to do a scenario and she wrote one based on a stage play she had acted in. She included all the dialogue as well as the action, and the results were unusable. A few days later she was asked to do a version of *Tom Sawyer* that would include only as much as they could shoot in one day:

> It was pretty dreadful, but it was what Marion and Olcott wanted. And I had caught the knack. From henceforth I was the mainstay of the Kalem Scenario Department.
>
> The woods were full of ideas. The surface had barely been scratched. A poem, a picture, a short story, a scene from a current play, a headline in a newspaper. All was grist that came to my mill. There was no copyright law to protect authors and I could, and did, infringe upon everything.
>
> We also traded on the name of successes, though the plot might be totally different. *Polly of the Circus* became *Dolly the Circus Queen*. . . . I sometimes wrote three complete scenarios, one-reelers of course, in one day. But that was when "inspiration burned." Generally I ground out one under pressure, at the last minute when the company was idle and waiting for a story—and how I hated it.[4]

For her first scenarios, Gauntier was paid twenty dollars per reel while the director was paid only ten dollars, an indication of the relative value the company placed on writers and directors.

In October 1907 Gauntier was asked by Kalem to do an adaptation of *Ben-Hur*. She was not familiar with the book or the play and had to sit up nights reading it to get the screenplay done in the required two days. The film was primarily the chariot race, shot at Sheepshead Bay Race Track. There was enough story left in the film for the publisher of the novel and the estate of the author to sue Kalem and win, establishing the copyright law in the area of film rights. The court decision, handed down in 1911, cost the company twenty-five thousand dollars in damages and another twenty-five thousand dollars in legal fees, making the film the costliest one-reeler of the time.[5]

Gauntier worked briefly at Biograph, not as an actress, but as a scenario writer and story editor at forty dollars per week. As the story editor she was allowed to buy outside scripts at fifteen dollars per script, but they nearly always had to be rewritten before they could be made.

Gauntier returned to Kalem in the fall of 1908 as a leading lady at thirty dollars per week and as a scenario writer at twenty dollars per script. That winter the Kalem company moved to Florida, and Gauntier found herself playing the leads in two films per week and writing two to three scenarios a week. She was terrified of doing stunts, "but for some inexplicable reason continued to write them. They never seemed so difficult when I was seated before the typewriter enthused about creating them."[6] She did a picture about

Belle Boyd, a real spy in the Civil War, and this led to a series of films about the character. Gauntier became so tired of the role she wrote a film that ended the war and married her off. The public wanted more films, so she wrote *A Hitherto Unrelated Incident of the Girl Spy.*

She was finding source material everywhere:

> I learned to dip into books, read a page almost at a glance, disentangle the plot in an hour; then lying face downward on the bed compel my mind to shoot off into the byways, twisting and turning the idea until it was as different as possible from the one that suggested it. Then to the typewriter to embroider the bare plot with details of "business," scenic suggestions and original personalities. During the next three years I do not believe I read a book through for mere pleasure.[7]

By December 1909 she was tired of the repetition. She wrote in her diary on the twelfth of that month:

> It looks as if there can be no excitement in a picture any more. It daily grows more difficult to write exterior stuff with no thrills and yet make it interesting. My mind has got to the point where it can think only of situations calling for "beautiful southern homes" (and we've used them down here again and again) breakfast and tea scenes and walks and proposals. I don't know which way to turn. And no matter how I plead, they never send down a scenario [from New York].[8]

Frank Marion suggested Gauntier try directing a picture as well as writing, so she wrote and directed *Grandmother.* She recalls, "The picture was successful but I did not care for directing, and refused Mr. Marion's offer for a unit of my own."[9]

In 1909 Gauntier suggested a European tour to make films, and in 1910 she, Olcott, and a cameraman went to Ireland and Germany. On the ship going over she wrote three screenplays they filmed. In 1911 they returned to Ireland, then Olcott and Gauntier continued on to Egypt, where she wrote and he directed *Captured by the Bedoins [sic], Fighting Dervishes of the Desert, A Tragedy of the Desert,* and *Down Through the Ages.* "There was," she recalls, "never a script in reserve; they were filmed as rapidly as I could turn them out."[10] It was on the trip through Egypt that Gauntier conceived the idea for what became *From the Manger to the Cross.* They started filming in Egypt with the flight into Egypt, then moved on to the Holy Land in April 1912. They decided more could be done with locations and decided to turn the film from a three-reeler into a five- or six-reeler. Gauntier's screenwriting fee was by now up to thirty-five dollars per reel per scenario. While Olcott went to London to get more actors, Gauntier stayed and supervised the building of the sets. During the three week pre-production period she was also writing each morning, and the company turned out two travel pictures to help with the expenses.

> Meantine I was working on the continuity of the scenario which was proving a more difficult task than I had anticipated. This was because many things which can be slurred over in literature and which are but dimly suggested in the Bible must be clearly defined and consistent when shown in pictures. . . . The idea I worked upon was to make a story of Jesus, the man, as he lived and walked and taught on earth; to show as little as possible of the supernatural.[11]

The year before, at a church in Charleston, South Carolina, Gauntier had seen a stained-glass portrait of the Virgin Mary in which the face was similar to her own. This suggested to her the possibility of playing Mary.

After the production was completed, Gauntier returned to New York. She helped not only with the titling of the film, but as was the custom of the time, with the cutting of it as well. The company wanted to release a film no longer than five reels. Her cutting was "mostly pruning" and the titles were "mostly quotations which must be searched for. These were simple and adequate and preserved the spirit of the picture—or so I thought then." Frank Marion unfortunately added informational titles that described in literal terms the accuracy of the physical production, which bothered Gauntier, even sixteen years later when she writes in her memoirs: "Now I ask you! Can materialism go further or be cruder?"[12]

The picture was an enormous hit and was shown for years. Kalem unfortunately did not wish to have any individual credits on their films, so Olcott and Gauntier resigned and formed the Gene Gauntier Feature Players Film Company. In 1915 they joined Universal, but Gauntier retired from films in 1918. She was a war correspondent in World War I, then drama and film critic for a Kansas City newspaper. In 1933 she published a novel, *Sporting Lady*, and she died in 1966.

Story Departments

Each of the film companies of the time established a story department with a story (or scenario) editor to run it. Beyond writing most of the scripts for the company, the scenario editor edited or rewrote scripts written by others for the company, as well as read materials submitted to the company.

The most detailed record of a story department of this period that we have is the Biograph story department logbook from 1910 to 1915.[13] For each entry there is the following information: date of purchase, title, author, price, finished (production of the film), released, and final title. Usually a story was bought one month, filmed the next, and released the month after, which indicates a continuing need for stories. The going rate for stories at the beginning of 1910 was fifteen to twenty dollars, with some getting as high as twenty-five dollars. By October 1910 a few stories were getting thirty-five dollars. In 1910 Biograph bought 162 stories, of which 114 were made (although some of them were not made until later years). Nearly all of the films of the year were one-reelers. In 1911 Biograph bought 117 stories and made 76 of them. In 1915, 238 stories were purchased and 158 made. By 1915 every story was getting thirty-five dollars, with some up to fifty dollars and a few a hundred dollars.

While Biograph bought stories from all over the country, most stories came from the New York area. Many came from people already connected with the company. Stories came from writers such as Stanner E. V. Taylor and Frank Woods, but some stories were purchased from actors on the lot, such as Mack Sennett, Mary Pickford, Mabel Normand, and Lionel Barrymore.

Gene Gauntier was not the only woman scenario writer of the period, nor the only story editor. Beta Breuil and Margarite Bertsch were story editors at Vitagraph at different times, and former (and later) newspaperwoman Louella Parsons worked briefly as the story editor for the Essanay company in Chicago. After selling a story to Essanay for twenty-five dollars in the early teens, Parsons was hired at twenty dollars a week to write scenarios and read material submitted to the company. She recalls, "Manuscripts came in on pencil tablets, torn envelopes and even on bits of wallpaper."[14] Parsons also assigned scripts to the Essanay directors. She had on her desk a row of boxes, each with the name of a director on it. "I would distribute the stories I bought indiscriminately down the line, and the directors made the stories I selected whether they liked them or not. Most of the time they didn't like them!"[15]

Another early screenwriter and story editor, this one male, was B. P. Schulberg. In 1912 he went to work as a scenario writer for Edwin S. Porter, who had left Edison and formed Defender Films. Schulberg describes to his son, Budd, the rhythm of early screenwriting:

> It was great fun, really easy and exciting. I'd think up a plot and write it on Monday. Porter would cast it, paint the sets, and pick out the location on Tuesday. He would shoot the picture on Wednesday, by which time I'd be ready with the next one, which he'd cast, plan and shoot by Friday. On Saturday our two one-reelers were shipped off to distributors. That was our routine, week in and week out, over the two years before you were born.[16]

Porter made Schulberg the scenario editor for the company, which meant he had to read the material sent in by amateurs. Schulberg remembers:

They came pouring in, mostly illegible scrawls, written on everything from postcards to butcher paper. Everybody who paid his nickel to see one of our shows thought it was easy money to dash off a movie. Most cf them were illiterate. Nearly all of them were godawful. . . . One in five hundred was acceptable. I told Mr. Porter that my job was cruel and unusual punishment. I would rather write all the scripts myself than plow through moronic mush like "A Widow's Revenge" and "The Black Sheep Reforms."[17]

William de Mille

William de Mille, the elder brother of Cecil B. De Mille, had been producing and writing for the theater for thirteen years when friends convinced him to try writing for pictures. In his 1939 memoirs, de Mille recalls what other friends thought of his move:

When I left New York for Hollywood in 1914, my friends unanimously agreed that I was committing professional hari-kiri; that I was selling my pure, white body for money, and that if my name were ever mentioned in the future, it could only be . . . by people lost to all sense of shame and artistic decency. This attitude on the part of my friends merely reflected the way in which motion pictures were regarded at that time by all legitimate writers, actors, and producers.

There were, of course, some who took exception to this point of view, a few members of the theatre who had begun to be frankly interested in the new medium. . . . [They thought] that the screen might, in time, reach the point of being accepted as entertainment by the better classes.

In 1914, no writers of name were working openly for the screen. Several well-known authors, it is true, had yielded to the temptation of jotting down a few elemental situations for use in the studios, but the writer, like the actor, trusted the sheltering anonymity of the screen to protect his reputation.[18]

Or, as one of de Mille's friends put it to him, "They'll pay you twenty-five dollars a reel, Bill. You can do several in a day, and they'll keep your name out of it."[19]

William de Mille agreed to come out to Hollywood after the success of his brother's film *The Squaw Man*, and de Mille went to work for the same company, the Jesse Lasky Feature Play Company. He was assigned an office at the end of a row of dressing rooms for the actors:

In construction it was exactly the same as the dressing rooms, except that it was double size. The idea may have been, those practical days, that if my highly adventurous training as a picture-writer should unfortunately result in my sudden death, a simple partition down the middle of my office would provide the company with two more dressing rooms. Whether intentionally ironic or not, the scene of my future labors was set in the midst of a lemon grove. For the next year most of my waking hours, and some of my sleeping ones, were spent in that little workroom with its plasterboard walls and tarred paper roof. Then, with the studio's further growth, I was moved to a new office supposedly outside the active section of the plant; but two years later the studio caught up with me again, and once more I had to fly before the march of progress. [20]

He was eventually made head of the company's story department. He asked a writer friend of his, Margaret Turnbull, to come out to be the second writer for the company. He then had the studio painter make him a sign that read Scenario Department, which he hung on the door. [21] After an argument with his brother, he was able to get a stenographer for the story department (there had only been one for the entire studio before). By the end of his first year as head of the story department de Mille had between six and eight writers working for him.

The company then decided the demand for new story material was so strong they would accept material from outside sources. De Mille estimates that within one year the department read ten thousand submissions from unknown writers. The company bought two, made one of them into a picture—and it flopped. They gave up reading outside material; it cost too much time and there was too little return on the investment. [22]

Scenario Fever

By the early teens motion-picture companies were looking for material wherever they could find it. In a publication from the Associated Motion Picture Schools entitled *How to Write Motion Picture Plays*, which appears to have been written about 1912, several story editors from various companies tell "What We Want." Biograph wanted "Problem stories in which effective contrast is made between the rich and the poor." The American Film Manufacturing Company "can now use Eastern and Western drama, melodrama, and comedy drama. All sorts of comedy subjects and an occasional costume play are purchased." The Bison Film Company recently "acquired the services of the Miller Brothers 101 Ranch Company of Indians and cowboys and is in the market for high class western and cowboy scenarios." The Eclair Company on the other hand did not want westerns, while Edison was more interested in "the particular plot than the classification." Kalem at this point wanted material that could be done in Southern California, and suggested writers keep in mind the personalities of their top stars, Alice Joyce and Carlyle Blackwell. Kalem did allow as how "an occasional railroad subject might be considered." Kinemacolor Company of America, an early attempt at making color films, wanted "open-air scenes as far as possible," while Majestic wanted "rural comedies or dramas of life on the farm." The Méliès Film Company was also looking for stories with Southern California settings, and were even more specific about their requirements: "The stories must not require military scenes or anything of a spectacular order. There may be a number of riders used in the picture, incidentally, up to the number of fifteen."[23]

Because the companies were opening themselves to outside submissions, there was a rush of books on writing screenplays. The majority of books about film published in the teens were screenwriting textbooks, with titles such as Eustace Hale Ball's *Cinema Plays, How to Write Them, How to Sell Them* (1917), J. Arthur Nelson's *The Photo-Play: How to Write, How to Sell* (1913), Catharine Carr's *The Art of Photoplay Writing* (1914), and the most successful of them all, Epes Winthrop Sargent's *The Technique of the Photoplay* (originally published in 1912, with a second edition in 1916, and a third in 1920).

Like Roy McCardell before him, Sargent began as a journalist. He was particularly noted as the critic "Chicot" covering the vaudeville world for the *Daily Mercury.* He worked for several other newspapers, and in 1898 sold his first story to the movies. He continued writing movies part-time while working full-time as a journalist and press agent. In 1905 he began writing for *Variety* and continued to do so until he died. In 1909 he became the scenario editor for the Lubin Company, and several hundred of his screenplays were produced by Lubin. One such comedy, a "split-reel" (only half a reel long), was written in forty-two minutes. He continued writing short stories as well, and for *Moving Picture World* he wrote a column on screenwriting that became the basis for his book.

Much of what Sargent writes is true of the screenwriting business both then and since. He notes that

> Few directors work from the script as written. Most of them make elaborate revisions and some of them reduce every script to the same dead level of mediocrity that represents their own ideas. Between the director and the cutting room the author has small chance of seeing his own work on the screen in the form in which it was written, though conditions in this regard are constantly improving.[24]

On the other hand, Sargent did not, in 1920, hold out much hope for talking pictures. "Although it is not to be supposed that the talking pictures will ever replace the silent drama, since it merely gives back a poor travesty on the speaking stage and the injection of dialogue defeats the end of the motion picture."[25]

What the books and articles by Sargent and the others did was create what would later be called "scenario fever." The companies at least paid lip service to the idea that they would read the material. B. P. Schulberg was only one of many who took a dim view of the majority of screenwriting textbooks and their authors. He tells his son

> Those fourflushers who had never been inside a film studio—such as they were—or had never seen a scenario were posing as old masters and pocketing fifty to sixty dollars a week, real money in those days. I would have to read these "corrected" scenarios and often they were worse than the originals.[26]

What became apparent to de Mille, Schulberg, and everyone else, was that screenwriting was becoming a craft, and to consistently get the best scripts it was necessary to have writers good at that craft.

Format

In *How to Write Motion Picture Plays*, the Eclair Film Company states, "We do not want single page scenarios nor suggestions, but neat, professional work, for which we are willing to pay well,"[27] but of the shooting scripts that survive from that period (the early teens) the single-page scenario *was* the professional format for a one-reel film.

In the J. Searle Dawley Collection of material at the Academy of Motion Picture Arts and Sciences Library, there are four shooting scripts from 1910–11. Dawley was a director for the Edison Company from 1907, and the scripts in the collection are his copies. The shortest is one page and the longest is four pages. All the scripts are typed. Each is attached to a heavy paper backing, so the script can be folded in thirds to fit neatly into the director's coat pocket.

The format of these screenplays, and the writing in them, is very simple. The following is scene 3 from the 1910 script *Homemaking*:

Gate Scene

Showing John bidding Nellie good bye. John has grip sack, etc ready to leave for the West to start a new life and make enough money to return and support the girl and eeeeee [sic] marry her

Other scenes are even less detailed. Scenes 14 and 15 are simply listed as "farm scenes" with no other identifying information. Scene 9 says only "Road Scene. Business with flowers between old maid and John."

In the 1910 scenario for *Railroad Picture*, the characters are not even named, and there is even less plot than in *Homemaking*. That Dawley and other directors of the time deviated from the scripts is not surprising. On the copy of the script for *Leaves of a Romance* (June 20, 1911), there are penciled notes of additional scenes shot, such as "Distant view of valley from Helen Hunt's grave" and "Waterfall at cascade," which suggest that Dawley was adding material on location. On two of the scripts, there are penciled-in counts of the footage shot for each scene.

Another collection of early scripts from the same period and slightly later is the Edison Company material at the Museum of Modern Art. The MOMA collection includes not only shooting scripts, but other materials about the films. These materials give us a clearer look at how closely the screenplays were followed. One of the earliest scripts here is a February 18, 1911, shooting script for a Revolutionary War drama entitled *Church and Country*. The screenplay is ten scenes long and runs only a page, the film being a one-reeler. Along with the shooting script is an "assembly," dated March 9, 1911, which shows that there were eighteen scenes in the "assembled," or edited, film. Scene 3 in the script is broken up by titles into three scenes in the film. The five additional scenes are all of George Washington, who did not appear in the script, although scene 5 is "Minister bringing his men to Valley Forge," which may have inspired the director to pad out a part for the Father of His Country.

In addition to the shooting scripts, the assemblies, and the post-production synopses of the stories, the Edison Company also had a printed form, Form 103, which was used as a rough draft for the editing of the picture. On this form are places for the number of the scene, a description of the action of the scene, and any comments on the quality of the scene, the photography, etc. A comparison of the shooting scripts and the post-production materials shows the scripts were followed, although often scenes that were a single scene in the script were broken up in the editing of the film by the insertion of titles. The comedies show the most changes from script to assembled films. In *Sticking Around*, a 1915 Edison film, the order of scenes is changed from the script to the final film, action within scenes is changed, portions of scenes are cut completely from the film, and in general the film moves more quickly than the script.

As can be seen from the quotations from and descriptions of these early scripts, they were not the carefully detailed presentations of everything that would appear in the films. The action of the film is very loosely described, and there were often changes within the scenes. The importance of the scenarios is that, from 1898 on, they provided the structure, or framework, for the films.

3

Griffith and Woods

David Wark Griffith worked in the theater for over a decade before he came to the movies. Primarily he was an actor, touring with a variety of stock companies in the East and Midwest, playing in everything from Shakespeare to the classic melodrama *East Lynne*. But he also wrote vaudeville sketches and plays. Richard Schickel, Griffith's biographer, says of Griffith's 1906 play *A Fool and a Girl*,

> If the overall design is absurdly melodramatic, individual scenes are well constructed; if the characters have more about them of the cartoon than they do of life, they are nevertheless determinedly colorful and occasionally surprising; if the tone of the writing is more pretentious or the product of an ear badly in need of tuning, there are nevertheless passages of some crude power and feeling in the piece. [1]

The same can be said for Griffith's writing, and directing, for the screen.

In late 1907 or early 1908 Griffith first approached the world of motion pictures, but not as an actor. He wrote an adaptation of the opera *La Tosca*, which he took to the Edison studios. The script was turned down, primarily because he used too many scenes to tell the story. He was however hired as an actor, and he subsequently went to work for Biograph as an actor.

Griffith began to sell Biograph scenarios, many of which he appeared in. Biograph's story editor at the time, Lee Dougherty, was also the head of advertising and publicity for the company. Griffith's wife of the time later wrote that Dougherty gave the stories the "once over" and hired writers. [2] One of those writers was Gene Gauntier, temporarily away from Kalem.

Gauntier's account of Griffith's move from acting and writing into directing follows in general outline and most specific details those accounts published elsewhere. Wallace ("Old Man") McCutcheon, the regular Biograph director, fell ill and a replacement was needed. Another writer was tried as a director. His name was Stanner E. V. Taylor, and he had been a journalist and a playwright. When his Broadway show *The Gibson Girl* closed, he was hired as a scenario writer at Biograph. Gauntier recalls that

> one day a desk was moved in beside mine and a slender, rather delicate looking

17

man, with small brilliant eyes and red spots on his cheeks, took possession of it. He was Stanner E. V. Taylor, and he had been engaged to write and produce one or two pictures a week entirely in exteriors, as well as furnish scenarios for the studio—all for thirty-five dollars a week. He was a pleasant, enthusiastic chap, an ex-newspaperman, and one of the most prolific writers of scenarios I have ever known.[3]

Gauntier remembered that Griffith at this time had talked to several people about directing, and when Taylor was given the opportunity to direct, Griffith said to her, "Why don't they give an actor a chance to direct? I wish I had Taylor's opportunity." Gauntier had mixed feelings about Griffith: "Griffith was twenty years ahead of his age, his ideas were revolutionary, stark, rude almost; but he was absolutely and innocently unaware of it and never dreamed that he had shocked me [with language that made her blush]."[4]

Taylor was not successful as a director, and Gauntier is unfortunately vague about the reasons. She wrote he was not incapable, "but rather because conditions under which he had to work were such that he could not show of what he was capable."[5] After a brief period away from Biograph he returned as a scenario writer and wrote twenty-five scripts Griffith directed for Biograph. He also wrote for many other studios, continuing as a screenwriter until as late as 1929.

Gauntier claims it was she who suggested to Henry Marvin, by now the general manager of Biograph, that Griffith be given the opportunity to direct, although other sources say it was Marvin's brother Arthur who made the suggestion.[6] She recalls that Griffith asked her for a scenario and she gave him *The Adventures of Dollie*, which had been written by Taylor. Mrs. Griffith describes the story as a "lemon,"[7] but Gauntier says it was "a simple, quiet story, all exteriors, with plenty of heart interest and easy to take."[8] What impressed Gauntier was that Griffith, rather than simply going out and shooting the script, took three days to "mull it over," in Gauntier's words, and then took another three days to shoot it, at a time when one-reelers were being shot in one or two days.[9] (Mrs. Griffith says they spent "almost a week working on" the picture, which may include the "mulling over.")[10] Gauntier was also impressed that Griffith had elaborated on the story, developing the six to eight scenes of the script into thirty scenes in the film.

The picture was enough of a success that Griffith continued to direct for Biograph. His directing methods in those days have been described by those who worked with him. He would gather the actors around him and tell them the story. He would describe the actions of the film, and then he would rehearse the actors, very often rehearsing different actors in different parts until he had decided on the casting. One aspect of his method that everyone who worked with him seems to agree on is that he never used a script.

It may well be true that he did not use a script on the set while working with the actors. It is a different matter to suggest that either there were no scripts from which his films were made or that there was no "screenwriting" involved. First, there was obviously written material that the films were based on. At the end of Robert Henderson's book on Griffith's days at Biograph, the author lists the fifty-seven different authors who provided material for Griffith's Biograph films. Granted many of those authors merely provided the "source material," such as Shakespeare and Tennyson, but there were also a number of writers on the staff who provided scripts for Griffith. Stanner Taylor wrote twenty-five originals from 1908 to 1911. After Taylor left, George Hennessy wrote thirty-five originals for Griffith from 1911 to 1913. The actors themselves provided stories. Lionel Barrymore wrote *The Burglar's Dilemma* in 1911, and Mary Pickford wrote *Madame Rex* in 1911 and *Lena and the Geese* in 1912.[11] Pickford's recollection is interesting in view of the legend that Griffith simply whipped movies up out of thin air:

> Surveying his squatters [actors sitting around the lot] one day, Mr. Griffith announced he needed a split or half-reel [a five-minute film].
> "Anybody got a story in mind?" he asked.
> Three or four of us dashed for paper and pencil and were scribbling like mad. During my first weeks at Biograph I had quite unashamedly sold Mr. Griffith an outline of the opera *Thais* for ten dollars. This time I ventured a plot of my own, and to the great annoyance of the men he bought it.[12]

And it should be remembered that Griffith himself, formerly a playwright, had written scenarios before he became a director and continued to do so after.

The scenarios were, by all accounts, as simple as those discussed in the previous chapter: ten to fifteen scenes, brief descriptions of the action. What they did, however, was provide a framework of Victorian melodrama and last-second rescues Griffith was familiar with from his days, or nights, on stage. Within those comfortingly familiar structures, Griffith could begin his development of the dramatic and narrative uses of film grammar. As Schickel and others have pointed out, what was important was not that he invented the techniques, which he did not, but that he used them for expressive purposes, i.e., to tell the stories the scenarios provided for him.

Frank Woods

Griffith scholar Russell Merritt describes Frank Woods as "the mystery man of the Griffith organizations,"[13] but that may be too exotic a description of this modest, overlooked man.

Frank Emerson Woods was born in Linesville, Pennsylvania, in 1869 or 1870. After publishing a newspaper in Erie, Pennsylvania, he came to New York in 1907 and became a reporter and advertising salesman for the *Dramatic Mirror*. To help get film advertising for the *Mirror*, he was allowed to write about the fledgling business. At the encouragement of Lee Dougherty, Woods began reviewing movies, apparently the first person to do so. Dougherty told him, "Fine, give us real serious reviews—tell us where we are wrong."[14] Woods signed the reviews "The Spectator," leading to one of his many nicknames, "Spec."

As a reviewer, Woods saw many terrible movies and became convinced he could do better, so he started selling "suggestions" to Biograph for Griffith to direct. Woods had begun reviewing the Biograph films in June 1908, a month before Griffith's first directorial effort was shown to the public. Woods was aware of the developments that Griffith made in film technique.[15] Schickel describes Woods's work as a critic of Griffith:

> He was a sensible and perceptive critic, perhaps the first more-or-less responsible journalist to comment more-or-less responsibly (and regularly) on the developing art of film. As such, his widely read column was largely responsible for spreading the reputation of Biograph films, building up Griffith in the process—a crucial element in the creation of a "genius," with immediate benefits and long-term hazards for his subject. . . . [Since he was selling scripts to Griffith] he had an undeclared interest in puffing Griffith.[16]

The Birth of a Nation

In 1912, after writing a number of scripts for Biograph and Griffith, Woods left and joined the Kinemacolor Company. One of the films Kinemacolor attempted but never completed was a screen version of the 1905 novel *The Clansman*. The novel was written by Southern sympathizer Thomas Dixon as a sequel of sorts to his 1902 novel *The Leopard's Spots*. Both books dealt with the Reconstruction from the Southern point of view, and both were roundly condemned by critics. Both novels were adapted by Dixon and theater producer George Brennon into a play in 1905 under the title *The Clansman*. The play toured the South and Midwest successfully for four months before arriving in New York. The play was denounced by the New York critics, but played with moderate success in New York and toured for another five years. It was, needless to say, particularly popular in the South.

Woods wrote the continuity for the Kinemacolor production, but technical problems prevented the completion of the film. After the failure of the company, Woods rejoined Griffith in time to do the scenario for his 1913 four-reel production *Judith of Bethulia*. In 1905 Griffith had worked for a company that had toured with Thomas Bailey Aldrich's 1904 play on the same subject, although Griffith did not appear in it. In April 1913 Lee Dougherty bought a scenario on the story by Grace A. Pierce so Biograph could avoid plagiarism charges. Blanche Sweet recalls that Griffith kept a copy of Aldrich's play on the set, and most likely suggested to Woods what details might be appropriated for his scenario.[17] For his jump into longer films, Griffith was using material he was familiar with.

In the fall of 1913 Griffith left Biograph and began to talk about doing an even-longer film than *Judith of Bethulia*. Woods recalls, "As I had joined him in charge of stories, he asked me what subject I could suggest. Naturally, I at once thought of *The Clansman* and proposed it to him."[18] Griffith had appeared in a stage production of Dixon's *The One Woman*, but was fired while the play was on tour, so Griffith sent Woods to negotiate with Dixon for the film rights, with instructions not to mention Griffith's past experience as an actor. Woods had lunch with Dixon and "I extolled Griffith as the sensationally great director of the time, which he was, but I carefully avoided reference to his previous experience as an actor."[19] Dixon's response was that he knew Griffith and his work well, both as an actor and director, and he would be happy to have him make the film.

Griffith and Dixon may have discussed the script for the film[20] but most of Griffith's discussions for the six months before production began in 1914 appear to have been with Woods. The story was expanded beyond the four-reel length of *Judith of Bethulia* and the three-reel length of the proposed Kinemacolor film. Griffith and Woods added considerably to the story. The novel of *The Clansman* begins at the close of the Civil War with Elsie and Ben meeting for the first time in the hospital after Ben has been wounded at Petersburg. Griffith and Woods have added all the prewar and Civil War material to the story.

Griffith and Woods have also changed material taken from the novel. In the book Ben has a Southern girlfriend, Marion, with whom he has been in love since before the war, and she is the one who, after being raped by Gus, jumps off the cliff to keep her reputation pure. The screenwriters have transformed her into Ben's Little Pet Sister of the film, and they have fortunately dropped the most ridiculous of Dixon's plot twists. Dixon has Ben discover Marion's body, and believing the old wives' tale that the image of whomever the person saw last before she died would remain for a short time in her eye, Ben uses a convenient microscope to look into Marion's eye and discover it was Gus who has driven her to this. The screenwriters simply have the sister survive the fall long enough to tell Ben.

The novel ends with the Ku Klux Klan riding to and fro around the countryside rescuing assorted people, most of whom have nothing to do with the story line. Griffith and Woods have shaped the ending so the rescues are mostly of important characters in the story.

The novel does not have the rich characterization Griffith brings to the film, and it does not have the historical sweep of the film. Dixon writes turgidly at best, and is more interested in politicking than telling a story. Griffith and Woods have removed most of the political speech making from the book and emphasize the melodrama (although in this they have probably been inspired by the play). They have also removed the most obvious racist statements of Dixon, which has the effect of making the film more subtly racist. The book's racism is overt and easy to dismiss, but the film's racism is built into the story. The implications of the story are that the blacks would be content as long as they stayed in their place, and that it would take the white Northerners to stir them up. We see in the film no black leaders, and the only leadership roles of anyone of color are taken by Silas Lynch and Stoneman's mistress, both of whom are mulatto, the implication being that blacks would only take any semi-intelligent action if they were part white.

The film was prepared and rehearsed in the same way Griffith's shorter films had been made, with scenes being rehearsed in detail and then shot. Griffith's biographer Richard Schickel suggests that this is perhaps one of the reasons that Griffith was unable, or unwilling, to step back and see the overall implications of the story. This is probably true, but it is also the reason why Griffith creates the extraordinary scenes he does. While Griffith had worked out as a screenwriter with Frank Woods the overall storyline, he had begun to think as a director, that is, in terms of scenes. This had always been part of his makeup; remember Schickel's description of his first play. The structure of *The Birth of a Nation* is a series of melodramatic last-second rescues, some of them successful (the raid on Piedmont, the rescue of Elsie at the end), some of them not (the death of the Little Pet Sister). What Griffith's working method gave him were brilliant scenes.

One of the most famous scenes in the film is The Homecoming. Ben, the Little Colonel, has been wounded in the war and returns to the family home. He stops at the gate and looks over the terrible condition of the house. He goes into the front yard and meets the Little Sister on the porch. There is a wide range of emotions that cross their faces before they embrace. Then they step to the door and the mother's arm comes out to gather in her son. It would be beyond most screenwriters to write in script form all the nuances Griffith, Henry Walthall, and Mae Marsh get into that scene. They are the kind of nuances of performance a good director and actors can work out in rehearsal, so it is likely that the scene was never discussed in more than general terms by Griffith and Woods. On the other hand, Griffith is careful in the scene to put the emphasis on the Little Sister, who will shortly die, rather than on the more obvious figure of the mother. So for all the intensity of the scene by itself, it is structured to connect with the rest of the film.

Woods recalls his collaboration with Griffith on the film:

> In this manner he rehearsed the entire continuity of the picture, going over it again and again, but at no time would he have a written script to consult. It was all in his head, developing as he went along. He frequently asked me to sit in on these rehearsals, and at one of the first of them I noticed that he had my old script of *The Clansman* in his hand, apparently consulting it. I remonstrated, saying that that script would be of no use as it was for a three-reel picture, and he was now contemplating a much more pretentious production. He replied that I was all wrong, that the script was very useful. The next time I came on the set, I saw him with the old script and again chided him about it. "That is all right," he replied, "I am consulting it frequently." "Then why," I asked, "are you holding it upside down?" He laughed and made no reply. However, that was the last I ever saw of my obsolete script of *The Clansman*.
>
> When the picture was produced Griffith had my name on the screen as co-author with himself in having written the adaptation, a credit to which I never felt that I was entirely entitled, although I had been in frequent consultation with him as production progressed.[21]

How often in the history of screenwriting do you find a director insisting a writer take cocredit with him on a film? And how often do you find a screenwriter willing to be so modest about his contribution to one of the most important films in the history of motion pictures?

Intolerance

Richard Schickel suggests that one of the reasons Griffith failed to see "the moral insensitivity" of *The Birth of a Nation* is because of his move to Los Angeles, i.e., away from New York City: "He became one of the first victims of its [California's] isolation from the main currents of contemporary thought and newly developing social consensuses."[22] The other side of this isolation, and part of the reason for many filmmakers' moves to California, was that it gave the filmmakers freedom from the restrictions imposed on them by the men who ran the companies in the East. One reason Griffith left Biograph was the limitations the company put on him in terms of length and size of films. For all the problems California may have brought Griffith, it also made it possible for him to indulge the experimental and more extravagant side of his artistic nature. It is possible that without the move to California, Griffith would not have been able to make the sweeping epics of both form and content he did in *The Birth of a Nation* and *Intolerance*.

Frank Woods was the earthy counterbalance to Griffith's extravagance. In addition to being screenwriter and story editor for Griffith, Woods, like others at the studio, filled a number of jobs. A white-haired man with horn-rimmed glasses, Woods acquired another nickname, "Daddy," because he became the unofficial chaperone for the young ladies on the lot. Lillian Gish calls him "the judge in all our disputes,"[23] and the other women remember him as a perfect gentleman around them. Karl Brown, on the other hand, tells us that Woods "loved a bawdy story, especially if it happened to be true."[24] Woods was the company's production manager, and he also handled publicity for the company. Karl Brown suggests Woods's personable way with members of the press helped the development of Griffith's "legend."[25]

Intolerance began as a small film entitled *Mother and the Law*, reputedly based on a newspaper story about a strike in a western town. As the furor and enormous financial success of *The Birth of a Nation* developed in the spring and summer of 1915, Griffith wanted to enlarge the story and attack what he felt was the lack of tolerance people were showing his film. Griffith added three other stories to the new film. Anita Loos, who had just come on the lot after having sold stories to Griffith at Biograph by mail, recalls that plans for what became *Intolerance* were a secret: "Daddy Woods, who wrote the script, and possibly Lillian Gish were in on D. W.'s secret, but it was perfectly safe with them."[26] Gish writes, "During this period, a typical day might start [for Griffith] with a story conference with 'Daddy' Woods."[27] Griffith and Woods undoubtedly discussed the storylines of the film, since they shared offices on the lot, but Woods himself in his recollections does not discuss the story development of *Intolerance*. What appears to have bothered Woods, with his modesty and his story editor's eye, was Griffith's plan to intercut the four stories. Woods says that Griffith "undertook to intercut all these four stories with the results in my opinion not so good,"[28] and that "frankly, he later admitted his mistake."[29]

Woods helped with the cutting of the film, especially in writing the titles. Anita Loos claims to have written the titles for *Intolerance*, including one stolen from Voltaire—"When women cease to attract men, they often turn to reform as a second choice."[30] She undoubtedly contributed to the titles, and so effectively that Griffith asked Woods to have her title other films on the lot, but there are many varieties of writing styles in the titles. It appears nearly everybody on the lot contributed to the titles. Joseph Henabery, for example, also claims to have contributed to the titles for the film. He objected to some of the earlier titles not being clear, and he discussed them with Griffith and Woods in their office: "I sat in there for about three hours. I hit the titles I particularly objected to. I made suggestions and they worked my ideas over and revamped the titles."[31]

Schickel describes how *Intolerance* grew "organically,"[32] growing as Griffith felt the necessity of developing scenes and sequences, but Karl Brown, the assistant cameraman, remembers it a bit less grandly: "We were forever going back to take more scenes of action that had been overlooked the first time around or had been thought up overnight."[33] Without a written script, Griffith was wasting enormous amounts of time, money, and the energy of his cast and crew. The first cut of *Intolerance* is reported to have run an unreleasable eight hours, and it became necessary to cut hours of material from the film. While we do not know specifically what was cut, there are sections of the film, such as the Huguenot and the Christ stories, that feel truncated.

A written script might not have cut down on the excessive footage shot, since directors always find ways to increase the coverage of a scene. A script could have cut down on the excessive storylines and could have made the film clearer to audiences. Griffith, Woods, and others did what they could in clarifying the story with titles, but given the intercutting between the stories, there was a limit to what clarification the titles alone could provide. The film was not a financial success.

Intolerance is indeed an extraordinary film. Almost anything one can say about a film one can say about *Intolerance*: it's too long, too short, sublime, silly, and one of the most influential films of all times. Griffith, however, never attempted anything like it again, probably because it took his method of filmmaking further than it could successfully go. *Intolerance* shows the best of Griffith in the sweep of the melodramatic stories complete with last-second rescues, some successful (the modern story), some not (the Babylon and Huguenot stories). There is also the intensity of the individual moments, the kind of scenes Griffith could work out with his actors in their detailed rehearsals.

For all the complexity of the editing, the story structure was still conventional, familiar, and melodramatic. By working without a detailed shooting script, Griffith made films that depended on the intensity and brilliance of moments, rather than on the sense of narrative flow that later became central to American films. It was Griffith's contemporary, Thomas Ince, who introduced the narrative structure that became the mainstream of American filmmaking.

As for Frank Woods after *Intolerance*, he supervised productions under Griffith's Fine Arts banner for Triangle pictures, although some other Triangle executives felt he "wouldn't recognize a good story if it knocked him over,"[34] an odd comment to make about the man who recognized the potential in *The*

Clansman for Griffith. What Woods was trying to do in the Fine Arts films were stories that were a bit more complex than Griffith did in his traditional melodramas. Kalton Lahue, in a book on Triangle, writes, "But for the most part, they [the films supervised by Woods] were program pictures with a psychological motivation which, while artistically done at times, failed to carry audiences along with them."[35]

In 1916 Woods joined Famous Players-Lasky and remained there until 1922. He was credited with the development of story conferences and a system of supervising producers, each with his own production unit, a forerunner of the major studio system. He died in 1939 at the age of seventy-nine. Griffith's biographer, Richard Schickel, wrote of Woods, "He is the kind of fellow my profession [journalism] turns out (alas, more rarely now than in former times) who are good companions, the bearers of much oral tradition and often, emissaries of literacy to the show biz crowd."[36]

4

Silent Comedy

M any of the earliest films were comedies. In the first group of productions from Edison's Black Maria was what was described as a "slapstick barbershop scene."[1] In a 1902 Edison film *Smashing the Jersey Mosquito*, a man and a woman are sitting on opposite sides of a table when they are interrupted by a gigantic spider sliding down an equally gigantic thread toward them. The humans take up weapons and destroy the spider, but only after destroying all the furniture in their "house." The action has obviously been structured to insure every piece of furniture is broken before the spider is killed.[2] Other one-shot films that survive also are structured gags.

One of the earliest filmmakers to move to a two-shot film was Edison's director Edwin S. Porter, and he constructed it to get a laugh, while perhaps making a serious point as well. In the first shot, a woman is shown cleaning an oven with kerosene. In the second shot, we see her tombstone.[3]

The collection of early scripts from the Edison Company at MOMA includes several scripts for comedies. The Edison comedy screenplays are even sparser than those for the dramas, which indicates the actors were expected to elaborate on the scene's action. The description in the shooting script *Pastry and Bombs* (retitled *All Cooked Up* when the film was released in 1915) for scene 2 is "Waiter and customer arguing over steak." The first scene in the screenplay, "Two cooks passing out pastry and arguing," becomes six scenes in the film. The storyline is laid out in the script, but the details of the action are left to the actors.

Mack Sennett

Mack Sennett, an ex-vaudeville performer, acted for Biograph. When he discovered the studio actually paid money for stories, he went home, copied a story out of a newspaper, and turned it in. It was returned to him with the notice that if he was going to steal, he should not steal from O. Henry.[4] Sennett wrote other stories for Biograph, including several Griffith directed, such as *The Lonely Villa* and *The Lonedale Operator.*

Sennett became a director of comedies for Biograph, and in 1912 with the financial assistance of two ex-bookies who were now successful film distributors, Baumann and Kessel, he founded Keystone, the studio most noted for its production of silent comedies. Now generally accepted as historical fact, the legend about Keystone is that Sennett hated scripts and would not allow directors to use them on his lot. The problem is that a collection of shooting scripts, as well as treatments and rehearsal notes, survives at the Academy of Motion Picture Arts and Sciences.[5]

Before examining the Sennett collection, another look should be taken at the sources of information about work on the Keystone lot. Keystone director Clarence Badger wrote in 1957:

> The stories for Keystone Comedies, as constructed by Sennett's writers, never existed on paper. They were simply "fished for," created by being built up bit by bit, and carried in the writers' heads. The director assigned always took part in the story conferences. It was up to him to memorize the story, the "gags" and situations agreed upon. Incidentally, a session of Keystone writers, in the heat of a "palaver," expressing their ideas with rhapsodical antics, explosive and salty exclamations, was likened to a gathering of badly deranged lunatics.[6]

Even Badger's statement, which mentions writers, begins to deconstruct the idea that Sennett's films were made up on the spur of the moment. (Though some were, the most famous being Chaplin's first appearance as the Tramp in *Kid Auto Races at Venice*.) In 1934, before the general putdown of screen-writers had begun in earnest, Gene Fowler devoted a chapter of his biography of Mack Sennett to the Keystone writers and how they worked. Badger's "a gathering of badly deranged lunatics" may well be referring to Fowler's wonderfully vivid descriptions of life on Sennett's writing staff. However, Fowler is also the first writer to mention that Sennett hired court stenographers to take down the gags and story details.[7]

In 1954 came Sennett's autobiography, *The King of Comedy*, in the form of "as told to Cameron Shipp," seemingly more a rewrite of Fowler's book in the first person, but eliminating most of his references to Sennett's writers. Sennett does allow himself one interesting comment:

> We found out that we could not make our best pictures without solemn and brain-beating preparation. A new theory of motion-picture economics smote us pretty forcefully. It was this: the more money we spent on the script, on writing the story, the less money it cost us to shoot the pictures when we put the actors to work. I thought that over and made motions to get all the work possible out of my writers.[8]

In 1915 Keystone became part of Triangle, and Harry Aitken, the founder of Triangle, wanted Keystone to produce a series of one-reelers to keep the company's distribution exchanges busy. Sennett resisted, on the grounds he and the company had moved up to two-reelers and to do one-reelers would be a regression. Aitken insisted and in 1916 Sennett set up a unit for which he told Aitken he would take no direct responsibility.[9] The head of the unit was Hampton Del Ruth, the head of Sennett's story department. Del Ruth, an ex-playwright, had written serious films for other companies. The script materials that do survive in the Sennett Collection are from the films produced by the Del Ruth unit.

Each folder in the collection represents a film or project (a few were not completed).[10] There are as many as thirteen items relating to the writing of a single film. In the folder for *Heart Strategy* there are, among other items: several story synopses showing changes in the development of the story; sets of notes on character motivation; a working screenplay dated September 22, 1916; a continuity dated October 5, 1916 (most likely prepared after the filming); and a printed Triangle-Keystone Complete Production Report. The Report is a printed form which has spaces for: "Scenario by _____" (in most of the folders in the collection that have this form, the blank is filled in with "department"), "Time on story————" (three days in the case of *Heart Strategy*), and "Rehearsing————" (no time listed for *Heart Strategy*).

Virtually every silent-film historian warned me before I started studying screenwriting in the silent film not to confuse a post-production script, or continuity, with a shooting script. However, in the Sennett materials, many of the items are dated. To take one example, in the *Her Candy Kid* folder, the first synopsis is dated December 30, 1916; the rough continuity, January 2, 1916; and a smoother continuity/screenplay January 3, 1917. The Complete Production Report shows the film began shooting January 5, 1917, and finished January 16.

It is also clear from the materials themselves what is pre-production and what is post-production. The pre-production materials tend to go from the general to the specific. The December 7, 1916, synopsis of *A Film Exposure* says the hero's father's "fad is calisthenics," but by the December 9 synopsis that has become a specific gag sequence with a set of Indian clubs. The continuities tend to be more literary. A scene that is just a fight in a working synopsis becomes "They get into a Willard-Johnson" in the post-production synopsis. What also becomes apparent from the post-production materials is the degree to which the script materials were followed. More than you would imagine; not completely—this is comedy after all—but closely enough to finish off, once and for all, the idea that Sennett's people did not use scripts.

The materials in the Sennett Collection do, on the other hand, confirm some of what has been written about work at Keystone. The synopses, and more crucially the stenographic records that occasionally accompany them, make a convincing case for the general descriptions of the writing process on the Sennett lot. The gags and storylines are constantly changing in the synopses, and very often complete sequences of what appear on paper to be usable gags disappear from one draft of the material to the next. The stenographic records of the story conferences do not necessarily confirm Badger's description of "a gathering of badly deranged lunatics," but that is probably because the stenographer's job was to get the words, the facts, and the gags down, but not necessarily the energy or the tone of the meetings. Reading the stenographic transcripts, one gets the sense of working profession-als trying whatever they think might play. And occasionally the freewheeling nature of the story conferences gets them into trouble. In a story conference on what became *Done in Oil*, the story gets more and more complicated until at the end of page 5 of the transcript Del Ruth tells Badger (who is telling the story), "Simplify it." Which they did in the next synopsis.

There are also new insights the collection gives us. Given Sennett's reputa-tion for making films that are nothing but gags, it is surprising to see the amount of time and energy that went into working out the details of the storylines. The number and variety of synopses for the films show that great effort was made to make a story work as a story. Perhaps there is more of a story in these films produced by Del Ruth because of his background as a playwright. Hal Roach, Sr., has said the difference between him and Sennett was that "Sennett stayed with the same kinds of gags without stories. I began hiring writers."[11] Sennett may have stayed with gags, but they were within the context of stories. Sennett and his writers did have a tendency to stay with the same kinds of stories and characters. In the development of *His Widow's Might*, the first draft synopsis is about a boy working at the beach with some bathing beauties. By the second draft, the heavy has become the traditional bogus count, and by the third draft the standard old-maid character has been introduced.

The time spent on developing the story could in fact be longer than the production of the film. The first synopsis of what became *A Dark Room* was done November 11, 1916, the next one May 24, 1917, and two more followed on May 30, with another one on May 31. On *Her Candy Kid* the total story time listed on the production report is sixteen days, while the shooting time is only eleven days.

Perhaps the biggest surprise of all is that time was spent on rehearsals. *Black Eyes and Blue* began with two synopses. These are followed by notes from a rehearsal a week later in which the storyline has been simplified and the action of the film begins more rapidly. *A Clever Dummy* was originally intended as a one-reeler, but it appears that after a rehearsal it grew into a two-reeler.

All this is not to suggest that the use of written screenplays on the Sennett lot was cut and dried. The synopses and scripts in the collection are very informal and not as detailed as, for example, the surviving scripts used by

Sennett's partner at Triangle, Thomas Ince. On any given Keystone-Triangle film there may be several drafts of the shooting scripts, or only one or more synopses. There are also frequently notes in pencil on the various scripts, synopses, and rehearsal continuities, which suggests that contrary to what Badger wrote, the directors did handle the written material. And post-production continuities do *occasionally* reveal discrepancies between the scripts and the films. One might also defend the "purity of the legend" by noting that these files come from films Sennett himself did not personally supervise. Nonetheless, these films were made at his studio, and what the files document is the writing process that those who worked there have described as having taken place at the Keystone lot.

Gene Fowler quotes Sennett as saying, "I don't want *what* they [writers] write. I want the brains that are behind their writing."[12] Sennett valued writers more than actors or directors. Fowler tells of two similar incidents in which Hampton Del Ruth wanted to direct and Raymond Griffith wanted to act and Sennett turned them down because he needed them as writers.[13]

Frank Capra tells the same story. When he asked Sennett to let him direct, Sennett replied, "A director? And lose a good gag man? You're nuts."[14]

Hal Roach and Harold Lloyd

Hal Roach, Sennett's competitor, says he used writers more than Sennett. He did not, but he did use them differently. The emphasis in the Roach films was more on story and character than it was in the Sennett films, even in those Del Ruth supervised, which tended to have stronger storylines than the other Keystone films. Perhaps this is why Roach's successful years extended longer than Sennett's. What also happened in the writing of the Roach films was that the development of the gags and the gag sequences were more complicated, if less freewheeling than the development of similar sequences in Sennett films.

This complexity of story and gag structure is particularly apparent in the films of Roach's most successful silent comedian, Harold Lloyd. Lloyd's brash, go-getter character depended on the quality and quantity of the gags. Lloyd describes for Kevin Brownlow the evolution of his use of gagwriters:

> When Hal and I started, we had to think up our own gags. When Hal went off [to direct another picture] . . . and I started my first picture with glasses, I had to think up all the gags myself. As the pictures began to make money, I hired as many idea men as I could get that I thought were good. . . .
>
> We had no script, but we made minute notes of the particular sequence that we were going to shoot . . . We built as we went along, like building a house. Building was of great importance.
>
> We'd have a certain number of pieces of business, gags, that we knew we were

going to do. They were called "islands." We knew we had to go there. But whatever we did between those was up to us. We would ad lib, make it up as we went along.[15]

In spite of Lloyd's final insistence that they would "make it up as we went along," it is clear that the "islands" and the "building" he describes provided the structure of the film.

Buster Keaton

Of all the silent comedians, Buster Keaton was most concerned with the story. In his 1960 autobiography he wrote:

Even when making my two-reelers I worked on the theory that the story was always of first importance. But one thing we never did when making our silent comedies was put the story down on paper. On the other hand I never would agree to start shooting until I had in my mind a satisfactory ending for a story. The beginning was easy, the middle took care of itself, and I knew I could depend on my writers and myself to come up with any gags we might need as we went along.[16]

Whereas Lloyd used up to six gag writers at one time, Keaton usually limited himself to two or three. The writers most often on Keaton's staff were Clyde Bruckman, Jean Havez, and Joseph Mitchell. Bruckman and Havez also worked for Lloyd, and Bruckman also directed (most notably his codirection with Keaton of *The General*). Bruckman also worked with Sennett, Laurel and Hardy, W. C. Fields, Harry Langdon, and later Abbott and Costello and the Three Stooges. Havez had written Broadway shows and was a songwriter. Joseph Mitchell had experience in both vaudeville and the legitimate theater.

Keaton would also include his technical staff in the story discussions to make suggestions for what might be accomplished on film. Their participation also meant that by the time shooting began, they would know the story as well as Keaton and the writers.

The result of Keaton's concern with story is the extraordinary narrative flow in his films. There are Keaton features, such as *College*, that are collections of gags, but in the classic features such as *The General* and *Steamboat Bill, Jr.* the storylines are strong enough to stand on their own, which strengthens the films. The gags work to enrich the story and the films, giving them a depth rare in any kind of comedy. Because of his concern for story, Keaton and his writers come up with gags that not only work by themselves, but also further the story.

In 1928 Keaton, at the urging of his partner and brother-in-law, Joseph Schenck, moved his operation to MGM, where he found himself surrounded by too many writers as well as executives who wanted to be gagmen. Keaton complains, "With so much talk going on, so many conferences, so many brains at work, I began to lose faith for the first time in my own ideas."[17]

As Keaton's career as a performer slumped, he did occasionally work as a gag writer for other comedians at MGM and elsewhere. He wrote gags for Harpo Marx for *At The Circus* (1939) and created some wonderful Civil War gags for Red Skelton in *A Southern Yankee* (1948), rejects one supposes from *The General*, but as good as Skelton is, Keaton would have been better doing the same gags.

Charles Chaplin

Keaton and Lloyd admitted to having gag writers and to having thought out the story lines of their films before they shot them. Chaplin admitted nothing.

At least later he admitted nothing. In 1913 when he first went to Keystone, Chaplin wrote to his brother Sydney, "And if you know of any little Ideas in the way of synaros [sic] etc. don't forget to let me have them."[18] A year later he wrote to Sydney about his films at Keystone, "I write, direct, and play in them."[19]

Chaplin also had people around to help on the writing of his films. In his days at Essanay and Mutual one of Chaplin's assistants was Vincent Bryan, who had written plays and vaudeville sketches for the theater before going to work for Keystone. On Chaplin's later films there were other writers with whom Chaplin "talked story," as the daily studio reports described the action. On the 1918 film *A Dog's Life* Chaplin consulted with Charles Lapworth, an English journalist who had originally come to interview Chaplin and stayed on briefly as a writer. Henry Bergman acted in Chaplin films and served as his assistant and story consultant through the early 1940s. Carlyle Robinson was Chaplin's press representative from 1917 to 1932 and as with other journalists helped out on scenarios with Chaplin. Eddie Sutherland was a director who took a pay cut to work as an assistant on *The Gold Rush* and he found that when he suggested a gag, Chaplin would dismiss it, only to come up with the same gag later. Sutherland says, "Now I know that Charlie didn't steal that from me. I planted it in his mind. He probably didn't hear it consciously. But subconsciously it stuck there."[20]

In a press release for his first film for Essanay in 1915, *His New Job*, it was allowed as how "Mr. Chaplin produced the play without any scenario whatever, although he had carefully thought out the outline of his plot beforehand."[21] From what Chaplin's biographer David Robinson has discovered in the Chaplin files, this was the way Chaplin worked for most of his films. Chaplin would work out the general outline of the story before shooting, often going through and dropping many potential situations and scenes in the process. The 1922 film *The Pilgrim* is the first for which notes and scenario materials survive, although Robinson points out

> it is possible, though not likely, that this kind of preparatory writing did take place on earlier films, but has simply not survived. The reduction of the periods during which production was halted for "working on story" and the extent of these notes would seem rather to indicate that Chaplin was moving away from his earlier method of creating and improvising on the set and even on film, towards a greater degree of advance planning on paper. [22]

We know from Kevin Brownlow and David Gill's astonishing excavations of the Chaplin film vaults[23] that Chaplin did in a sense "write on film," improvising, repeating, developing the gags. What Robinson's work in the "paper" side of the archives shows is that the *story* elements were worked out in advance, first in Chaplin's head and in discussion, later on paper, but that the details of the gags were worked out on film. Robinson points out that the scenes shot and reshot nearly always appear in some form in the final films, since there are usually story elements in them.

Chaplin's genius, however, was not in the storylines, which unlike Keaton's, were often awkward but serviceable. As with Griffith, what one loses in Chaplin in story terms, one makes up for in the brilliance of individual scenes. Chaplin was as brilliant as Griffith, if not more so, in creating through rehearsal and improvisation dazzling scenes: the eating of the shoes and the dance of the rolls in *The Gold Rush*, the end of *City Lights*, the feeding-machine sequence in *Modern Times*, and many others. One would include the dance with the globe from *The Great Dictator* in that list except that it was thoroughly detailed in the script before it was shot. [24] Like Griffith's films, Chaplin's are often more satisfying in parts than as complete films. To borrow Andrew Sarris's useful phrase, both Griffith and Chaplin are screenwriters for anthologies. Or anthology films.

5

Titles

A subdivision of screenwriting that eventually developed in silent films was the writing of titles. The first films, however, did not have "intertitles", or titles within the films themselves, since either the action of the film or the main title of the film itself explained the action. Kemp Niver, in his examination of early films, has concluded that Porter's 1903 film of *Uncle Tom's Cabin* has the first intertitle in American films.[1] *The Great Train Robbery*, which followed *Uncle Tom's Cabin*, has no titles beyond the main title, and it appears that titles did not become commonplace until the longer story films became popular.

J. Stuart Blackton writes about how he decided to use titles for the first time. Vitagraph did an adaptation of the successful play *Raffles, the Amateur Cracksman* in 1903 in which no titles were used, and the audience found the action confusing. Shortly thereafter Blackton did an (unauthorized) adaptation of Booth Tarkington's *Monsieur Beaucaire* in which he claims to have used the following descriptive title:

> *The Ambuscade*
>
> Determined to win the hand and affections of the Fair Lady Mary, the Duke waylays her with his ruffians in a lonely spot. Beaucaire, single-handed, gallantly comes to her succor, but is outnumbered and falls desperately wounded from a cowardly stab in the back, delivered by the Duke, who abducts the Lady Mary and throws Beaucaire into a foul dungeon.

This title stuck in Blackton's memory because a Midwest exhibitor wrote to complain to the company, "What do you mean by 'succor' the Lady Mary? We don't like such suggestive language in our neighborhood houses."[2]

By 1905 descriptive titles were in general use, and by 1909 certain titles had become conventions. Historian Terry Ramsaye recalls that in 1909–10

> in many establishments, notably, the IMP [Independent Motion Picture Co.], big rolls of stock titles which could be used in most any drama were kept on hand, ready printed. The stock title list included all such vital expressions as, "The next day," "Ten years elapse," "Happy ever afterward," "Forgiven,"

"Wedding bells," and "One hour later." The titles were hauled down by the
yard and inserted where needed, by Jack Cohn, IMP's film editor.

Ramsaye reports that in 1909–10, there were only an average of 80 feet of title
per 1000 feet, whereas by 1926 the average had risen to 250 per 1000. [3]

Titles soon attempted to duplicate literature, or at least steal from it. In the
1912 Edison production of *The Charge of the Light Brigade* most of the titles
are lines from the poem on which the film was based. When Griffith
produced *Judith of Bethulia*, his first four-reeler, in 1913, he wanted something more elaborate in the titles, so Frank Woods "phrased the captions in the
style of language of the day," according to Mrs. Griffith. She also notes,
"However, it proved too much of a strain for the exhibitors, for they afterward
fixed up the titles to suit themselves in good old New Yorkese." [4] It is unlikely
that the exhibitors went to the expense of making their own titles, but it is
possible Biograph did some retitling.

As pictures got longer and more elaborate, so did the titles. Griffith and
Woods's titles for *The Birth of a Nation* include not only dialogue and
description, but historical background, complete with footnotes and nudges
to the audience to let them know that specific scenes were based on historical
paintings of the events. The titles for that film underwent several revisions in
phrasing and punctuation, according to Karl Brown, who had to photograph
them. [5]

Anita Loos

The titles for *Intolerance* were contributed to by many people. One of them
was Anita Loos, a young writer from the Biograph days. She sold her first
story to Biograph by mail in 1912, when by her account she was only
nineteen. She subsequently wrote several more stories for Biograph, as well as
sketches for vaudeville. When she actually met Griffith and his company in
1913, they were astonished at her youth. She contributed stories to the
Griffith company, as well as writing titles. Her break as a writer came from
her skill at writing titles.

Griffith had imported from New York two stage actors, John Emerson and
Douglas Fairbanks. According to Loos, Griffith could not figure out what to
do with them, and to get them off his back, he had Emerson look through the
story files to try to find something for Fairbanks to star in, with the understanding that Emerson would direct it. What Emerson found was a number of
Loos's stories. He told Griffith, "I've found a gold mine of material for
Fairbanks. A lot of stories by some woman named Anita Loos."

Griffith replied, "Don't let that material fool you because all the laughs are in the lines; there's no way to get them onto the screen."

"But why couldn't the lines be printed on the screen?"

Griffith said, "Because people don't go to movies to read. They go to look at pictures." Emerson asked Griffith why he bought so many stories. "I like to read them myself. They make me laugh."[6]

Emerson talked Griffith into letting him do a picture entitled *His Picture in the Papers* starring Fairbanks. Loos was intrigued by Emerson's determination to use her gags as written titles. Griffith was not pleased at the five-reel results, feeling there were too many titles. Fortunately, the picture was inadvertently shipped to the Strand Theatre in New York when a scheduled film did not arrive, and it was an enormous hit. While as Richard Schickel points out Fairbanks's screen personality was seen in films before his collaboration with Emerson and Loos,[7] it was their film that made him a star. More importantly, it was the series of films that Loos now wrote for him and Emerson directed that confirmed his star status. Loos also went on to write a series of star vehicles for Constance Talmadge in the late teens and early twenties, which were also marked by her skill at titling.

Frank Woods, writing in 1922, points out that title writing was the one area of screenwriting where writers of a more literary bent could function successfully, especially if they had some newspaper experience.[8] The value of a newspaper background is also stressed by Katharine Hilliker, one of the best title writers of the silent films. She writes:

An excellent training camp for the embryo titler is the local room of a newspaper office, for there as nowhere else he is taught to prune his garden of literature—his mental sunflowers are cruelly cropped—and the faculty of being able to express much in little is one of the first rules of the titling game.

She also states

it is also vital that the most readable and easily understood terms be employed.

I remember well the consternation with which the word *propinquity* was greeted in my first set of titles. The producer who had ordered them shied away from it like a skittish colt. He swore that not ten people in an average audience had ever seen the word, much less knew its meaning.

Hilliker made the producer agree to test the word on ten people in the office, five picked by her, five by him. Only two knew the word.[9]

Dialogue Titles

Titles showing what the characters were saying appeared as early as Porter's 1904 film *The Ex-Convict*, but they did not become commonplace until around 1910, when titles became either description or dialogue.[10] From 1910 to the midteens, there were very few dialogue titles written in the scripts, since the titles were written and added to the film later. The Sennett screenplays, from 1916–17, include very little dialogue. Most of the title writing on the Sennett films came from someone, most likely Hampton Del Ruth, reviewing the rough cut of the film and suggesting where the descriptive and dialogue titles should go. On *A Finished Product* one of the projection-room notes indicates a place for "Des [the studio abbreviation for descriptive title] intro father and the maid," which becomes in the film "Father's idea of advance is to make advances to the maid," a typical Sennett title.[11]

Tricks of the Trade

Title writer Gerald Duffy recalls one of the trickiest jobs he had and his solution for it:

> In Mary Pickford's *Through the Back Door,* one particular title had a burden to bear. It had deftly to insinuate that Mary was eloping—but it couldn't say it because she wasn't. We simply wanted to deceive the audience into thinking she was. Also, it had to suggest that her mother was contemplating a divorce. Moreover, the last time we had seen the characters they had been on Long Island. Now we were to show them in a New York hotel—and it was necessary that we tell the audience that it was a New York hotel.
>
> Another vital point was that the title had to be funny. Writing that title was a staggering undertaking. But the furniture in the picture saved me. My title read, "If it were not for New York hotels where would elopers, divorcées, and red-plush furniture go?" Seventeen words told everything.[12]

One of the legends of silent-film history is that films were constantly changed completely in the writing of the titles. Many writers from and about the period claim it happened, but one of the only instances of a writer actually claiming to have done it on a specific film comes from screenwriter and playwright Elmer Rice. Rice was working for Samuel Goldwyn in the late teens and early twenties, and the studio had made a picture of Wallace Irwin's *Trimmed in Red,* a satire of "parlor Bolshevism." The picture was bad and Goldwyn asked Rice to see what he could do. Rice noticed there were outtakes of the silly heroine's hobby of collecting animals. There were lovebirds, canaries and cockatoos, white mice and chameleons, fish and frogs, even a baby alligator in the bathtub. Brooding over this zoological abundance I threw out parlor Bolshevism entirely and invented a new religion; Neo-Pythagoreanism, which posited the transmigration of human souls into the bodies of animals. The story now dealt with the excesses into which the lady's adherence to this exotic creed led her. I recut the whole picture, eliminating all political scenes and restoring scenes in which animals appeared. Then I wrote a series of explanatory introductions and appropriate bits of dialogue, none of which bore any relation to the original story, but which managed to suggest the new plot. It was still a bad picture, but was now releasable. It must have brought in many times my total earnings at the Goldwyn studio.[13]

A wonderful tale, but the review of the picture in *Variety*[14] makes it clear that the Bolsheviks remained in the film, as well as the Neo-Pythagoreans.

William Hornbeck, a film editor who started with Sennett, also claims to have been involved with a retitling job:

> We had one we considered too bad to ship, so we held it back. The company wasn't doing too well; we were at the end of our contract with Pathe, and the contract hadn't been renewed. Pathe didn't think we were making good enough pictures. Eddie Cline got the idea of making fun of the picture. We overdid the title and made the name of the picture *The Gosh-Darned Mortgage*. We still felt it was horrible. We finally shipped it to New York. When the review committee saw it, they gave it the highest rating of all our films and gave us a new contract for the coming year. "Now this," they said, "is the type of film we want."[15]

Pictures were probably not completely changed through retitling as often as legend would have it, but they were frequently improved, or doctored, by title writers. The best known and most successful of these title doctors was Ralph Spence. Screenwriter Clara Beranger notes that

> when *Helen of Troy* (a 1927 release also known as *The Private Life of Helen of Troy*) was made it was not very good and the producers said, "What are we going to do with it?" What they did was call Mr. Spence in to write the titles for it. They were really funny and put the picture over.[16]

By the end of the twenties Spence was earning ten thousand dollars a picture and in 1926 he ran an ad in *Film Daily Yearbook* that said, "All bad little films when they die go to Ralph Spence."[17]

As we have seen with Gene Gauntier, Frank Woods, Anita Loos, Elmer Rice, and Ralph Spence, the work of writing titles for silent films also involved the writer in the editing of the film. While the director is primarily concerned with getting the scene, the writer is by nature and training concerned with the overall structure of the film. Therefore the writer knows what fits into that framework and what does not. A scene a director loved to shoot may simply not work in the film. The director may be proud of his coverage of a particular scene, not noticing that it does not make the story point it needs to if the film is to make sense.

Anita Loos and John Emerson in their 1920 book *How to Write Photoplays* state that the author of a scenario may be called in to cut and condense the picture. They imply it was common practice for the writer to be provided with a hand-cranked projector to run the film so he or she could select scenes to use as he wrote and rewrote the titles for a film. They suggest that directors will often reshoot scenes a writer might suggest at this post-production stage. They state

> Many sub-titles have to be written during the cutting. Frequently the wording must be changed with a view to how it will appear on the screen, not how it sounds when read aloud. Illustrated subtitle cards can be planned in detail at this stage of the game. [18]

The writer's involvement in these early, informal days of moviemaking covered more than just scribbling a few notes before production began. The writers were involved throughout the production and post-production phases of filmmaking. What this led to in later years was the writers becoming not only directors, but also producers and even the heads of production at many of the major studios.

6

Ince and Sullivan

Thomas Ince was born in 1882 and went on the stage at the age of six. After his own stock company flopped, he started acting in motion pictures in 1910, and began directing in December of that year. In the fall of 1911 he accepted a position as director for Baumann and Kessel's New York Film Company and moved to their studio in Edendale, a suburb of Los Angeles. By June 1912 the studio staff had so increased in size that Ince decided to form a second production unit under director Francis Ford. But Ince did nearly everything on the films he made—he wrote, directed, and edited—and he wanted a way to maintain control over the second unit. His chosen method of control was the screenplay. Working with the head of the story department, Richard V. Spencer, who wrote over six hundred original scenarios by 1917, Thomas Ince developed a more detailed continuity scenario than had been used before.

The screenplay, often finished weeks before production began, helped in the production planning of a film. From the detailed script it was possible, as Ince's people did, to make a list of scenes that could be shot together on the same sets or locations. This list could be used to make a more efficient schedule for shooting the film. A list of the cast of characters could be made so casting could be handled in an organized manner. Lists of the props, costumes, animals, and special effects could be made. Costs of all of these could be planned for each film.[1]

Ince also controlled the action of the film. Here is the opening scene of the 1914 script for *Satan McAllister's Heir*, cowritten by Ince and screenwriter C. Gardner Sullivan:

SCENE 1: CLOSE UP ON BAR IN WESTERN SALOON

A group of good Western types of the early period are drinking at the bar and talking idly—much good fellowship prevails and every man feels at ease with his neighbor—one of them glances off the picture and the smile fades from his face to be replaced by the strained look of worry—the others notice the change and follow his gaze—their faces reflect his own emotions—be sure to get over a sharp contrast between the easy good nature that had prevailed and the unnatural, strained silence that follows—as they look, cut.

Needless to say, the cut is to Satan McAllister. The action necessary for the story is laid out in a clear manner and any "improvisation" by the director or actors would take away from the clarity of the scene.

In addition to the description of the action in the above scene, there is also the typical Ince touch of instructions to the director, here in the "be sure to get over," etc. The Ince scripts are, in effect, letters to the production team, including but not limited to the director. In Sullivan's 1916 screenplay *The Dividend*, there are a number of college scenes. In a scene for a reception, the instructions are: "Nice set for this. The idea to be conveyed is that of an afternoon tango tea. Have lots of pretty girls in this scene, and see that the men wear correct afternoon dress."[3] Sometimes Sullivan and/or Ince cannot hide their enthusiasm for what they hope for. Scene 66 of *The Dividend* begins, "HERE IS A CHANCE FOR A FINE SCENE."

C. Gardner Sullivan

Ince's most prolific and valuable screenwriter, and the most important screenwriter of silent films, was Charles Gardner Sullivan. Born in Stillwater, Minnesota, in 1885, he was a newspaperman who sold sketches to vaudeville and his first film story to the Edison Company in 1911. He found himself attracted to the western and adventure films Ince was producing and began to sell stories to him.

Ince brought Sullivan to California in 1914, where he became the mainstay of the Ince writing staff. He wrote quickly, vividly, and clearly. One can imagine exactly how the opening scene of *Satan McAllister's Heir* will look on the screen. Sullivan also wrote scripts on a great variety of subjects, such as drug addiction, prostitution, and adultery. It was for his western scripts that he was best known, particularly those for a star Sullivan, as much as anyone, created: William S. Hart.

Hart, a classical stage actor, had joined the Ince company the same year Sullivan did. Sullivan created in his writing, and Hart created on the screen, the character of the "good badman," the western outlaw who, usually as the result of his romance with a good woman, turns to the right side of the law in the last part of the film. Sullivan wrote twenty-two of Hart's sixty-seven films, most notably *The Passing of Two-Gun Hicks* (1914), *On the Night Stage* (1915), *The Aryan* (1916), and *Hell's Hinges* (1916). Even after Hart and Ince parted company, Sullivan continued to write for Hart, including Hart's last great western in 1925, *Tumbleweeds*. As Anita Loos (and John Emerson) were with Douglas Fairbanks and Constance Talmadge, Sullivan was a screenwriter who was crucial to the establishment and development of a major star.

When Ince's company became part of Triangle in 1915, Sullivan became head of the story department, and by 1917 he was earning $52,000 a year. In 1917, as Triangle fell apart, Ince and his crew moved to Paramount, where Sullivan worked with a variety of directors and stars. By 1925 Sullivan was earning a reported $150,000 a year.[4] He wrote and produced for Cecil B. De Mille's company, and continued writing in sound films until 1940, then worked as a script consultant for studios such as Fox. He died in 1965.

In 1920 he wrote a "vamp" drama for Louise Glaum entitled *Sex*, and it is one of Sullivan's silent films for which both the screenplay and film have survived.[5] The introductory scenes are full of Sullivan's usual "A good study as she gazes at Adrienne."[6] In one scene of the innocent young woman, Daisy, Sullivan notes, "(Be very careful in the characterization of Daisy not to lay too much emphasis on her innocence, it is rather one of ignorance and her desire to be one of this select company which is to be gotten over)."[7] This is after Sullivan has emphasized her innocence in several shots. The scenes, including the one the note is on, are all considerably condensed in the film.

There is in fact a lot less detail in the film than in the screenplay, which suggests that the director, Fred Niblo, simply could not get across all Sullivan suggests in the script. This is most noticeable in scene 180. Overman, the married man who has been having an affair with the "vamp," Adrienne, has now been thrown over by her. Sullivan describes the scene outside her door afterwards:

> Overman comes through the door, he pauses a moment and stands there as he seeks to regain his balance; Naturally he cannot help being humiliated, but at the same time the calm manner in which Adrienne had disposed of him after he had proposed to her, appeals grimly to his sense of humor, and he exits with an ironic smile.

One can imagine what a sensitive director (one with Griffith's talent but a more sophisticated sensibility) with a good actor could do with that stage direction. In the film the shot begins with him outside the door, and the actor, William Conklin, gives a slight grimace and walks off. This is typical of the loss of emotional detail from script to film, not only in this film, but in other films Sullivan wrote. And in films by other screenwriters. It is in fact a continuing problem in American films: the directors are often not up to the quality of the screenwriters.

Scripts vs. Films

The legend about Ince and his development of detailed shooting scripts is that once he approved the script, it was marked with a rubber stamp that said,

"Shoot as written." None of the film scholars who have looked at the collections of Ince scripts have found the stamped warning. There are occasional typed warnings that scenes should be shot as written, but no rubber stamp.[8] There is also more than enough evidence to conclude that Ince did not consider the completed screenplay the end result, but merely the first step in the process of making a film. It was not necessary to follow the script exactly, as historians have assumed Ince's directors did. Having the original written plan, however, it was then possible to see how changes affected other portions of the plan, thus maintaining (as Griffith's method often failed to do) a balance in the overall structure. This could in turn lead to more complex and sophisticated methods of storytelling on film, which is exactly what happened in Ince's films.

With the few Ince scripts for which the films also survive (and the great portion of Ince's films have been lost), it is possible to follow the path from screenplay to completed film. The screenplay was used throughout the process. As noted, it was used for production planning. The screenplay was also the most detailed telling of the story, as indicated by the notations in pencil (and sometimes in pen) on scripts, which call for cuts and condensations in the action. The handwriting of these notes varies, but it is assumed by most scholars that the majority of them are in Ince's hand. Many of these notations were probably made in pre-production meetings Ince is known to have had with the directors and writers of the films.

One of the standard notations in the Ince screenplays is a penciled "O.K." that appears next to or written over each scene. The general assumption among scholars has been that this was Ince's O.K. of the written scene, but there are other possibilities. If Ince was approving the script in full, why would he mark each scene as O.K.? The "O.K.s" appear on production copies of the scripts, as indicated by the production notes in pencil on them. It is possible the checks were for the footage as it was shot, and that Ince was approving the scene as photographed. But often the "O.K.s" appear as if most were written in a row at one time, rather than at different points as the footage came in. Another possibility is that the "O.K.s" were part of the post-production process and were Ince's approval of rough cuts. In the absence of firsthand accounts of how this checkoff system worked at the Ince studios, we cannot say for certain what the "O.K.s" refer to, but they are representative of the use of the script as part of the process beyond a simple approval as typed.

In addition to the "O.K.s" there are a variety of other notes on the Ince screenplays. Ince's notes both break scenes up into more shots than are indicated in the typed script and condense scenes into single shots. "Thus," Edward Azlant observes, "by both segmenting and condensing scenes, Ince imparts a distinct rhythm to the screenplay, with some sequences becoming widely and slowly spectacular, and others close and fast."[9]

One of the screenplays Azlant discusses in detail is the 1918 script by C. Gardner Sullivan, *Keys of the Righteous*. It is 121 pages long, with 396 scenes. The script is even more detailed than earlier Ince scripts, so there are less handwritten notes about production matters (sets, camera angles, etc.). The notes do outline many condensations of shots and scenes. Azlant counts over thirty such condensations in the second half of the script, which he points out changes "the ending from a personal emphasis to as much plot activity as Ince can extract from a courtroom."[10]

Keys of the Righteous is one of the Ince-Sullivan films that has survived, although Azlant did not look at the film. A comparison of the script to the film is even more revealing, for it demonstrates how the Ince script-to-film system worked and how a film could change from the original script.[11]

Scene 38 calls for a typical Ince-Sullivan "great study of Joh [*sic*, although the character's name is John] here," and the director, Jerome Storm, complies with a wonderful establishing shot of the character laughing (although we have no idea what he is laughing about). On scene 45 a penciled note says scene 56 taken here' with 41 and 45, which suggests notes written by the director for the film editor (script girls, who later kept track of such matters, were only beginning to be used at this time). Scene 63 and the following scenes, part of a flashback, have been cut from the film so the flow of the story is smoother. Scene 68 has some playful business between the heroine Mary and her father Peter and Uncle John that is nowhere to be found in the script, or in any penciled notes on the script, except that the retake of the scene, which appears to include this action, was taken under the number 68A.

The action in scenes 77, 78, and 79 is simplified and some material apparently shot for the opening of the film is inserted here as a transitional device, which allows the titles to be dropped. Titles are also dropped from scene 85. Scenes 94 to 103 are dropped completely. A scene in a police court (104) has several people in the screenplay, but only the three necessary characters in the film, which again simplifies the action and makes it clearer. Scenes 160 to 170 are rearranged in the film, and there are fewer titles. There is also a title in this sequence that was penciled out in the screenplay but used in the film. Scene 233 is a fight scene between Peter and John, and it is extended in the script by penciled notes indicating scenes 233 ins (an abbreviation for insert), 233 ins A, and 233 ins B. Three insert scenes are also added to 235 and 236.

The title for scene 244, which reads "Ore City, clinging stickily to the west shore of Lake Superior," and the title for scene 246, which reads "The Street of Crimson Blotches, St. Croix Avenue—ironically christened the 'straight and narrow way,'" are condensed into one title in the film, which reads "Ore City, St. Croix Ave—the street of Crimson Blotches." Scene 264 takes place in a saloon and the saloon singer is described by Sullivan as "a fat, painted ghoul," and the bar as "in short, this is vice in its cheapest most sordid aspects; use great types for the waiters, all of them being good burly men who look like ex-yeggs." Unfortunately those details do not survive in the film. The types picked were not "great," the singer becomes a rather ordinary vaudeville act, and some of the business described in the screenplay between Mary and the denizens of the saloon has been dropped from the film, although there is an exchange between Mary and a pimp that is not in the script. While the final courtroom scene has been condensed in terms of scenes, nearly all the action remains in the film, although not as detailed as in the script.

There are similar changes in other Ince scripts and films. The 1921 Ince production *The Bronze Bell* is an entertaining adventure tale set in India, a pseudo-Kipling cross between *Gunga Din* and *The Prisoner of Zenda*. There are many scenes added in pencil, usually with the main scene number circled and penciled lines drawn to smaller circles with inserted scenes indicated by number. Nearly all of these additional scenes are close-ups of the actors. There are many scenes, particularly in the first part of the script, that have been x-ed out in pencil and may never have been shot, since no trace of them appears in the film. Other scenes were shot and condensed in the editing. There are also the usual Ince production notes in the script. For an establishing shot of a Calcutta hotel that was not used in the film, Ince adds, "NOTE: USE the front of the Ocean Park bath-house for this scene. Do not forget to convey the humidity and heat in all India scenes." For a street in the Oriental Quarter of Calcutta, the script suggests a street "used by Mr. J. Parker Read— at Universal City—for his Bermuda sequence in the *Leopard Woman* story will most probably suit us here."

A scene in a Portuguese bar has been eliminated completely from the film, which meant creating new titles to make the transition between the scenes before and after it. One reason the bar scene may have been eliminated was that it served to introduce an Indian Secret-Service man. In the film several of his subsequent scenes were cut. He does finally appear in the film, demonstrating the most astonishing change from an Ince script to a film. In the script he is an Indian throughout the film; in the movie it is revealed shortly after he appears that he is in fact Henry Knowlton of the British Secret Service, disguised on this mission as a Hindu. This change may have been made late in the production. In the final shoot-out in the Temple of the Bell, Knowlton appears to be played by a different actor than in previous scenes.

Another surprising change from script to film occurs in the 1921 film *Beau Revel*. The film is a sophisticated drama about a playboy father who attempts to seduce his son's girlfriend, telling the son it is a test of her faithfulness to him. The girl eventually leaves both father and son, and the script ends with the son, Dick, walking out on his father as well. The film continues with scenes that are not in the screenplay, either in the typed original or in any penciled notes. The film intercuts between Dick and the girl, Betty, making up while Revel has hallucinations of his various other women, who go away when he tries to move toward them. Revel considers shooting himself, then jumps out the window and has a short death scene on the steps below. The new ending, unfortunately, is overly moralistic in comparison with the sophistication that has gone before, although Lewis Stone's excellent performance from the rest of the picture carries this final segment.

The rest of *Beau Revel*, one of the best of the Ince films, is a clear demonstration of how much careful scripting of a film could add to the storytelling capabilities of filmmaking. In an early sequence Revel is discussing his skill at seduction, and the script suggests that this scene be intercut with a scene in which Revel's current lover and her husband are arguing, "because that is the place for it, because it fits with the action." Whoever wrote that line is right, and it helps the director, John Griffith Wray, maintain an emotional balance in the two scenes so that the scenes play off each other when cut together. This is not simple D. W. Griffith crosscutting for suspense, but rather crosscutting to comment on the characters and their emotional states. This intercutting is indicated in the screenplay and extended in the film itself. By planning that kind of cutting, it is possible to make a more precise match in the cutting on a regular basis than Griffith manages in his catch-as-catch-can style of shooting. The use of the script makes possible a more subtle and complex kind of storytelling than Griffith ever used.

Ince's Influence

Most film historians tend to dismiss Thomas Ince's influence on American film by saying that his system of organizing production became the pattern for major studio production, thus implying it cut down on the "creativity" of the "geniuses" (usually directors) who were free to shoot whatever they wanted before the studio system came in. Directors, with a few notable exceptions, were never "free" from scripts, or at least from the necessity of developing a story. The studio organizational system, which had existed in embryo form before Ince, but which he perfected, did come to dominate American films for more than thirty years, and many of the best directors worked in it, some contentedly, some less so. Ince should be rightly noted for that contribution to American film history.

Ince, however, made another contribution that may be even more important. He also perfected the narrative style of filmmaking, which became the native American style. Just as Griffith took Porter's beginning experiments in story telling and crosscutting and elaborated and developed them, so then did Ince take Griffith's techniques and apply them to the story film. Griffith's "screenwriting" style created films that were brilliant in moments and scenes but sometimes awkward in continuity. What Ince did was use the screenplay as part of a style, as well as a process, of filmmaking that emphasized a smooth flowing continuity. The scripts, the notes on the scripts, and the cutting of the films all add up to films that told stories clearly and cleanly. There are seldom the brilliant moments in Ince's films there are in Griffith's. What Ince's films do, at their best, is catch the audience up in a story and propel the viewer through it.

Ince, along with C. Gardner Sullivan (both when he was with Ince and later as a free-lance writer) and perhaps Frank Woods when he was supervising the Triangle dramas for Griffith's company, were beginning to use the grammar of film to make films that appealed to the mass audience that wanted to see, and later hear, stories. Ince, Sullivan, and Woods were setting the pattern, not only in industrial organization, but also in narrative, that would become the mainstream of American filmmaking.

If Griffith was the forerunner of the "dazzling genius" school of filmmakers that might be said to include Erich Von Stroheim, Orson Welles, and Robert Altman, Ince (in spite of his untimely death in 1924) was the forerunner of the narrative filmmakers like John Ford, Howard Hawks, Henry King, Darryl F. Zanuck, Irving Thalberg, George Lucas, and Steven Spielberg.

And the writers who wrote their movies.

Part 2
The Studio Period
1920–50

7

Silent Studios

As a result of the enormous success of *The Birth of a Nation* and other features, the companies of the Motion Picture Patents Company, which had banded together in 1909 to try to control the business, were going out of business. The opposing independent companies were willing to give audiences what the conservative members of the Patents Company were not: stars and feature films (the move to both stars and feature films increased the need for writers, since stars needed scripts tailored to them and features required more story material; however, an industry observer of the period, Benjamin Hampton, felt the emphasis on stars helped devalue writers, since writers were then only thought of as hacks whose job was to twist any material into a star vehicle).[1] By the late teens, the independent companies began to form what were to become the major studios, which would dominate American film production for the next thirty years and distribution for at least another thirty years. The late teens and early twenties saw the establishment not only of large-scale production facilities in Lòs Angeles, but also an increase in the number of distribution exchanges around the country and the world and a spree of buying or building theaters. To feed the distribution and exhibition sides of their operations, the major studios needed not only the production of a large number of films, but needed those films in an orderly pattern.

The best-organized method of production the fledgling majors saw was the system established by Thomas Ince. The system called for, in typical industrial style, a division of labor. Ince had begun to break down the various functions in the making of a film so that writers wrote, directors directed, and editors edited. Not only was this more efficient than having everybody do everything, it also provided a way for the head of the studio to maintain control over the filmmaking process. That process was planned, and the plans, which existed on paper in a variety of forms, were subjected to oversight (or interference, depending on one's point of view) by managers. A manager could be, as in Ince's case, the head of the studio, or he could be a supervisor, or production supervisor, or producer. And one of the written forms the producers used as a method of control was the written script.

This system of course did not spring full-blown from the head of Thomas

Ince. There had been elements of it from the beginning of movies, but Ince perfected it and made it the most visible model for the majors to use. It was not adopted without adjustments and problems, especially for screenwriters, as the remaining sections of this chapter will show.

Eminent Authors

From the beginning of movies, the writers hired for films had experience in the other popular arts. With a few exceptions (the Edison Company in 1909 hired well-known "authors"), the "serious" writers of plays, novels, and short stories avoided the films because of the lack of intellectual status accorded films. The makers of the earliest films did not think of film as art or themselves as artists. The controversy over *The Birth of a Nation* established that motion pictures could move and upset audiences the way other art forms could. There was an increased critical awareness of movies as a potential art form by the late teens when the movies also became a big business. In the division of labor writers were now identified as such and not simply as general collaborators. In such a climate it was only natural the heads of the companies would begin to consider hiring "serious" writers.

The most famous, disastrous, and influential of these attempts was a plan announced by Samuel Goldwyn in 1919. Goldwyn had recently had bad experiences with stars Pauline Frederick and Geraldine Farrar, and he decided to put the emphasis on stories rather than stars. Within his own company he formed a group entitled Eminent Authors, Inc., to be headed by novelist Rex Beach (one of the writers hired by Edison ten years before), who was in charge of selecting authors to write stories for the Goldwyn films. Those Beach selected in the first group were Gertrude Atherton, Mary Roberts Rinehart, Rupert Hughes, Basil King, Gouvernor Morris, and Leroy Scott.[2] (Adolph Zukor and Jesse Lasky, Goldwyn's former partners, thought he might have the right idea, so they hired Elinor Glyn, Arnold Bennett, and even Somerset Maugham.)[3] To help these prose writers dramatize their stories, Goldwyn also hired playwrights Charles Kenyon, Cleves Kinkhead, Thomas Buchanan, and Elmer Rice.[4]

Since the Belgian playwright Maurice Maeterlinck was on a lecture tour of the United States, Goldwyn hired him as well, even though he did not speak English. Maeterlinck spent three months writing a story, then another three months having it translated. Goldwyn's reaction when he read it was, "My God, the hero is a bee." It was an adaptation of Maeterlinck's novel *The Life of the Bee*. Maeterlinck returned to Belgium, with Goldwyn settling his contract for fifty cents on the dollar. Goldwyn also accompanied him to the train station and told him, "Don't worry, Maurice, you'll make good yet."[5]

Maeterlinck was not the only author who had problems; nearly all of them did. As Goldwyn wrote (or had ghostwritten for him) a few years later:

> The great trouble with the usual author is that he approaches the camera with some fixed literary ideal and he cannot compromise with the motion picture viewpoint. . . . This attitude brought many writers whom I had assembled into almost immediate conflict with our scenario department, and I was constantly being called upon to hear the tale of woe regarding some title that had been changed or some awfully important situation which had either been left out entirely or else altered in such a way as to ruin the literary conception.[6]

The general historical view is simply that the authors were unable to see things in visual or dramatic terms, or were perhaps unable to see the difficulties of translating their language into film. These attitudes are apparent in the recollections of one of the Eminent Authors, Mary Roberts Rinehart:

> The stubborn resistance he [Goldwyn] met was not in the authors, most of them humble in their ignorance of a new art; but in his own organization. If authors could arrange in what sequences their stories were to be developed, leaving to mere technicians the details of that development, the high-salaried scenario department would become superfluous.[7]

Rinehart obviously had very little sense of what was required to translate a prose story into a script and a film.

Her complaints about the scenario department, however, were not unfounded. There was a resentment against the Eminent Authors from the writers who had learned the craft of screenwriting. The head of Goldwyn's story department at the time was John Hawks, who had worked for Ince. Elmer Rice describes Hawks as an "eccentric, unlettered, likeable, alcoholic extrovert, well versed in all the routines and clichés of filmmaking, and not without a certain instinct for dramatic construction."[8] Rice found Hawks and his staff too much to deal with:

> I had accepted Goldwyn's offer largely on the strength of his promise of free creative scope. But he had reckoned without the scenario department's entrenched bureaucracy. The practitioners of the established patterns of picturemaking saw in the invasion from the East a threat to their security. Beneath the surface affability there was a sort of struggle for power.[9]

The leaders of the opposing sides were Hawks and playwright Thomas Buchanan, but Rice notes Hawks

> had the advantage of status and a supporting organization.

Nor did the stars and directors take kindly to Goldwyn's concept of the writer's importance.

The proposed revolution in writing came to nothing. All story material was channeled through Hawks, who vetoed every innovation with the comment that it was "not pictures."[10]

While Hawks may have been vetoing truly inventive cinematic ideas, more likely he was right in asserting that what the Eminent Authors were writing was "not pictures." Goldwyn had invested a great deal of money and even more, his own prestige, in the idea, and if it was simply a question of his bureaucracy throwing a wrench in the works, he could have stopped it. Goldwyn, for all his legendary troubles with the English language, was not a stupid man, especially in the area of filmmaking.

Because of the publicity given Goldwyn's Eminent Authors plan, its failure was equally well-known. This unfortunately did not stop other studios from following Goldwyn's lead and hiring more literary types with equal lack of success. The most damaging consequence of those schemes to screenwriters (real screenwriters, not literary slummers) was the growing intellectual put-down by the New York literary establishment not only of the movies, but particularly of screenwriters. There had always been a tendency in the New York establishment to deprecate the movies, but it increased with the move of the movies to Los Angeles (and therefore out of the control of the New York establishment) and with the sudden increase of the movies' influence on American life. The Eminent Authors, both Goldwyn's and the others', who returned to the literary scene added fuel to the fire.

June Mathis

A complete division of labor did not begin instantly and it was still possible for writers to continue to contribute to a film in more than just the writing of it. The most interesting example of this was one of the best-known screenwriters of the early twenties, June Mathis.

As a result of short stories Mathis wrote she became Metro's regular scenarist in the teens. On her own, Mathis discussed the film possibilities of the novel *The Four Horsemen of the Apocalypse* with its author Vicente Blasco Ibáñez. The studio was at first unconvinced, but Mathis persuaded Richard Rowland, the head of the company, to pay twenty thousand dollars for the rights in 1919. Mathis did the adaptation, and pushed Rowland to hire Rex Ingram to direct the epic production, although Ingram had only directed small films before. Several people, including Ingram, claimed credit for the discovery of the film's leading man, but it was Mathis who made the decision to cast the little-known Rudolph Valentino in the part that made him a star.[11]

After a dispute at Metro, Mathis and Valentino went to Famous Players in 1921–22, then Mathis left to run the Goldwyn story department a year later. She was with Goldwyn during the merger of Metro and Goldwyn into Metro-Goldwyn-Mayer. In addition to a film editor assigned to cut Von Stroheim's twenty-four reels of *Greed* into a less impressive but releasable ten reels, June Mathis was also assigned to supervise the editing and do the retitling.[12]

Klaw and Erlanger, the theatrical producers, had been suspicious of movie people interested in *Ben-Hur* since the illegal Kalem version. Mathis, however, used her persuasive powers on Abraham Erlanger. He not only sold the rights to the Goldwyn Company, but part of the deal was that she was the only person who could write the screenplay for it. Unfortunately, she was not as successful with this production as she had been with *The Four Horsemen of the Apocalypse*.[13] She insisted the film be shot in Italy, but Italian filmmaking skills were simply not up to the requirements of the film.[14] Mathis was removed from the film, as were the leading actor and director she had chosen, and the picture was completed in Los Angeles. Mathis returned to work for Valentino, but had a quarrel with his wife. She worked briefly at First National before her sudden death in 1927.

June Mathis extended into the studio period the practice of screenwriters being involved in all aspects of production. Her work, along with that of writer-producers Frank Woods and C. Gardner Sullivan, laid the groundwork for the later development in the studio system of screenwriters into producers.

Writers vs. Directors: Round One (of Many)

One of the side effects of the division of labor in the making of motion pictures was an increasing tension between the screenwriter and director. One of the best perspectives on the early stages of this never-ending story is provided by a man who saw firsthand all sides of the issue: William de Mille. De Mille began his work in movies as a screenwriter, then became head of the story department, and eventually was a director himself. He recalls that as a writer and head of the story department, he tried to be as insistent as possible the script be shot as written. He did have to admit that when a director came to him to complain about a script, the director may have been right, if only because in the midteens the directors tended to have more experience in making films than the newer screenwriters did. Even before he became a director, de Mille noted that the director is

the most important single factor in putting a story on the screen. . . . If the writer is too exact in defining every move of the camera, every cut and every angle, he robs the director of freedom in his own proper field; he ties the director's hands to the point of cramping his cinematic style and preventing his use of the camera as an instrument for emphasizing dramatic values instead of merely recording action.

The director of a motion picture plays a more important creative part in the finished work than does the conductor of a symphony; for the director not only conducts but, to a large extent, orchestrates the composition. . . . Screenwriters, unlike composers, cannot completely orchestrate their work on paper. . . .

They [writer and director] are both creating the picture, and I, for one, cannot lay down an exact line of demarcation, or find the spot where the writer ends and the director begins. That is probably why so many fine results have been achieved by writer and director working in close collaboration, each conscious of the other's field of creation, but reinforcing rather than limiting each other.[15]

While such close collaboration is the ideal in theory, in practice there are difficulties. De Mille notes that often directors did not have a good story sense. He writes, "They thought in terms of individual scenes rather than integrated plot, and showed an almost unquenchable desire to stop the story in order to develop what they thought was a good incident."[16] As head of the story department, he was frequently called upon to intervene in disputes between writer and director. When de Mille himself became a director, he discovered that "the director's point of view was not nearly as unreasonable as I had supposed."[17] De Mille saw that the problem began when the writing and directing functions were split between two (or more) people, noting that "the two crafts became theoretically separated but never actually untangled."[18]

William de Mille also accurately saw that part of the problem came from the increasing dependence on stories and story films. This inevitably meant a dependence not simply on directors who could use the grammar of film to tell stories, but on writers who could provide and construct the stories the directors were to tell. De Mille felt that the battle began in 1914, about the time he got into movies: "As the importance of the story value and story construction began to be realized, it was inevitable that a conflict of authority should develop between writer and director."[19]

But without writers there was nothing to direct.

8

Sound

Sound films did not capture the public's imagination until the 1927 film *The Jazz Singer,* although the producers of that film had been trying for some time. Warner Brothers, the controller of the Vitaphone (sound-on-record) process, began making Vitaphone films in 1926. The process was used either for music scores to silent films *(Don Juan)* or for programs of Vitaphone shorts. The first programs of Vitaphone shorts were primarily musical, although the second program of Vitaphone shorts did include a comic monologue by George Jessel, but it was overshadowed by Al Jolson's singing.[1] It is not surprising that Warner Brothers eventually replaced Jessel as the proposed star of *The Jazz Singer* with Jolson.

The early sound shorts from other companies also relied on music and poetry readings. Warners, however, discovered that there was less audience interest in musical shorts and more in sketches and short plays that emphasized dialogue.[2]

The Jazz Singer was not originally conceived as a film with dialogue. The film was to be a conventional silent film in most of its scenes, with the Vitaphone process used to provide both a musical background score and in a few sequences songs. The emphasis was to be on the novelty of the songs within the dramatic film. Alfred Cohn's screenplay for the film includes instructions of where the songs are to be performed, but the dialogue of the story is rendered in numbered titles, as was one of the conventions of silent screenwriting.[3]

There were, as the film approached production in mid-1927, some thoughts among the Warner Brothers executives about the possible use of dialogue in a few scenes. The first, and most famous line of dialogue, was ad-libbed by Jolson in his first musical scene. He sings "Dirty Hands, Dirty Face" in a nightclub, and when the audience applauds, Jolson says, "Wait a minute! Wait a minute! You ain't heard nothin' yet. Wait a minute, I tell ya, you ain't heard nothin'." He then sings the upbeat "Toot, Toot, Tootsie." His ad-libbed line had a startling impact on the audiences of 1927, because they knew they had not heard anything yet. The line, and Jolson's song, made it clear to the audience that a performer could come to them on film as much through his voice as through his look.

As strong as the impact was of Jolson's line, sound might have remained only a novelty if it were not for the other dialogue sequence in the film. Jakie Rabinowitz, now Jack Robin, is on his way to becoming a Broadway star, and has stopped off at home to see his mother. Jack (Jolson) sits down at the piano and plays and sings "Blue Skies," which he interrupts to talk to his mother to tell her how he is going to move her up to the Bronx when he is successful. Although the mother has a few lines, the scene is mostly Jolson's. There is no indication of it in the script, and nothing substantially like it either in Sampson Raphaelson's original story "The Day of Atonement" or the play *The Jazz Singer* Raphaelson adapted from it. The scene was apparently ad-libbed, as legend has it. Here is dialogue being used for the first time in American films as part of the story and to help show character. What is even more crucial to its impact is the end of the scene. Jack's father, who has objected to his son's going on the stage, comes into the room at the end of the song and says, "Stop!" which is recorded in the Vitaphone process. This sets up a dramatic scene, which is then played out as a *silent* scene, complete with subtitles. Even watching the scene now, one can feel the frustration the audiences of the time probably felt: the screen could tell its stories with spoken dialogue and then suddenly it went back to the old way of filmmaking. American films have always been narrative films, and this scene in *The Jazz Singer* showed how dialogue could improve narrative filmmaking.

Roy Pomeroy

The introduction of sound did not cause as much chaos in the industry as legend has it. There was certain disruption in production methods, as well as unease among actors, directors, cameramen, and screenwriters, none of whom knew if they could adjust to sound. But the industry made concentrated efforts to work out the problems as quickly and efficiently as possible. Some of these efforts were successful, some less so.[4]

In early May 1928, for example, the newly formed Academy of Motion Picture Arts and Sciences held a meeting for the members of the writers' branch of the Academy to discuss the problems of writing for sound films. Unfortunately, the man who did most of the talking at the meeting was not a writer. He was Roy Pomeroy. Pomeroy had been a special-effects technician (he helped devise the parting of the Red Sea in Cecil B. De Mille's 1923 version of *The Ten Commandments*) who had taken the time to go to the laboratories of Western Electric and study the technology of sound. For a period of about a year, he dominated the movie business, simply because for that year he was able to convince people he knew what he was talking about.[5]

It was in this role as the master of sound that he talked to the Academy writers.

Pomeroy told them it would probably take a full year to shoot an entire feature film with sound, although some two months after this meeting, Warner Brothers released their first all-talking film *The Lights of New York*. That film had taken much less than a year to make because Warners had the experience of the Vitaphone dialogue shorts behind them. Pomeroy talked about the time and expense necessary to conceal the microphones on the sets, although soon microphones would be put on booms over the heads of the actors. He insisted there should be a lapse of time between two people talking so that audiences could turn from one character to another. He said that characters should never be photographed from the back while they were talking, since the audience would not be able to tell who was speaking.

Also present at the meeting were several writers, whose questions and comments indicated a more practical bent. Anthony Coldeway, a writer at Warners, described the policy at that studio, which was to try to lay out the story and exposition in the dialogue at the beginning of the script, and then let the action carry the story, with an "occasional spoken title."[6] Coldeway said at Warners the procedure was to write the screenplay first without dialogue, and then send it to the title writers, who were expected to write the dialogue. He added, "Yes, the use of sound devices will make title writing more important,"[7] meaning the writing of the "spoken title," or dialogue.

An example of the format problems screenwriters faced can be found in script materials prepared in 1929 for an attempt to turn what remained of Von Stroheim's *Queen Kelly* into a partial sound film.[8] On page 5 of the March 9, 1929, script for this effort, what little dialogue there is to be spoken is typed out in the same way that written titles were done in silent screenplays: "TITLE: Patricia, the Mother Superior wishes to see you immediately in the Library." On page 12 there is simply the line "Patricia sings the 1st verse of the song IN SOUND." On page 16 and following pages, the dialogue is identified as: "SPOKEN TITLE." The formats that eventually evolved within the industry were a combination of the silent-screenplay formats with the standard stage-play formats, in which the speaker of the dialogue is identified in capital letters centered in the page, with the speaker's dialogue underneath it.

The change in formats soon brought a change in the kind of writing needed for films. In the silent-film scripts, the majority of the writing was in descriptions of actions and what the camera would see. What the sound films needed was dialogue, and by the early thirties, the look of American screenplays had changed drastically. There was by then much less description of the action (and what there was was certainly not in the elaborate literary style of the writers of the silent film), and the screenplays consisted mostly of dialogue.

Dialogue and Dialogue Writers

The assumption, as we have seen at Warner Brothers, where the scripts were sent to the title writers, was that the screenwriters who told the story were somehow incapable of writing dialogue. This was not true and the studios should have known it. Scriptwriters had been writing dialogue in screenplays since the early teens, and not just dialogue that would be replaced by fancier titles. Frances Marion recalls how she got started as a dialogue writer for silent films. In 1913 she was working as actress/extra for director Lois Weber. Weber overheard producer Oliver Morosco's amazement at watching a scene from a film of *Macbeth* being filmed in which the extras were saying lines like "I'll be hornswoggled if it ain't my old pal Macduff." She wondered what lip-readers might make of that, and Weber, after thinking about it, asked Marion to write lines for the extras. She gave Marion the script, and told her:

> Note where the mob scenes are. You'll be in costume and move among them. But your principal job is to write snatches of dialogue, pick out individual types you can depend on, and rehearse them so we won't have any more such expressions as "I could kick a dog in the face" to register surprise, or "Let's kill them frog-eatin' bastards" when a crowd is clamoring for the death of Marie Antoinette.[9]

Marion was not the only writer writing dialogue for silent films. Most of the surviving screenplays from the later silent period have many lines of dialogue in them in addition to lines identified as titles. The dialogue was written to help the actors get into the feel of the story. Even Chaplin gave his actors lines to say in his silent films.[10]

The dialogue written by the silent-title writers was not necessarily good spoken dialogue. Title writers had to compress much information into as few words as possible. Sometimes these lines could be spoken, sometimes not. The most famous example of unspeakable dialogue from the period is found in the screenplay for John Gilbert's first sound feature *His Glorious Night*, written by Willard Mack.[11] The screenplay is an adaptation of Ferenc Molnar's play *Olympia* but the dialogue, which was so damaging to Gilbert's career, is pure silent-film titles, as in the line, "Princess—my Princess—I love you—I love you—I love you." When delivered in Gilbert's intense tenor, the line produced audience laughs and the beginning of the end of Gilbert's career.

When the title writers' dialogue proved to be too literary or too unspeakable, the studios naturally turned to people experienced in writing dialogue: playwrights. Frances Marion's first "talkie" assignment found her forced to collaborate with playwright James Forbes, "an unctuous little man." She and Forbes kept rewriting each other until the dispute finally had to be settled by the head of the studio.[12]

In addition to disliking Forbes, Marion did not care much for the other "dialogue writers" brought into the industry:

> At first, almost all the screen stories were turned over to them. The results were not satisfactory. Unaccustomed to the swift pace necessary to keep scenes from becoming static, they could not move their pawns on the chess board. All action ceased while actors faced each other and talked longer on any subject than women at a club meeting. Baffled, the producers finally permitted the scenarists to become humble assistants to these dialogue writers. We did not relish the chore but obeyed implicitly, our eyes on our paychecks.[13]

It was not long after the debacle with Forbes that Marion was working on screenplays by herself.

Nor was she alone. The legend of course is that actors, directors, and screenwriters were thrown out of work in large groups. It was not true for actors (Ronald Colman, W. C. Fields, Joan Crawford, Laurel and Hardy, and Garbo managed the transition) nor directors (Ford, Hawks, Capra, Vidor, Henry King, and others), and it certainly was not true of writers. Of the writers previously written about here, many had careers that spanned both the silent and sound films successfully. William de Mille continued, mostly as a director, but also as a writer, into the late thirties, with his last writing credit coming in 1939. Clyde Bruckman, who wrote as well as directed for Buster Keaton, went on in the sound era to write on the sound films of Harold Lloyd, as well as those of Abbott and Costello. Chaplin was successful in the sound era, even when he finally began to talk. Anita Loos, after giving up screenwriting for a time in the twenties, returned to work at MGM in the thirties and wrote such films as *San Francisco* (1936), *Saratoga* (1937), and *The Woman* (1939). C. Gardner Sullivan's sound films include *Strange Interlude* (a 1932 adaptation of the Eugene O'Neill play), *The Buccaneer* (1938), *Union Pacific* (1939), and *Northwest Mounted Police* (1940), the last three for Cecil B. De Mille. Frances Marion had written many of the Mary Pickford films of the late teens, then in the sound era wrote *The Big House* (1930), *Min and Bill* (1930), *The Champ* (1931), *Dinner at Eight* (1933), and *Camille* (1937).

There were others who made the transition as well, such as Jules Furthman, who began selling stories to movies in 1915 and writing scenarios in 1917. Ben Hecht wrote *Underworld* in 1927 before going on to a career in sound films. Bess Meredyth and Sonya Levien were two women screenwriters who were successful in both silent and sound films. The screenwriters (like, to be sure, the actors and directors) were smart enough to learn the new craft of writing for talking pictures. The new craft, in fact, was not all that different from the old. The American film was still, more than ever, a narrative film, and the silent screenwriters who survived the transition were the storytellers.

9

Visitors from the East

There are generally considered two waves of writers from the East who came to Hollywood and the movies.[1] The first wave consisted of Goldwyn's Eminent Authors in 1919, which was discussed in chapter 7. The second wave is thought to be the wave of playwrights and others brought out after the introduction of sound. For reasons suggested in the previous chapter, the writers brought out at the very beginning of the sound period were not successful. Alexander Walker notes that

> by mid-November 1928, about 75 per cent of the writers brought West by Fox for a three-month trial period in the talkie workshops were repacking their cases, paying their bar bills and preparing to catch the train back to New York on 1 December. Of the twenty-five per cent of the survivors, it was significant that the majority were composers and librettists. Other studios had similar experiences.[2]

The playwrights who came west simply did not know the craft of writing for the screen, and few of them seemed to bother to learn that craft. What was being demanded of the writers of dialogue for the sound films was not theatrical dialogue, but a more realistic kind of dialogue. Not surprisingly, many of the men (and women) who became the best screenwriters of the time had previous newspaper experience, which gave them experience not only with having written how people talk, but also in writing for tyrannical editors. Both kinds of experience were helpful in working for the movies.

On the other hand, many of the best-known writers who went to Hollywood in the second wave were from the literary world. Compared to the debacle of the Eminent Authors plan, the second wave of visitors from the East were of much more value to American motion pictures. Unfortunately, their experiences continued and compounded the problem of the image of the screenwriters that the Eminent Authors had begun.

The reasons the studios wanted the Eastern writers are clear. First of all, they needed writers who could write dialogue, and at least some of the writers brought out in the late twenties and early thirties had achieved some reputation for dialogue in their plays, short stories, or novels. Second, the studios, like Mack Sennett before them, wanted the writers' minds. Third, the writers were often simply the literary prizes that the studios sought.

Why did the writers come? The obvious answer is money. While there was a certain prestige in writing novels and short stories, there was often very little money in it. This was particularly true of the magazine market for short stories, which declined sharply in the early years of the Depression. Novels, particularly literary ones, often only brought in a few hundred dollars in royalties. Compared to this, the studios were paying not merely hundreds a week, but often thousands.

Money was not the only answer. The Depression had hit New York, but did not hit the film business until the early thirties, primarily because of the success of the novelty of sound films. The climate was better in Los Angeles, and many writers found their friends in Hollywood as well. The second wave might more legitimately be said to have begun with Herman J. Mankiewicz's famous 1925 telegram to Ben Hecht: WILL YOU ACCEPT THREE HUNDRED PER WEEK TO WORK FOR PARAMOUNT PICTURES. ALL EXPENSES PAID. THE THREE HUNDRED IS PEANUTS. MILLIONS ARE TO BE GRABBED OUT HERE AND YOUR ONLY COMPETITION IS IDIOTS. DON'T LET THIS GET AROUND.[3] In addition to Hecht, Mankiewicz can also lay claim to having brought out to Hollywood such other writers as his brother Joseph and Nunnally Johnson. Johnson himself describes the gathering of his friends in Hollywood in a 1934 interview: "In fact, it is about the only place now where I can find my friends. They're all out there. A party looks like the old *Herald-Tribune* room. No, it looks more like a speakeasy."[4]

There was also another, more complex reason. When a writer wrote in New York, or rather in the literary forms that were based in New York (plays, novels, short stories), the writer was open to direct criticism of his work, since the literary establishment, or at least the critical side of it, was also based in New York. For a writer, the movies offered critical anonymity. If the creators of a film were mentioned in reviews, it was most likely the director, the actors, and sometimes the producer, but almost never the screenwriter. Partially this was because the director had developed the reputation as the creator of the film, but it was also because screenwriters tended to be credited in groups, so it became impossible for critics to tell which of the many writers contributed what to the film. (At some studios, most notably MGM, there were often several directors who worked on a picture, but the tradition was to give only one screen credit.)

Such anonymity had its price, since it went hand in hand with the alienation the screenwriters felt from the product they were creating. Their work was often changed so much they would not recognize it. In the literary world, their work was relatively untouched (at least in comparison with what happened to it in Hollywood), and they could legitimately claim it as their own. That was not true in Hollywood, and to make matters worse they were paid large sums of money for the privilege of having their work changed. It is not surprising that the writers of the studio days came to feel they were prostituting their talents, and it is unfortunately this image that came to be the dominant myth about writers in Hollywood.

Like most myths, there is some truth behind this one, and there are many writers whose careers might be made to fit into the pattern of "destroyed literary talent." John Schultheiss[5] considers Edwin Justus Mayer as one of the early examples of a promising Eastern writer whose literary output declined after his arrival in Hollywood in the late twenties. Mayer was the author of the 1924 Broadway success *The Firebrand*, a biographical play about Benvenuto Cellini, and towards the end of his life he was planning a book about Pitt the Elder, but it was never completed. The intervening time was spent in Hollywood, but his screenplays included *Desire* (1936), *A Royal Scandal* (1945), and his best and best-known, *To Be or Not To Be* (1942).

Another writer from the twenties who came to Hollywood was Samuel Hoffenstein.[6] He made his literary reputation with a 1928 book of verse *Poems in Praise of Practically Nothing*, and followed that by another volume in 1930, and then wrote nothing in the traditional literary forms until 1947. His screenplays, however, include *Dr. Jekyll and Mr. Hyde* (1932), *Tales of Manhattan* (1942), and *Laura* (1944).

Daniel Fuchs is another example Schultheiss gives of the literary decline of an Eastern writer.[7] In the thirties, Fuchs wrote three critically acclaimed novels about life in Brooklyn: *Summer in Williamsburg*, *Homage to Blenholt*, and *Low Company*. Fuchs began his screenwriting in 1942 with *The Hard Way*, then also wrote *Criss Cross* (1949), *Panic in the Streets* (1950), and *Love Me or Leave Me* (1955), the last of which probably inspired John Updike's disguised putdown: "his favorite Jewish writer was the one who turned his back on his three beautiful Brooklyn novels and went into the desert to write scripts for Doris Day."[8]

What becomes apparent in looking at these, and other careers, is that while the literary and theatrical worlds may have lost from these writers' Hollywood activities, the movies gained from them. In each of the careers mentioned above, there are films that could be considered the equal of their more conventional literary work.

In addition to the writers who showed some sort of literary decline as a result of their Hollywood experiences, there are also writers who gained, either in terms of subject matter for future material or extension of literary technique. William Faulkner spent a total of four years working in Hollywood, spread out over a period of twenty-three years. His Hollywood output is noted particularly for his collaborations with director Howard Hawks on *The Road to Glory* (1936), *To Have and Have Not* (1944), and *The Big Sleep*

(1946). He was not particularly good at the craft of screenwriting, and his work had to be rewritten, or at least revised, by his screenwriting collaborators, which included more accomplished screenwriters like Nunnally Johnson and Joel Sayre on *The Road to Glory*, Jules Furthman on *To Have and Have Not*, and Furthman and Leigh Brackett on *The Big Sleep*. Tom Dardis, studying Faulkner's Hollywood period, has suggested, however, that Faulkner's experience in writing the World War I screenplays *Today We Live* and *The Road to Glory* helped inspire him to write the novel *A Fable*, which has a World War I setting.[9]

After his Broadway success in 1935 with *Waiting for Lefty* and *Awake and Sing*, Clifford Odets went to Hollywood in 1936, primarily for financial reasons. Among the films he wrote were *None But the Lonely Heart* (1944, which he also directed), *Humoresque* (1946), *The Sweet Smell of Success* (1957), and *Wild in the Country* (1961, which starred Elvis Presley, who turned out to be surprisingly adept at Odets's dialogue). Odets felt very much that he had sold out and dealt with the subject in vivid terms in his 1948 play *The Big Knife*, which was made into an equally vivid film in 1955.[10]

Nathanael West wrote the novel *Miss Lonelyhearts* before he began writing for Hollywood; in fact, it was the critical success of the novel that brought him to Hollywood. Unlike most of the other literary figures who came West in the thirties, West did not work for the major studios. His screenwriting days were spent in the smaller studios: Republic, Monogram, and RKO. There are no major films in his filmography, although there are some interesting B pictures, such as *Five Came Back* (1939). Tom Dardis describes what West got out of Hollywood:

> West was perhaps more at home than some in grinding out the rather stupefying plots that his employers at Republic, Universal, and RKO demanded of him, for his usual attitude toward the work was one of amusement, even sustained, gleeful amusement. It was junk all the way, but it supplied him with the money to keep on writing when nothing else would, the writing that in *The Day of the Locust* finally turned into an examination of the entire junk world of which he was now at the center. No American writer got as much out of Hollywood as did West; the creation of the curious atmosphere of that book is a triumph. No writer was ever as successful as was West in simultaneously destroying the old romantic myth of Hollywood glamour and replacing it immediately with a brand-new one—the one of sinister decay in blazing sunlight.[11]

The most famous of all the Eastern writers who came to Hollywood was F. Scott Fitzgerald, and it is the stories by and about him in Hollywood that formed the legend of the visitors from the East. Fitzgerald had an early interest in the movies. Some of his short stories were sold to films in the early twenties, and in his 1922 novel *The Beautiful and Damned* one of the characters is a novelist who after a first great success ends up writing trashy movies in Hollywood. In 1924 Fitzgerald wrote a treatment for Famous Players of his novel *This Side of Paradise*, but the film was never made. Fitzgerald did go out to Hollywood from time to time in the twenties and early thirties, partially for social reasons, sometimes working on unproduced screenplays, such as *Lipstick* in 1927 and *Red-Headed Woman* in 1931.

When he returned to Hollywood in 1937, Fitzgerald's literary reputation had already begun to decline. His agent had been unable to sell any of his stories to any magazines for a year, and his 1936 earnings from *all* his books was $81.18.[12] The minor success in 1934 of *Tender Is the Night* had provoked some interest in Fitzgerald on Hollywood's part, but that had diminished by 1937.[13]

Fitzgerald unfortunately ended up at MGM, the studio that was in many ways the least hospitable to him and his talent. He had worked at MGM in 1927 and 1931 and, like most writers, had been charmed by the head of production at MGM, Irving Thalberg. By 1937 Thalberg was dead, but his system of using many writers on a single project continued under the producers who survived him. Fitzgerald faced two problems. The first was that he did not collaborate easily with either producers or other writers, and his time at MGM in the late thirties was one of recurring conflicts resulting from the collaborative nature of screenwriting at that studio.[14]

The second problem Fitzgerald had was that he was a prose writer, and the examples of his screenwriting work that have been published and/or excerpted show the problem. Fitzgerald writes, as he does in his novels and his short stories, in a fluid, elegant style, not a style that is particularly appropriate for treatments or screenplays. A reader frequently reads one of Fitzgerald's wonderful phrases, then asks himself how that phrase is going to be shown on the screen. Two recent writers on Fitzgerald's period in Hollywood[15] both suggest that as Fitzgerald's years in Hollywood passed, he was beginning to learn the craft of the screenwriter. After reading Fitzgerald's screenplay and treatment work, both published and unpublished, such a conclusion is unwarranted. The last screen project Fitzgerald worked on was an adaptation of Emlyn Williams's *The Light of Heart*, and his 1940 screenplay was not used when the film was made two years later under the title *Life Begins at 8:30*. The screenplay for the film was by Fitzgerald's friend Nunnally Johnson. Fitzgerald's script is darker, while Johnson's is more sentimental. Fitzgerald's story and scene construction are competent but not unique, and his writing is tired and heavy, while Johnson's script has the smoothness and grace normally associated with Fitzgerald's prose.[16]

Even though Fitzgerald was not particularly successful as a screenwriter, he was not particularly unhappy in Hollywood. As with other writers, he found a number of his friends out in California, and he was making good money, which he needed at the time. Tom Dardis has shown that Fitzgerald was in the higher earning brackets among screenwriters of the time (Dardis indicates that not more than eighteen other writers were paid more in 1938).[17] Dardis also discovered, in interviews with those who knew Fitzgerald in Hollywood, that he was not the broken-down drunk that legend has it.[18]

There is also *The Last Tycoon*, the novel Fitzgerald was working on when he died. Even in its uncompleted form, it is still rightly considered one of the best novels ever written about Hollywood. Certainly its scenes of the Thalberg-inspired Monroe Stahr on the lot give us the best-observed look at a head of a major studio at work in that period of time. In addition, the romantic scenes between Stahr and Kathleen are as good as any Fitzgerald wrote. The novel, as we have it, is hardly the work of a destroyed talent.

How did the myth of Hollywood as the destroyer of literary talent start, and why has it continued? The movies themselves were looked down on by the other arts from the movies' earliest days, but it was only with the Eminent Authors plan that the disdain for films in general turned to screenwriters and the screenwriting profession in particular. Before the twenties, screenwriters came from popular journalism and the popular arts, and the movies were generally seen as one of those popular arts. By the twenties, the movies had come to be perceived as much more powerful and much more influential than had first been thought. Which perhaps would not have been a problem if the movies had remained in New York.

What we have here is an example of New York provincialism. New York tends to think of itself as, if not the center of the universe, at least the center of cultural activity in the United States. There is some truth to this self-image, since both publishing and the theater are strongly concentrated in New York. By the twenties, the American theater had begun to develop serious plays, only to see the movies steal popularity from the theater. And the movies were made in California, which was generally assumed not to have any culture at all. An example of the New York attitude of the time toward movies and Los Angeles can be found in Edmund Wilson's infamous 1941 essay on California writers, "The Boys in the Back Room." After criticizing the school of hard-boiled novelists and short-story writers as "preeminently the poets of the tabloid murder,"[19] Wilson complains that San Francisco's potential as an artistic center was hurt by the 1906 earthquake,

> and that thereafter the great anti-cultural amusement-producing center, Los Angeles, grew up, gigantic and vulgar, like one of those synthetic California flowers, and tended to drain the soil of the imaginative life of the State. (It is a question how much the movies themselves have been affected by the California

atmosphere: might they not have been a little more interesting under the stress of affairs in the East?)[20]

In an effort to match the work of publishing and the theater, the heads of the companies tried to compete by hiring the writers who were well-known in the other media. It did not work with the Eminent Authors plan or immediately after the introduction of sound. Many of the writers who came to Hollywood from the East in the twenties and thirties found it difficult to adjust. They could not, or would not, learn how to write for films. The writers from the literary world often found it impossible to collaborate in the extensive way filmmaking required. The writers from the theater found a different kind of dialogue was required by films. Those writers found it easier to return to New York and complain about conditions in Hollywood. Their complaints were supported by those who had remained in New York. The New York provincialism of the artistic and literary community assumed that there could only be one cultural headquarters per country and that New York was it. Those people forgot the lessons of the Italian Renaissance, where there were thriving cultures in several cities. Movies were a different kind of artistic activity and needed a different kind of writer. It is those writers who became the important screenwriters of the major studio period.

The "New York" attitude, however, affected the screenwriters, both in how they viewed themselves and how they were viewed by others. From July 1946 to August 1947, Hortense Powdermaker, an anthropologist, conducted a study of the Hollywood community, subsequently published as *Hollywood the Dream Factory* in 1950. While many of her perceptions of the movie industry are accurate, her views on the writers are colored by those conventional attitudes, in some cases communicated to her by the writers she interviewed. She discusses how screenwriters are isolated in Los Angeles, and softened by the money.[21] She goes into accurate, if somewhat-misleading detail, on how writers are deprived of power, although by the time she was studying the situation writers had found a variety of ways to combat those problems.

Powdermaker realized years later that had she gone into the research with a "holier-than-thou" attitude toward screenwriters,[22] and writes, "Today I am critical of the Hollywood field work, more so than any of my other field experiences."[23] She adds, "Although closer by temperament and profession to the writers than to any other group in Hollywood, I failed to identify with them or to get inside their roles."[24]

That attitude of superiority on the part of the intellectual community dominated thinking about screenwriters until it was changed, decades later, by the films of a single screenwriter.

10

Metro-Goldwyn-Mayer

Metro-Goldwyn-Mayer was known as the biggest and the best of the major studios. It had the most stars, and it had the most glamorous costumes and sets. It had the prestige that comes with being the best. MGM also hired the most well-known writers, such as William Faulkner, F. Scott Fitzgerald, Aldous Huxley, George S. Kaufman, and Moss Hart. These writers were not necessarily the best screenwriters, and the way the studio used writers was certainly one of the worst in the industry. Unfortunately, because of MGM's position in the business, the image of the screenwriter in Hollywood became that of the screenwriter at MGM.

The head of the studio from 1924 to 1951 was Louis B. Mayer, who was determined to make MGM the best. He knew the business, and he knew how to find stars, but he was not much of a reader. For the screenwriters at MGM, the most important figure in Mayer's office was not Mayer himself, but what screenwriter George Oppenheimer called "the lady storytellers, the Metro troubadours."[1] Mayer had the stories told to him, and the primary troubadour during his years at MGM was Kate Corbaley, an ex-librarian who had worked for Ince until his death, then came to MGM. Samuel Marx, a story editor at MGM, recalls, "She soon won his [Thalberg's] devotion as well as that of Mayer, who loved to listen to her. Without doubt, she reminded Mayer of the time his mother read stories to him."[2] Screenwriters at Metro learned to make sure Corbaley, or whoever was telling Mayer the story, understood and even liked the story she was telling to him. Screenwriter Donald Ogden Stewart recalls that on one occasion Mayer complained that Stewart did not follow the novel MGM had purchased for a high price. Stewart knew Mayer had not read the novel, but figured it had been told him wrong. After that, Stewart would arrange for the storyteller to tell the story to him first so that Stewart "would know the gospel according to her before attempting any of my own interpretations."[3]

Irving Thalberg

The head of production at MGM from 1924 to 1933, and the man who did the most to define the MGM style of screenwriting, was Irving Thalberg.

Unlike Mayer, Thalberg was a reader, and at Universal before he came to MGM he developed the reputation of having an excellent mind for stories. He would not only listen to Kate Corbaley's versions of the stories, but read the original material if he thought there was a potential film in it.[4] He wanted the best writers around him, and he was willing to pay the best prices. It is perhaps therefore not surprising to discover Thalberg liked writers. It is somewhat surprising to discover writers liked Thalberg.

On the surface, one can see why they liked him. He was charming, sensitive to the interests of others, and intelligent about the filmmaking process. He was good at suggesting ways a story could be developed for the screen, and he was excellent at critiquing a screenplay or a completed film.

On the other hand, as kind as Thalberg could be to writers, he was brutal with and about their work. It was Thalberg who took Ince's system and divided the labor of screenwriting even more. For Ince a writer wrote and a director directed, but Thalberg instituted the practice of having several writers or even teams of writers at work on the same script without, supposedly, the other writers knowing it. Most screenwriters who worked at MGM in the thirties and forties have stories of discovering, usually over lunch in the commissary, that another writer was working on the same project. Sometimes a writer did not even have to get all the way to the commissary. George Seaton, then a young writer, was working at MGM with Robert Pirosh on a scene for A *Night at the Opera*:

> We were in our little cubbyhole and we were talking about it and we stopped, paused trying to think, and we heard something in the next office. In those days, that little Writers' Building had tissue paper walls. We heard somebody talking about the same scene. So we put our ears to the wall, and sure enough, whoever it was, they were working on the same scene. We didn't know who it was, so we waited until they came out and it was [Bert] Kalmar and [Harry] Ruby. We introduced ourselves and I said. "We were told to work on this thing" and they said, "So were we and we heard you talking through the walls, too." So the four of us got together after that and worked on the scene as quartet, and it was a pleasure to work with them. Harry Ruby . . . was one of the sweetest men in the world but he was a baseball nut and all during our conferences he would pretend to be pitching. Bert Kalmar was a magician, as a hobby, and to keep his fingers supple, he always used to roll a half dollar from finger to finger on both hands. So here we were with one fellow pitching all day long and another fellow rolling half dollars. The only defense we had was to bring in a putter and a ball and start putting. That's the way we worked together.[5]

As writers worked, Thalberg and/or his producers shuffled their scenes into a shooting script. Nor was the shooting script the end of the writing on a film. After the film was shot and cut together, there would often be retakes of substantial portions of the film, which were rewritten after the films were viewed either at the studio or at sneak previews. The number of writers who worked on a single film could be surprisingly high. *The Wizard of Oz* had ten screenwriters who worked on it at one time or another,[6] while A *Night at the Opera* had eight and A *Day at the Races* had six.[7] To compound the insult to screenwriters, the writers given credit by the studio on the film tended to be those who worked last and who often had done not much more than a polish job or added some dialogue. It is not surprising that the first stirrings of what led to the development of the Screen Writers Guild began at MGM.

Thalberg also divided the labor of producing. Thalberg developed a group of production "supervisors," or producers, each one responsible for a number of productions each year. Many of these people were talented in their own right, but they often were incompatible with the writers assigned to them. Buster Keaton's difficulties upon his arrival at MGM came at least in part from having to deal with his "supervisor," Laurence Weingarten, whose previous expertise was in making Biblical films and who it was generally agreed had not much of a sense of humor.

Other writers found other supervisors difficult to deal with. Screenwriter William Ludwig discovered that producer Carey Wilson was trying to sell as his own a story Ludwig had told him, since Wilson got a bonus of five thousand dollars for every story the studio bought from him.[8] Donald Ogden Stewart recalls the problems with Hunt Stromberg, who

> had one further touchstone by which he tested all [story] values. I would bring to his office a tender love scene. He would read it, then pick up a riding crop and stride back and forth, spitting freely as he moved and more fiercely as he talked. "Son," he would say, "I like it [spit]. I think it's a fine scene [spit]. But how about that dumb Scranton miner? Would he understand it?" Hunt had never been in Scranton and I don't think he'd ever seen a miner, but every bit I wrote had to get the commendation of that mythic creature sitting in a Scranton movie house. Charlie MacArthur and I once tried to get a friend in Scranton to send us out a real miner, but he claimed he couldn't find one dumb enough. Every producer, incidentally, seemed to have some similar signature-tune for use in conferences with writers. Irving would constantly toss and catch a coin. Others would have their nails manicured, their shoes shined, or their hair trimmed. It was very impressive.[9]

The Freed Unit

Thalberg's system of producers continued after his death in 1936. One of the most successful examples of that system did not begin producing until the early forties. Arthur Freed had been at the studio since the late twenties as a songwriter. As a result of the success of *The Wizard of Oz*, a production Freed had encouraged, Freed's friend Louis B. Mayer made him a full producer on the lot. Freed's unit produced such musicals as *Meet Me in St. Louis, Showboat, An American in Paris, Singin' in the Rain*, and *Gigi*.[10]

The development of the 1944 film *Meet Me in St. Louis* is typical of how Freed's unit worked in the heyday of MGM. It was screenwriter Fred Finklehoffe who suggested to Freed that a film could be made out of stories by Sally Benson. Freed had the story told to Mayer and the other MGM executives by Lillie Messinger, one of the "Metro troubadours," and Mayer became enthusiastic about the project.[11] The material was purchased by the studio in 1942, and Benson, Sarah Mason, and Victor Heerman all tried without success to develop a script.[12]

Freed assigned Finklehoffe to do the screenplay, and Finklehoffe insisted on having Irving Brecher to help him. Finklehoffe thought highly of Freed:

> That was the thing I liked about Arthur. He didn't want to write the script himself, he just wanted you to do it. That's why he was always so successful— because he was immensely cognizant of creative people and treated them as such. All the rest of those alligators thought they were creative: they weren't. They were in the salmon business and didn't know it.[13]

Originally the film was not conceived as a musical, but as the script developed, Freed saw how it could become one, and he talked to a skeptical Mayer. Mayer finally said, "Well, Arthur, go ahead. Either you'll learn or we'll learn."[14]

Vincente Minnelli, just at the beginning of his career, was brought in to direct, and Brecher describes working with him:

> I'd read a scene and act it out for him. He'd listen with his eyes closed . . . a very bright, sensitive, talented person. He would nudge me into a better line of dialogue, a better curtain line here and there. He was particularly helpful in a couple of love scenes, especially the one between Esther and John after the Christmas party, under the tree out in the snow. He made me write that scene as it is now in the picture, and I was very grateful for his help.[15]

Judy Garland had not originally wanted to do the film, but Freed arranged for her to hear Brecher read the script, which changed her mind.[16]

Writing for Stars

The studio was the leader in finding and developing stars, and the writing staff was just as much a part of this activity as the makeup and publicity departments were. One reason Thalberg used so many writers was that he was constantly under pressure to keep his high-salaried stars at work.[17] One time screenwriter Lenore Coffee was working at home and got a call from Thalberg. A big speech a star was to deliver in a scene was not working, and Thalberg had Coffee dictate a new speech to Thalberg's secretary. Coffee did not even know what film the scene was in.[18]

Thalberg thought the development of the story for the star was crucial to the star's development. As in the silent days, there were writers who specialized in writing for individual stars. Frances Marion suggested Marie Dressler for a part in the 1930 film *Anna Christie*, which helped revitalize Dressler's career. Marion then went on to write *Min and Bill* and *Dinner at Eight* for Dressler.[19]

Jean Harlow was in films from 1929, usually in small parts, occasionally in starring roles in *Hell's Angels* and *Public Enemy*, but she did not become a star until John Lee Mahin wrote *Red Dust* in 1932. The character in the play being adapted was rather depressing and Mahin suggested making her funny. Mahin told director Victor Fleming how to have her say the comic lines that he wrote for her:

> She's crying, she's cleaning the parrot cage, and she says to the parrot, "What have you been eating, cement?" I thought if she isn't crying, it won't be funny, it'll just be unpleasant if she says it angrily to the parrot. But if she's crying at the same time, if she's brokenhearted, then it's funny and sweet.[20]

The wisecracking blonde Mahin created for Harlow in this film defined her image as a star, and Mahin went on to write several more films for her, including *Bombshell*, *China Seas*, and *Riffraff.*

It was also Mahin who suggested another MGM contract player, Clark Gable, play the male lead in the same film.[21] It helped establish Gable as a star as well, and Mahin worked on the writing of other Gable films, including *Too Hot To Handle*, *Test Pilot*, *Gone With the Wind*, and *Boom Town.*

Examples of the problems of constructing a script for a star in the MGM method can be seen in the development of the 1938 film *Marie Antoinette*. In the early thirties MGM bought a novel about Marie Antoinette, and after nine weeks of writing under another producer, Thalberg took over the project.[22] Thalberg intended the film to be a major prestige picture to star his wife, Norma Shearer, and to be directed by the studio's director of such important films, Sidney Franklin. Since Shearer and Franklin had a success together on *The Barretts of Wimpole Street*, Thalberg decided to team them with the screenwriters of that film—the English Claudine West, the Hungarian Ernst Vadja, and the American Donald Ogden Stewart. Stewart however wanted out of Hollywood at the time (1933) and Thalberg let him go. Stewart returned the following year and

> I resumed daily conferences with Sidney Franklin, Claudine West and Ernst Vadja, with hopes that in six months at the most I would be back at work on a play of my own.
> This hope was on the optimistic side. Fourteen months later the head of Queen Marie was still firmly on her shoulders and I was still consulting with my colleagues as to the best way of explaining the French Revolution in terms that would not lose audience sympathy for Norma Shearer.[23]

The screenwriters did what they could. At the beginning Marie is a bright and bouncy young girl. She is then forced into a marriage with the man who becomes Louis XVI, who is seen in the script as rather shy and bumbling around her. She is willing to make the best of the marriage, but is faced with the antagonism of the others at court, particularly Madame Du Barry. Du Barry is portrayed as a caricature of how most people think of Marie Antoinette: rich, spoiled, and nasty, so Marie is seen as better by comparison. Marie has a love affair with the Danish count Axel de Fersen, but renounces it to do her duty. She also gets a large number of close-ups indicated in the script, and a terrific farewell scene with her husband and her children.[24]

The writers tried hard to make Marie Antoinette sympathetic, but the film[25] overpowers most of their efforts. Shearer is not at her best being bright and bouncy in the opening scenes. While the casting of the young Robert Morley is intended to make Louis XVI unsympathetic, it has the opposite effect. Because he seems so delicately lost in the court politics, our feelings are drawn to him. The differences between Marie and Du Barry seem more of degree than of kind. When Marie turns down the purchase of a necklace on the grounds that people are starving, it is more than a little ridiculous, simply because the MGM production values are so lavish and so prominently displayed. The entire MGM studio style of filmmaking works against the writers' efforts.

The MGM Screenwriting Style

A very distinctive MGM studio style of screenwriting came out of Thalberg's system. MGM films tend to be very episodic. For all of Thalberg's legendary story sense, what he eventually worked his way toward was a style that was in practice uneven and often disjointed. Partially this came out of his determination to find scenes that worked, that played. Sometimes there are connections between the scenes and sometimes there are not. Often moments built up to either never appear or else go by very quickly. After Thalberg's death, there are also scenes that are supposed to work in the Thalberg tradition, but do not particularly, since the other producers did not necessarily have Thalberg's feel for the way a scene would work.

In the MGM films, there is also the problem that the original idea for a script may not be well developed. In the John Lee Mahin script for *Boom Town*, Gable and Tracy are cast as two oil roughnecks, and people who remember the film most likely remember the funny fight in the mud between the two stars in the beginning of the film. What is not remembered is that halfway through the film the two roughnecks hit it big and spend the second half of the film sitting around in plush MGM sets talking about the problems of being rich. In the same manner, the Mahin-Laurence Stallings script for *Too Hot To Handle* establishes Gable as a daredevil newsreel cameraman, then does not do much with the situation.

What Thalberg's approach does give are scenes for the stars to play. What we tend to remember are the great scenes from the MGM films: Gable looking at Harlow in the barrel in *Red Dust*, Harlow and Dressler going into dinner at the end of *Dinner at Eight*, Charles Laughton terrorizing the crew in *Mutiny on the Bounty*, the earthquake in *San Francisco*, the stateroom scene in *A Night at the Opera*, and Garbo's death scene in *Camille*.

Or Garbo in any scene in any film, for that matter.

11

Twentieth Century-Fox

Twentieth Century-Fox was formed in 1935 by a merger of the Fox Film Corporation and Twentieth Century Pictures. Throughout the teens and twenties Fox depended on the drawing power of such stars as Theda Bara, William Farnum, and Tom Mix, although Jules Furthman, later an important screenwriter, worked at Fox as early as 1918 and steadily at Fox in the early twenties. The company went into receivership in 1931 and limped along with occasional successes until 1935, when the company and Twentieth Century Pictures arranged a merger. Twentieth, a much smaller company, had only been in existence for two years but it had Darryl F. Zanuck.

Darryl F. Zanuck

Zanuck started selling stories to the movies in the early twenties and was soon working for Warner Brothers, writing stories for their big star, Rin Tin Tin. Zanuck's Warners career will be discussed in the next chapter, but in 1933 he resigned and with Joseph Schenck formed Twentieth Century Pictures, which was an immediate success. Two years later the company was merged with Fox, with Zanuck taking over as head of production, a job he held for the next twenty-one years.

Zanuck's approach differed from Thalberg's. Thalberg was given the stars by Louis B. Mayer and found the material to suit them. Zanuck started out at Twentieth Century-Fox with very few stars. He had only Shirley Temple, who soon grew up, and Will Rogers, who died shortly after the merger. Zanuck was not particularly interested in stars, and while the machinery was in place at Fox to develop stars, that was not Zanuck's top priority. Because he thought of himself as a writer, he paid more attention to the story than the stars. People who worked with Thalberg talk of his ability to work out problems with a scene, but Zanuck's concern was the movement of the story. Screenwriter Nunnally Johnson says:

> I always thought Zanuck had a Geiger counter in his head. Darryl was a great editor. He'd read a script and the minute it got dull, or didn't move, or went off the track, tick-tick-tick, he said, "It stopped. Now where did this start?" He'd go

back, two pages, three pages, and then he'd figure where the movement stopped, or the movement went wrong. So when you came in to talk to him, he had exactly where it wasn't moving right.[1]

If the emphasis in the screenwriting style at MGM was on scenes for the stars, which lead to an episodic structure, the screenwriting style at Twentieth Century-Fox under Darryl Zanuck was on the narrative line, the "movement," as Johnson describes it. This gives the Fox films a smooth flow that the MGM films do not have. At its best, this style gives the films a narrative movement no other studio can match.

The negative side of the Fox style is that it could often not be as powerful and emotional as the MGM style, or as insistent and driving as the Warners style. Zanuck would occasionally cut the more interesting moments from the scripts (and the films, which would infuriate the directors) in an attempt to keep the story moving. Like Ince before him, Zanuck would cut away the fat to the narrative bone, leaving out the emotional moments Thalberg made the heart of the film. The scenes in the Fox scripts did not tend to glorify the stars but to move the story forward.

Under Zanuck, scripts were developed for their story properties, not shaped around the stars, so the stars at Fox incline not to have as well-defined images as those at MGM and Warners. On the other hand, once Zanuck found a story that was particularly useful for a star, he tended to stick with it. There is a sameness about the films of Alice Faye and Betty Grable that comes in some cases from their being remakes of earlier films.[2]

Zanuck differed from Thalberg in other ways. Zanuck did not have teams of writers working on the same script at the same time. While there were often several writers credited on the final film, they worked serially rather than simultaneously. Zanuck did not keep writers and others waiting to the degree that Thalberg did, but he did tend to begin story conferences at about eleven at night. Present would be Zanuck, the writer, the producer, a secretary to take notes of the conference, and often one or two hangers-on. Nunnally Johnson once asked Zanuck why he had one particular person at the conferences, and Zanuck replied, "You notice every now and then I'd say to Al, 'What do you think of that, Al?' And Al would answer. I'm just trying to find out if it was clear to Al. If it's clear to Al, it'll be clear to everybody in the United States."[3] Zanuck would throw out plot suggestions rapidly, and writers who stayed at Fox for a long time came to learn that Zanuck did not expect every one of them to be followed. When Philip Dunne took over as the writer on *Forever Amber*, he read the conference notes from the previous writers' works. He discovered one writer had included a scene in a draft exactly as Zanuck had dictated it in the previous conference. Zanuck's note on the scene in the next conference read, "The scene beginning on page 82 is the worst scene I ever read in my life." Dunne says, "He knew that was the scene he'd dictated, but he didn't want that scene, he wanted the writer to write a scene along those lines."[4]

While Thalberg was personally kind to writers, he was not particularly kind to their work. Zanuck was not as personally charming, but he was ferocious in protecting the script. This was not necessarily a single writer's script, but the script Zanuck had worked out with however many writers it took to get a satisfactory screenplay. Zanuck, like Ince, was insistent on the screenplay being shot as written, and there are in the Fox scripts from time to time notes that are *very* insistent on this point. Also like Ince, Zanuck was very involved in the cutting of the films to insure that the story was told well and clearly, and like the Ince films, there are Zanuck films where, even though the screenplay was worked out in very thorough detail, there are scenes cut from the final film.[5] Zanuck's Fox films have the same narrative flow that Ince's do.

Because Zanuck was so concerned about the storyline, and because of his involvement in the scriptwriting process, Twentieth Century-Fox can be considered, more than any other, the studio of the writer. Zanuck had three writers that he particularly depended upon, the three screenwriting princes of Fox: Lamar Trotti, Philip Dunne, and Nunnally Johnson.

Lamar Trotti

Lamar Trotti was the most versatile of the three major Fox screenwriters. One observer of Trotti's career broke down his output into the following categories: four musicals, nine costume melodramas, six war films, nine comedies, ten social dramas, eleven biographical films, and ten films of "Americana."[6]

Born in Atlanta, Georgia, in 1898, Trotti worked for the *Atlanta Georgian*, where he became one of the youngest city editors in the county. Jason Joy hired him as a publicist for the Motion Picture Producers and Distributors of America in 1925, and when Joy went to Fox in 1932 as part of its story department, he took Trotti with him.

Trotti had an idea for a film about Chicago Mayor Chernak, and Joy sent him to the head of the Fox B-picture unit Sol Wurtzel, who in turn sent him to Dudley Nichols, then just beginning his long and distinguished career as a screenwriter. Nichols liked the idea, as did Wurtzel, who wanted Nichols to write the script. Nichols recalls several years later:

> Very softly, Trotti asked if he could sit in and learn how a screenplay is written. I took him on as a collaborator. It was a fairly good script and it made money, though the direction was faulty. . . . I enjoyed the collaboration— something I had never done before and hardly done since.[7]

The film, *The Man Who Dared*, was the first of six collaborations between Nichols and Trotti, films that included *Judge Priest* and *Steamboat Round the Bend*, both directed by John Ford. In 1939 Trotti wrote two films directed by Ford, *Young Mr. Lincoln* and *Drums Along the Mohawk*. Ford was reluctant to direct the first of the two[8] since there had been two Broadway plays in the last two years on Lincoln's early life, but Zanuck bullied him into it. Trotti's script captures both the awkwardness of the young Lincoln and the hints of greatness in the man, without forcing the latter on the audience, as so many biographical films do. *Drums Along the Mohawk*, set in pre–Revolutionary War New York state, was an adaptation of the Walter Edmunds novel and a rousing look at frontier life.

Trotti was frequently assigned the big pictures, such as the Irving Berlin musical *Alexander's Ragtime Band* or Fox's answer to MGM's *San Francisco*, *In Old Chicago*. It is indicative of the differences in screenwriting styles of the two studios that while the earthquake sequence in the former is the more spectacular sequence, the Chicago fire in the latter is the better scene. The earthquake is a wonderful collection of special effects and cutting, while the fire involves the actions of the major characters in the film and carries the story forward.

Zanuck made Trotti a producer in 1942, and Trotti pushed Zanuck into letting him make *The Ox-Bow Incident* in 1943, an antilynching western Zanuck opposed. It is a strong script, if somewhat schematic in laying out the issues and characters. The film, shot on soundstages rather than on locations, looks artificial and it is to the credit of Trotti's script it remains as powerful as it does.

Trotti also continued to write big pictures for Zanuck, such as *Wilson*, Zanuck's Fourth-of-July-parade version of the life and work of Woodrow Wilson, and *The Razor's Edge*, an adaptation of Somerset Maugham's best-selling novel that Trotti explained this way to Philip Dunne: "Basically it was an anti-heterosexual picture."[9]

Trotti's best picture, and one of his last, was *I'd Climb the Highest Mountain*, an adaptation of a novel about a circuit-riding preacher in his native Georgia at the turn of the century. It is a warm, delightful look at American life of the period. It was perfectly directed by another southerner, Henry King, who directed eight of Trotti's screenplays and who called Trotti "one of the most brilliant writers that it has ever been my pleasure to work with."[10] Trotti died of a heart attack in 1952, a year after the release of the film.

Dudley Nichols, six years after Trotti's death, writes of his onetime collaborator:

> He was a quiet, shy man, but very strong inside, and morally strong. He was imaginative, and full of humor of the right sort, the quiet sort which grins or

chuckles but doesn't laugh loudly. And he had a great affection for children and people, which was perhaps the source of his strength as a writer. Zanuck held him in high esteem.[11]

Philip Dunne

Philip Dunne was the most literate and intelligent of the three Fox princes. One day Zanuck blew up at him in a projection room and said, "You know what your trouble is? You think you're God." Dunne replied, "This from you? I know who God is around here. I'm just one of the Apostles." Dunne says, "It was a great compliment to have Zanuck tell you that you thought you were God. He admired arrogance and I had my share."[12]

Dunne was the son of the great American humorist Finley Peter Dunne, the creator of "Mr. Dooley." After attending Harvard and working on Wall Street, Dunne became a reader for the old Fox studios, then wrote screenplays for MGM and United Artists before signing a contract at Twentieth Century-Fox in 1937. He remained at the studio for twenty-five years.

Zanuck liked historical films (which led the studio to be nicknamed Nineteenth Century-Fox), and since Dunne considered himself an "historian manqué"[13] Zanuck put him on the historical films. When Dunne complained that the other writer on *Suez* had created a fictional love affair between Empress Eugénie and Ferdinand-Marie de Lesseps, Zanuck replied, "Look, it's movies. Forget it. We're not writing history, we're making a movie."[14] Dunne was able to get at least some accurate historical information into the films he wrote.

Dunne was also noted for the literacy of his screenplays, particularly in his adaptations of such varied writers as John O'Hara, Louis Bromfield, John Galsworthy, and John P. Marquand. This literary quality, which led one film historian to describe his screenplays as "relentlessly literate,"[15] made him the perfect choice to adapt Richard Llewellyn's novel of a Welsh coal-mining community *How Green Was My Valley*. Dunne was originally opposed to doing the film at all, since he felt the first screenplay by another writer was "just a bitter [pro-]labor diatribe."[16] Zanuck assigned Dunne to do the screenplay and he wrestled with trying to get the scope of the novel into a manageable length. The novel had the boy Huw grow up and the first draft Dunne wrote followed that story. It was not until Dunne and William Wyler (who was then scheduled to direct) saw the screen test of Roddy McDowell that they decided to tell the story with Huw remaining a boy. Later events in the novel, such as the sister's return to the village, were put in at earlier places in the story.

After service with the Office of War Information during World War II,

Dunne returned to the studio intent on doing more modern and realistic films about current social conditions. Zanuck instead assigned him to adapt *Forever Amber*, a lurid, best-selling novel about the London of Charles II. Dunne and his cowriter cut Amber's husbands from four to one, her children from three to one, and her many lovers to merely four.

Dunne did have an opportunity to write one of the postwar films Zanuck produced about social problems. Dudley Nichols had done a first draft of a screenplay called *Pinky*, an adaptation of a novel about a young black nurse who passes for white in the North, but returns to her hometown in the South. In Nichols's version the question was, as it had been in the novel, whether Pinky would become a radical or not. Dunne suggested that the question should be whether she would live as a black or as a white person. The film was the second highest grossing film of 1949.

In 1951 Dunne wrote *David and Bathsheba*, one of the most literate and intelligent of all the Biblical films. Originally the script was to deal with three areas of David's life, but Dunne and Zanuck decided to focus only on the David and Bathsheba story, since it meant, as Dunne said, "You could tell a story which you could not normally tell because of censorship, but it would be sacrosanct because it was out of the Old Testament."[17] The film, and Dunne's Biblical dialogue, was so convincing that some people in the audience tried to find David's final prayer in the Bible. When they couldn't find it and wrote to Fox, the studio sent them mimeographed copies of the speech Dunne had written.

Dunne frequently worked as a script doctor, fixing scripts other writers had begun. Zanuck sent him scripts for his comments, and Zanuck sent his scripts to other writers:

> I know he sent mine to Lamar Trotti. I used to get Lamar's scripts and I'd call up Lamar, "I've got your script." We'd talk about it. This was very helpful. I think Zanuck thought I was just reading it and making a comment, but actually I'd talk it over with Lamar. I didn't want to suggest anything that might upset his work, that I might not know about. Several times we were able to improve the script. I said, "I'll tell Zanuck I talked to you," and he said, "No, just send it in as your idea, and then I'll allow him to persuade me."[18]

Dunne thought he was called in to doctor scripts because he was a fast writer. He wrote, or rewrote, *Anne of the Indies* in one week when the production was all ready to go and Zanuck decided the script needed revision. Dunne recalls:

> I think Lamar did a lot of this, too. I think Zanuck trusted us. Lamar and I walked into the dining room one day. He had a private dining room. He had

some people from off the lot there. He said, "Now these are my old pros." This was the feeling. It was a nice feeling. We were sort of dependable.[19]

Nunnally Johnson

Nunnally Johnson was the best of the three major screenwriters at Fox. Zanuck described him as "a Rock of Gibraltar."[20]

Johnson was born in Columbus, Georgia, in 1897. In the early twenties he was a humor columnist for various New York newspapers and later in the twenties he sold short stories to two magazines with totally different views of American culture, the *Smart Set* and the *Saturday Evening Post*.

When the depression hit the *Post*, he moved to Hollywood permanently in 1932. He worked briefly for Paramount, then was hired by Zanuck for the new Twentieth Century Pictures in 1933. F. Scott Fitzgerald later told Johnson he should leave Hollywood because it was destroying his talent.[21] Fitzgerald was wrong. Johnson's talents for dramatic storytelling, scene structure, and sympathetic characters were more suited for screenwriting than for short stories, and his scripts are considerably better than his short stories. His was a gift for screenwriting that Zanuck saw and helped develop. It is possible that if Johnson had stayed at Paramount, he might have written more comedies, which were never Zanuck's strong suit, but Johnson was appalled at the way writers were treated during his days at Paramount. He found Zanuck's concern for the importance of the script much more to his liking, so we will just have to make do with the comedies Johnson did write: *Roxie Hart, How to Marry a Millionaire*, and *The World of Henry Orient*, to name a few.

Zanuck started Johnson writing dramas with *The House of Rothschild*, a 1934 film about the banking firm and one of Twentieth Century's early hits, oddly successful given the view most people had of banks in the thirties. After the merger with Fox, Johnson wrote *The Prisoner of Shark Island*, the first of three of his scripts directed by John Ford.

In 1939 Johnson wrote one of the most entertaining westerns of the period, *Jesse James*, a glamorized, full-bodied view of the Missouri outlaw. In *Jesse James*, Johnson managed to balance rousing action, human drama, a large cast of wonderful characters, and unself-conscious populism.

Johnson followed *Jesse James* the next year with his adaptation of John Steinbeck's *The Grapes of Wrath*. Working with more serious material than he had dealt with before, Johnson managed to cut down the five-hundred-plus pages of the novel into a script that Steinbeck told him was "more dramatic in fewer words than my book."[22] Johnson eliminated elements like Steinbeck's biological imagery, which would not fit in a narrative film of the kind Zanuck wanted to make, and used material from the more editorial interchapters that he adapted as scenes for the major characters. Johnson also changed the dramatic shape of the story in the second half, making it rise from the low point of the first California camp the Joads stay in until the final scene. That final scene, which finds the Joads on the road looking for work, Johnson adapted from two different scenes in the novel. Zanuck later claimed to have written that scene,[23] but the Fox story files prove that the scene is in Johnson's scripts from the first draft on.[24]

After a brief period away from Fox in the midforties, Johnson returned to write and produce such films as *The Gunfighter*, *The Desert Fox*, *How to Marry a Millionaire*, *The Man in the Gray Flannel Suit*, and *The Three Faces of Eve*.

At the memorial service after Johnson died in 1977, fellow screenwriter George Seaton said:

> In 1971, because of illness, the curtain fell on Nunnally's activity as a filmmaker. He said it was just as well because he couldn't understand the new wave. Scripts without construction, without believable characters, without form or substance and dialogue filled with copulative verbs and excremental nouns made him feel that he was "just a saddle maker in the age of Detroit." If only we had more saddle makers like Johnson.[25]

Other Writers at Fox

Because of Zanuck's interest in strong scripts, other major writers worked for him at Fox at some point in their careers. Sonya Levien, whose career extended back into silent films, worked with Lamar Trotti on *In Old Chicago* and *Drums Along the Mohawk* and cowrote the 1945 musical version of *State Fair* with Oscar Hammerstein II. Ben Hecht worked on the screenplay for *Tales of Manhattan* and did the final version of the swashbuckler *The Black Swan* (because Zanuck considered that Hecht "is great on pirate stories and knows more about piracy than anybody on earth").[26] Dudley Nichols wrote *Man Hunt*, *Swamp Water*, and the first drafts of *Pinky*. Jules Furthman even returned to the studio he had worked at in the silent days and wrote one of Fox's best films noirs of the forties, *Nightmare Alley*.

12

Warner Brothers

According to the famous quote, Jack Warner, the head of the Warner Brothers studios, thought that writers were "schmucks with Underwoods."[1] Fortunately Jack Warner was smart enough to employ as heads of production two men who thought a little more highly of writers. The first was Darryl Zanuck, and he was replaced by Hal Wallis.

Zanuck at Warner Brothers

Jack Warner suggests in his entertaining if not completely creditable memoirs that one of the reasons they hired Zanuck as a writer for Rin Tin Tin in 1923 was that he was so good at acting Rinty's part.[2] Zanuck was so fast at coming up with stories, for humans as well as dogs, that he soon was writing under three pen names in addition to his own: Melville Crossman, Mark Canfield, and Gregory Rogers. Zanuck assigned the names arbitrarily to stories, but for some reason Crossman's stories seemed to be the most successful. MGM wanted to hire Crossman away from Warners, but by then Zanuck had become a "supervisor."[3]

Zanuck was promoted to head of production for the studio at the time of production of *The Jazz Singer*, which he supervised. Under Zanuck's command, Warners began a series of historical films with *Disraeli* in 1929 and the Busby Berkeley musicals with *Forty-Second Street* in 1933. Zanuck's most distinctive contributions to the early Warners sound films, however, were in the stories that he described as "torn from today's headlines."

The first of these was the 1930 film *Little Caesar*, based on a novel by W. R. Burnett. The first draft of the screenplay was by Robert N. Lee, and the final draft by Francis E. Faragoh, a former drama editor for *Pearson's Magazine* and playwright. The differences between the two drafts show Zanuck's influence, as the story becomes more linear and more the step-by-step rise of Rico.[4]

Zanuck followed that film with another classic gangster film, *Public Enemy*. The basis for this film was a three-hundred-page unpublished novel called "Beer and Blood" by two Chicago writers, John Bright and Kubec Glasmon. Zanuck noted in his first story conference that the novel contained five stories and the film could only tell one.[5] The screenwriter assigned to the film was Harvey Thew, and the emphasis was shifted to the story of Tom Powers, with much of the social observation of the original novel put in the background, a result of Zanuck's desire to tell a story.

The third major social-comment film Zanuck did at the time was the 1932 release *I Am a Fugitive from a Chain Gang*. The film was a slightly fictionalized account of the life of Robert Elliot Burns. Burns's story appeared in newspapers in 1929 when his wife turned him in as an escaped prisoner and in 1930 when he escaped again. The storyline of the film followed the story Burns sold to Warners in February 1932 for $12,500, which was developed in outlines and treatments in April 1932. The first temporary script was completed in May, followed by two more drafts in July, with each draft reviewed by Zanuck.[6]

The direction of the film was assigned to Mervyn LeRoy, who had directed *Little Caesar*. In 1974 LeRoy wrote his memoirs, and in the fashion of directorial memoirs, he lays claim to many things in the film. For example, he writes:

> I tried to show brutality without being brutal. There was a scene of [Paul] Muni being flogged by sadistic guards. Instead of dwelling on the actual beating, I focused my cameras on the shocked and horrified faces of the other prisoners who were witnessing the beating, and on the shadows of the beating playing on the wall. I am convinced that this made a more terrifying sequence than actually showing a whip landing on flesh.[7]

It *is* more terrifying, which is why Zanuck and the writers included it in the script before LeRoy was ever assigned to the film.[8]

LeRoy also claims the authorship of the visual ending of the film. As scripted, the escaped convict is asked by the girl, "How do you live?" and he replies, "I steal." In the film he pulls away from the girl into the darkness and the line is heard coming from the dark. LeRoy says the scene was being rehearsed in the light when a fuse on one of the lights blew. The electrician promised it would not happen again, but LeRoy experimented with the effect and decided a slow fade would be better.[9] The character's fading into darkness at the end of the scene is in the script.[10] As the script and story files of the studios are opened to scholars, directors are going to have to show a little more restraint than they have in the past in interviews and memoirs. They may even have to remember the truth.

Hal B. Wallis

While Zanuck was writing screenplays for Rin Tin Tin, Hal Wallis was writing press releases about the dog star. Wallis later became a producer, eventually moving up to head of production when Zanuck left Warners in 1933.

Under Zanuck the Warners' films had been tough and short (*I Am a Fugitive from a Chain Gang* runs seventy-six minutes, and *Public Enemy* runs only seventy-four minutes). Zanuck's output tends to have the more linear approach of his later Fox films. Wallis began to change the look and the pace of the Warners' films, at least partly because Warners had begun to exhaust the genres the studio had created. The change also came from a difference in Wallis's taste. Both at Warners and later as an independent producer at Paramount and Universal, he was interested in more literate prestige pictures. Under Wallis Warners continued to turn out some of the kinds of pictures it had under Zanuck (*The Roaring Twenties* [1939] is a summing up of the Warner gangster films of the thirties, and *Confessions of a Nazi Spy* [1939] certainly fits into the stories-torn-from-today's-headlines style) but with Wallis there was a renewal of interest in the historical films Zanuck had started with *Disraeli*.

John Huston was one of the writers on such a film, *Juarez* (1939), and he recalls the complexity of the writing collaboration:

> [Aeneas] MacKenzie, [Wolfgang] Reinhardt and I worked in complete harmony. Wolfgang had a scholar's knowledge of Europe during the period of Napoleon III and the Hapsburgs; I was a Jeffersonian Democrat espousing ideals similar to those of Benito Juarez; and MacKenzie believed in the monarchical system—perhaps even to the point of defending the Divine Right of Kings. Thus the actual writing, when MacKenzie and I go to it, was by way of being dialectic. We worked on the screenplay for almost a year. Warner Brothers always kept a day-by-day account of script progress and how their writers were doing, but, thanks to Henry Blanke [the producer of the film], we were spared the customary surveillance. Nothing was shown to the front office until the last line had been written. After we turned it in, I got a call from Hal Wallis, followed by a note saying it was the best script he had ever read.[11]

Huston was disappointed in the film when rewrites had to be made to accommodate Paul Muni, who insisted that as Juarez he had to have more lines and refused to do the film unless the script was rewritten. Huston recalled, "The studio had lent itself to the creation of his ponderous prestige; now it had to pay the consequences."[12] The consequences in this case were that many scenes of Muni were shot that were not used in the final film.

Wallis, perhaps more than Zanuck, was concerned about more aspects of the film than just the story line. It is difficult to imagine Zanuck caving in on the demands of a star for a change in a script, but Wallis was in the business of building up stars at Warner Brothers, and the stories were tailored to the stars. Warners was second only to MGM in its development and protection of stars, although the Warners stars, and therefore the stories selected for them, tended to be rougher and less genteel than those Thalberg and his producers developed at MGM.

Robert Lord, a writer-producer at Warners in the thirties and forties, has been quoted as saying that the first rule for screenwriters at Warners was, "Don't bore the audience, anything goes as long as it's entertaining and interesting."[13] While the MGM films of the period can be defined as big scenes for big stars, and the Fox films as smooth-flowing stories, the Warners films might be described as examples of "piling on." There always seem to be more characters than needed just to tell the story, more relationships between the characters, and more plot complications.

Casey Robinson

The master of the Warner Brothers style of screenwriting, and the best of all the Warners writers, was Casey Robinson. A man he met while working on the New York World later got him a job in the movies.[14] Robinson came to Hollywood in 1927, and spent his first screenwriting years writing B pictures for Paramount. When Harry Joe Brown, a director who had filmed one of Robinson's previous scripts, went to Warners as a producer, Robinson followed him.

Robinson's first big success for Warners also was the first big success for its star. The film was Captain Blood (1935) and the star was Errol Flynn, and Robinson's script set the tone for the Warners swashbucklers and for Flynn's screen personality. Two years later Robinson wrote the first of six films he did for Bette Davis, It's Love I'm After, a bright, bitchy comedy. Robinson said later that it helped to know which actors he was writing the screenplay for: "You see the actor's voice—yes, you actually see it as well as hear it, just as you hear [Richard] Burton, you hear Bogart as I used to hear him, and Bette Davis, how I heard her voice!"[15]

In 1939 he wrote Dark Victory for Davis. It was based on an unsuccessful play Tallulah Bankhead had performed on Broadway. Robinson recalls:

I read the play in a hot bath after a walk in the bitter cold winter weather [in New York] and suddenly the whole concept and approach to the screenplay came to me. It happened just at a time when Bette Davis had been turned over to me at the studio and I knew Dark Victory was for her.

It was a very peculiar time at Warner Brothers when practically all the films being made were very masculine, here was a girl who was being treated like a man on the screen. . . . It was an altogether wonderful experience because for the first time I was able to present Miss Davis in a truly feminine role which launched her into that orbit of success at the box office which her talent so richly deserved.[16]

In 1941 Warners released Robinson's *King's Row*, an astonishing job of adaptation. Robinson describes the problems, calling the film

one of the most satisfactory films on which I worked but which was a nightmare in the beginning. I was given this volume as a going-away present when I left for an eight week vacation in the Philippines and the Orient, and as I began to read it en route, I realized it was a book of high literary standard at the same time the material itself was thoroughly frightening.

We were in the middle of the censorship era and here was a book with 11 or 12 different kinds of insanity, miscegenation, incest (both, of course, verboten) and the author had seen fit with his view of the world that any character he portrayed with qualities of goodness came to a bad end, and vice versa.

I finished the book on shipboard. . . . I then thought it [adapting it into a film] was an impossible task.

I took the book and threw it as far as I could into the Sulu Sea, saying to my companion, "Nobody else will read this book as far as I am concerned," but just as it hit the water, the whole solution of transferring it to the screen came to me. And so there I was for six weeks, stuck out in the Orient with no copy of the book and dying to get my hands on it.[17]

Robinson's solution was primarily to focus on the young idealistic doctor who fought the old corrupt establishment. He also softened or eliminated many of those elements mentioned, but at the same time managed to keep the tone of Henry Bellamann's novel, and the result is one of the darkest visions of American small towns to be presented in American films of that period, only matched, if at all, by *The Magnificent Ambersons*.

Robinson was also helpful in dealing with the censor over the problems of adapting *King's Row*. Before any script of the novel was even sent to the Breen Office, Joseph Breen wrote to Warner Brothers saying the picture could not be made and if it was made, "It is likely to bring down the industry as a whole."[18] Jack Warner, David Lewis (the producer of the film), Hal Wallis, and Robinson went to see Breen personally. Wallis recalls, "Casey carried the brunt of the argument and I could see Joe Breen was impressed."[19] Breen agreed to consider the possibility and it took four drafts of the script by Robinson to win him over.

Robinson's skills at adapting potentially censurable material were challenged the following year when he wrote the Bette Davis vehicle *Now, Voyager.* Robinson managed to make the love affair romantically compelling while avoiding the restrictions of the Hays Office. Robinson's skill at romantic scenes is also apparent in the Paris flashbacks in *Casablanca*. The writing of that film is typical of how the entire screenwriting process at Warner Brothers worked.

Casablanca

In 1941 Hal Wallis had his contract revised so he would only have to supervise his own productions, not the entire production output of the studio. For his second film under the new contract, he sent a note to the Warners story department about the unproduced play they had covered entitled *Everybody Comes to Rick's*. The note said, "I want it."[20]

The play was written by Murray Burnett and Joan Alison. It was inspired by a small café in a resort town in France Burnett had visited in the summer of 1938.[21] He and Alison started writing the play in the summer of 1940, basing the plot on the fictional creation of "letters of transit" and "exit visas." No one, in New York or Hollywood, ever questioned the reality of the letters and visas, although one writer Wallis approached objected to the melodrama of their use.[22] The legend is the play was terrible, but both Robert Sherwood and Ben Hecht told the producers who had optioned the play it did not need a major rewrite. The writers' agent suggested that the writers sell the play directly to the movies, since that is "where the real money is."[23] The play was sold to Warners for twenty thousand dollars, the highest price until then for an unproduced play.[24]

Jerry Wald, a writer-turned-producer at the studio, suggested the play could make a romantic melodrama in the mold of *Algiers*, a 1938 hit.[25] What appealed to Wallis was the contrast between the melodramatic plot and the bright dialogue, some of which was obviously in the original. To carry through on that concept, Wallis hired the twin brothers Philip G. and Julius J. Epstein to write the script.

The Epsteins had been in Hollywood since the midthirties, when Julius had been writing screenplays in collaboration with Jerry Wald.[26] With *No Time for Comedy* in 1940 and *The Man Who Came to Dinner* in 1941, the Epsteins developed the reputation for witty dialogue that made Wallis choose them for *Casablanca*.

The Epsteins were also gifted storytellers in person, which helped Wallis get over a particularly difficult problem in adapting the play. In the play the leading woman is Lois Meredith, an American woman, and from the beginning there were problems foreseen with the censors about having an American woman sleep with an old lover to get the letters of transit for her current lover. (This problem was one reason the play was not produced in New York, since it was felt such a character would not be sympathetic to the audience.) Wallis and the writers married the character to Laszlo and made the romance with Rick take place when she did not know Laszlo was alive. Wallis also thought that if the woman was European, American audiences might be more willing to accept her behavior. The obvious choice then for the part was Ingrid Bergman, and early in the writing of the script, Wallis sent the Epsteins over to tell David O. Selznick, who had Bergman under contract, the story.

There are at least three versions of the meeting with Selznick. In the legendary version, the Epsteins told him a wonderful tale, got Bergman, then could not remember what they had told him. In the second version, they were ushered into Selznick's office and told him that the story was a romantic melodrama with a "sinister atmosphere. Dark lighting and a lot of smoke." On the basis of that alone, Selznick gave them Bergman.[27] The most accurate version is probably that they told him the story of the play, finishing up with the line quoted above.[28] Whichever version is closest to the truth, the value of screenwriters as storytellers was demonstrated.

The Epsteins, however, had already agreed to go to Washington, D.C., to work on the *Why We Fight* propaganda films series. They were replaced by Howard Koch, who came to Warner Brothers after writing for Orson Welles's radio program *The Mercury Theatre of the Air.* For that series Koch had written "The War of the Worlds," the program that scared the East Coast into thinking Martians had landed. The Epsteins did some work on the script while in Washington[29] and they left Koch the beginnings of a script (Wallis felt that by mid-May 1942 they had forty good pages, or enough to start)[30] and some of their patented crisp dialogue. The exchange between Rick and Renault about the reason Rick came to Casablanca ("For the waters." "Waters? What waters? We're in the desert." "I was misinformed.") was written by the Epsteins.[31]

It fell to Koch to deal with Humphrey Bogart. Bogart was not happy with the character of Rick. He felt Rick was too much of a weakling crying over a lost love, and he wanted the dialogue for Rick improved. It was improved. In the original screenplay, Rick's line is "Of all the cafés in all the towns in the world, she walks into my café." As a result of Bogart's complaining, the line was changed to the now-classic "Of all the gin joints. . . ."[32]

Some of the lines from the play did not need the Epstein or Koch touches. The first-act curtain line is Rick saying to Sam, "Then play it," referring to the song that had been in the play from the beginning, "As Time Goes By."[33]

Koch wanted the flashback in the middle of the film to be about Rick's fighting the fascists, but Wallis wanted the flashback to be about the romance, and he had Robinson write it, along with some suggestions from another screenwriter, Albert Maltz.[34]

With all the writers working on the script, there was still the problem of the ending. In the play Rick helps Lois and Laszlo get away, then turns himself in. One suggested ending was that Strasser should kill Laszlo, then Rick and

Ilsa could be together, but Wallis turned that down.[35] The debate at the studio was whether Rick would have to pay for breaking the law, as was conventional in films at the time, and a requirement of the Production Code. The Epsteins meanwhile had returned to work on the script, and they suggested the ending as it now stands in the film. Other writers were working on other endings, but the Epsteins' was shot first, and everybody seemed satisfied with it at the time.[36]

And ever since.

13

Paramount

Paramount never had a single figure who dominated the screenwriting process for the length of time Thalberg, Zanuck, and Wallis did at their studios. The closest Paramount came to a definable screenwriting style was with the witty comedies of the thirties and forties, but that was also the period when Cecil B. De Mille was producing and directing films not particularly noted for their wit. There were, however, studio executives, producers, and writers who contributed to the screenwriting process at Paramount.

After his time as a writer and story editor for Edwin S. Porter, B. P. Schulberg worked for Famous Players (a forerunner of Paramount), United Artists, and Louis B. Mayer. Schulberg rejoined Paramount in 1925 as the general manager of the Hollywood studios, a job he held until being forced out of the company in 1932.[1] It was during his reign at Paramount that the Marx Brothers were brought to the movies, as was Herman J. Mankiewicz.

Herman J. Mankiewicz and the Marx Brothers

Alexander Woollcott called Mankiewicz "the funniest man in New York," and Robert Sherwood said he was "the truest wit of all."[2] He contributed to both the Algonquin Round Table and the first issues of the *New Yorker,* and he wrote plays as well as sketches for Broadway reviews. In 1925 he came west to write for MGM, and the following year he returned to Hollywood, this time for Paramount. Mankiewicz became noted as a titler of silent films, writing such gems as "Paris, where half the women are working women . . . and half the women are working men."[3] Schulberg was the first of a long line of producers and studio executives who were both impressed and aggravated by Mankiewicz. While the other writers on the Paramount lot worked in the writers' building, Schulberg had Mankiewicz put into an office near him in the administration building.[4] Mankiewicz was often called upon by Schulberg to advise on the recutting of films after their previews.

In 1929 Paramount signed the Marx Brothers to make films for the studio. The first two, *The Cocoanuts* and *Animal Crackers,* were filmed plays the brothers had appeared in on Broadway and both were shot in the Paramount studios on Long Island. By 1931 the brothers moved to Hollywood, and the producer they were assigned at Paramount was Herman J. Mankiewicz.

There were already five writers hired to write *Monkey Business* when Mankiewicz was assigned to it. Will Johnstone, a cartoonist for the *New York Evening World*, had started writing material for the Marx Brothers for the 1923 review *I'll Say She Is*. While the Marx Brothers were doing *Animal Crackers*, they were hired to do a radio program, and Johnstone was hired to write it, since he had never written for radio. At this time Groucho met S. J. Perelman, who was just beginning his career as a cartoonist, and since he had never written a radio show either, he was hired to collaborate with Johnstone. Except that the idea they came up with, the brothers as stowaways on an ocean liner, seemed to the brothers too good to waste on a radio show, and since they owed Paramount a third film. . . . Meanwhile Nat Perrin, a young law student, had stolen some stationery from a large agency and written a letter to the brothers praising a sketch Perrin had written that turned out to have a good part in it for Chico. Perrin was hired as a gag writer for Chico, and Groucho decided *he* needed a gag writer as well, so he hired a Chicago newspaper columnist named Arthur Sheekman. This left Harpo without his own gag writer, so a mild-mannered newspaper cartoonist named J. Carver Pusey, who did a cartoon about a boy who did not talk, was hired for Harpo.[5] The writers worked for seven weeks on their own while the brothers were off on a real ocean liner. The writers read the script to the brothers on their return; Groucho announced, "It stinks," and the writers, the brothers, Mankiewicz, and sometimes the director, Norman McLeod, sat around for another five months rewriting.[6]

Mankiewicz supervised, if that is not too grandiose a word for it, one and a half more Marx Brothers films at Paramount. The one was *Horsefeathers*, and the chief writers on it were two songwriter/screenwriters named Harry Ruby and Bert Kalmar. Joe Adamson, who has studied the genesis of the Marx Brothers scripts and the writers who wrote them as closely as anybody, writes:

> Harry Ruby affirms that when you sat down to write a script for these clowns, you went about it like nothing else in the course of human events. To prepare material for comedians he alternately describes as "iconoclastic" and "*meshuggeneh*," one, he insists, finds oneself going through mental contortions unrecognizable even to schizophrenics. The results of Kalmar and Ruby's efforts in this direction (*Horsefeathers* and *Duck Soup*) are without a doubt the weirdest things even the Marx Brothers ever tried to do—even weirder when you hold them up next to Kalmar and Ruby's efforts in other directions: their Wheeler and Woolsey or their Clark and McCullough scripts, where all the cute and careful contriving is right there where it should be. *Horsefeathers* and *Duck Soup* almost look like parodies of everything else Kalmar and Ruby wrote.[7]

The half film that Mankiewicz supervised was *Duck Soup*. He began the production of it, supervised some of the writing, and then was removed by the studio, which he subsequently left. More will be heard of Mankiewicz later. He had, however, left his mark on the Marx Brothers films. Their first two films, *The Cocoanuts* and *Animal Crackers* were filmed stage plays, but with the three films he had worked on, the Marx Brothers film style had been set. While producers at other studios, like Thalberg, Zanuck, and Wallis, were working out storylines, Mankiewicz was deliberating avoiding plots. He once said, "If Groucho and Chico stand against a wall for an hour and forty minutes cracking jokes, that's good enough for me."[8] What he and the writers brought out was the anarchic spirit of the brothers, which they did by finding the simplest structures necessary for the collection of gags. When the Marx Brothers left Paramount after *Duck Soup*, and went to Thalberg and MGM, the energy and the wit became, as would be expected with Thalberg, tamer and more refined. The Marx Brothers were contained in scenes, some of them great, to be sure, but ultimately, in Joe Adamson's phrase, joy became laughter.

Cecil B. De Mille and Jeanie Macpherson

Cecil B. De Mille's films were not as funny as Herman Mankiewicz's. At least not intentionally. De Mille did have some success in the early twenties with a series of semisophisticated comedies, many of them starring Gloria Swanson, but he was noted more as a director of spectacular films.

Given De Mille's interest in melodrama and spectacle, two staples of the silent film, it is not surprising that he continued using screenwriters in the thirties and forties who had begun their careers in silent films, such as C. Gardner Sullivan and Waldemar Young. Young, yet another former newspaperman, had begun writing for films in 1917. In the early thirties he wrote four films for De Mille.[9]

The writer who stayed longest with De Mille, from 1913 until her death in 1946, was Jeanie Macpherson. De Mille recalls in his autobiography that when he met her she "was then an actress, a lovely, petite girl, sensitively feminine, but with the high spirits of one descended from a clan whose heart could see the noble Scottish title, the Macpherson."[10] De Mille thought she would work better as a screenwriter, so he dictated four short scripts to her, then asked her to come up with a fifth. She did, but De Mille did not like it, so she kept trying until he did.[11]

In 1922 Macpherson wrote *Manslaughter* for De Mille, and as part of her research, she had herself arrested and spent three days in the Detroit jail.[12] She later told friends she had tried to escape, but was caught.[13] She wrote De

Mille's 1923 version of *The Ten Commandments*. De Mille's original idea was to cut between the modern and ancient stories, as Griffith had done with *Intolerance*, but Macpherson found this approach "bumpy. It started and stopped, ran and limped."[14] It was Macpherson's suggestion, which De Mille followed, to tell the Exodus story first, then the modern story.[15] Macpherson also contributed without credit to *The Crusades*.[16]

The screenwriting style of the De Mille films is just as suited to his star-director personality as the style of the Marx Brothers films is suited to their star-actor personalities. There is the emphasis on the spectacular elements such as the destruction of the temple in *Samson and Delilah* (1949) and the train wreck in *The Greatest Show on Earth* (1952). The writing in the De Mille films, no matter who did it, tends to be rather pompous and self-important. The writing is often surprisingly clumsy, which most likely comes from De Mille's use of so many writers on noncomedic material. It is the kind of clumsiness seen in the MGM films as well. Occasionally there is a crude energy, as in the script for *Union Pacific*, but mostly the writing is simply melodramatic.

William LeBaron

After B. P. Schulberg left as head of the studio, the position of general manager was filled by a number of people. The dominant figure at Paramount from 1935 until he left the studio in 1941 was William LeBaron.

LeBaron was an experienced writer. While still in college LeBaron collaborated on four musical plays, one of which ran for several months on Broadway.[17] LeBaron was the managing editor of *Colliers Magazine* and his sense of story selection was such that his publisher, William Randolph Hearst, asked LeBaron to take over as general manager for Hearst's Cosmopolitan Productions in 1919.[18] LeBaron was with Famous Players-Lasky from 1924 to 1927, then was head of RKO during its first two years. He was a producer at Paramount before taking over as head of production.

It is not surprising that William LeBaron ended up as head of production at Paramount in the thirties. He appears to have had a particular affection for comedians. It was LeBaron who gave W. C. Fields his first substantial film role in the 1924 Cosmopolitan film *Janice Meredith*, and LeBaron's name keeps popping up as a producer throughout Fields's film career. LeBaron produced *The Old-Fashioned Way* and *It's a Gift*, both for Paramount, then continued producing Fields films while head of production.

LeBaron was also the producer of two of the early Mae West films, *She Done Him Wrong* and *I'm No Angel*, which she wrote herself. Under LeBaron's reign at Paramount, the *Big Broadcast* films were produced, including *The Big Broadcast of 1938*, which introduced Bob Hope to the screen. It was also during LeBaron's tenure that the Hope-Crosby *Road* films were begun in 1940 with *Road to Singapore*. LeBaron also supervised the Jack Benny films done at Paramount in the later thirties.

William LeBaron was not just sympathetic to performers, but to writers as well. It was LeBaron who finally allowed a major screenwriter at a major studio to direct his own script. The writer was Preston Sturges.

Preston Sturges, the Screenwriter

Preston Sturges's father was a traveling salesman. His stepfather was a successful stockbroker. His mother was a companion to Isadora Duncan. No wonder Preston Sturges became a screenwriter.

Sturges was a playwright first, writing a 1929 Broadway hit, *Strictly Dishonorable*. He began writing for the screen in 1929 at Paramount's New York studios. Although he received credit only for the dialogue, his complete scripts were used for the films, *The Big Pond* (1929) and *Fast and Loose* (1930).[19] *Strictly Dishonorable* was filmed by Universal in 1931, and on the success of the film, Sturges went to Hollywood to write for that studio in 1932.

Sturges wrote a screenplay on speculation and sold it to producer Jesse Lasky, who made the film for Fox in 1933. *The Power and the Glory* told the story of a railroad tycoon who, in spite of all he has, commits suicide. The story was told in a series of flashbacks by the hero's best friend Henry and Henry's wife, but the flashbacks are not presented in chronological order. Not only was the structure of the film revolutionary, so was Sturges's deal with Lasky. The script would be shot as written, with any changes to be made only by Sturges, and instead of being paid a flat fee, Sturges would get a percentage of the gross. Such a deal scandalized the industry, and produced editorials and letters in the trade papers either acclaiming the deal or denouncing it. It is hard to tell whether studio executives were more upset over the percentage arrangement or the idea that the script should be shot as written.[20] While the picture garnered excellent reviews and did good business in New York, it was not successful in the rest of the country, and Sturges made nothing on his percentage.

In 1936 Sturges returned to Paramount, and his first assignment was a typical Paramount film, a vehicle for George Burns and Gracie Allen. He wrote material similar to their radio routines and he jokingly told people that if he had to, he could always get a job writing for radio.[21] Sturges was also briefly assigned to a De Mille picture, *The Buccaneer*, but lasted only until De Mille realized Sturges was turning Napoleon into a comedian.[22]

Sturges's best script from the late thirties was *Easy Living*, a screwball comedy about a girl and a mink coat thrown out of a window that lands on her. She tries to give the coat back, which turns out not to be that easy. Sturges surrounded the heroine, played by Jean Arthur, with a gallery of funny supporting characters, a hallmark of Sturges's later scripts. After several more conventional scripts, including two that featured Bob Hope, Sturges returned from gag comedy to comedy of character and situation.

The Great McGinty began as a Sturges screenplay in 1933 under the title *The Vagrant*. He revised and retitled it over the years, emphasizing the comedy rather than the drama in the story of a dishonest politician who rises to the governorship and turns honest, only to be destroyed because of it. The final rewrite, which was the shooting script, was dictated in two days and two nights.[23] Sturges also persuaded LeBaron to let him direct the film. The result was a smash hit in 1940, won Sturges his first Academy Award, and started the landslide of writers turning director.

In the early forties, Sturges followed *The Great McGinty* with hit after hit, and in himself he had found the director best suited to bringing out the comic richness and energy of his own screenplays. Sturges had always had an idea for casting, although as the writer on the film his advice was seldom taken. Now he was able to build a stock company of actors and he could write directly for them, knowing what they would sound like and that they could deliver his kind of dialogue. He knew as director he could set the proper if frenzied pace his scripts required. There is a perfect match between screenwriter and director in *The Lady Eve*, *Sullivan's Travels*, *The Palm Beach Story*, *The Miracle of Morgan's Creek*, and *Hail the Conquering Hero*. As will be seen from the films Sturges did after he left Paramount there was also a match between screenwriter-director and studio.

Paramount after LeBaron

William LeBaron's replacement at Paramount, when he left in 1941 to go to Fox, was songwriter-producer B. G. "Buddy" DeSylva. The humorist H. Allen Smith, who spent six months trying to be a screenwriter at Paramount in the forties, called DeSylva "the best audience on earth,"[24] because he laughed so easily at jokes and scripts, but Smith admitted that other screenwriters found it difficult to work with DeSylva because he would laugh all the way through the story, then tell the writers, "It stinks."[25]

DeSylva was supportive of his writers. Billy Wilder and Charles Brackett wanted to do *The Lost Weekend*, but DeSylva's boss, Y. Frank Freeman, thought the book was terrible. While Freeman was out of town, DeSylva bought the book because, as he told the head of his story department, William

Dozier, the fact that Wilder and Brackett liked it was good enough for him.[26] DeSylva would have been overruled by Freeman except that Freeman was overruled by *his* boss, the president of the entire company, Barney Balaban.

DeSylva left the company in 1944 because of ill health and was replaced by Henry Ginsberg. Under DeSylva and Ginsberg Paramount developed in the forties a system of executive producers not unlike that at MGM, and screenwriters found themselves dealing more and more directly with the individual producers.

14
Columbia

While the major studios dominated Hollywood in the thirties and forties, there were many smaller studios. Some only lasted a few years. Some lasted longer. Only one became a major studio, and that was Columbia. Perhaps the most important reason Columbia succeeded where other smaller studios did not was that the studio made a point of hiring *and keeping* good screenwriters.

The first Columbia features were made in the twenties under restrictions similar to those of other Poverty Row studios. The emphasis was on outdoor films, since indoor sets cost money to build. Columbia, like the other minor studios, did not own its own theaters, so it was forced to make better films to compete for theater bookings with the lesser efforts of the major studios. This situation led Harry Cohn, the head of the studio, to an early appreciation of the value of a good script, and it led to certain story-construction elements. In a 1928 interview Cohn talks about his philosophy:

> The producer who makes a good picture can always get distribution for it. . . . This is why we work on our stories a long time before we put them into production.
> We have learned, too, that big circuit bookers look at a reel or two of a picture, and if they are not astounded by the revelations of the early footage, they never finish looking at the picture. The result is that, like newspaper writers, we put a punch in the first reel of our picture that demands immediate respect and attention, and then go on with our story, building, building, building. . . .
> Our scenarios run about two hundred and seventy-five scenes. The big studios use five hundred scenes in their scripts. We never waste time and money filming scenes we don't really need.[1]

All of the above is certainly not to suggest that the relationship between Harry Cohn and the writers at Columbia was sweetness and light. Cohn was suspicious of writers, as indicated in the most famous of all Harry Cohn-and-screenwriters stories. One day Cohn was walking along outside the writers' building, and he realized he heard no sound coming from the open windows. He yelled, "Where are the writers? Why aren't they working? I don't hear a sound. I am paying you big salaries, and you do nothing. You are stealing my money!" The air was filled with the sounds of typewriters. Cohn yelled, "*Liars!*"[2]

Screenwriters at Columbia began (and many ended) their careers by being directly intimidated by Harry Cohn. After the writer had been working at the studio for two weeks, Cohn's office called and asked the writer to send over the work he had been doing. The next day the writer was sent into Harry Cohn's imperial office and heard Cohn tear the script apart. If the writer caved in to Cohn and began to grovel, he was soon fired. If the writer fought back, he stayed. The writer could make additional points with Cohn if he could prove that Cohn had not in fact read the script at all.[3] Cohn was awed by writers and what they did, but he would be damned if he would show it. The curious thing is that the writers who could survive Cohn, and deal with him, often had long and distinguished careers at Columbia. That is true of the two major writers at Columbia in the thirties and forties, Sidney Buchman and Robert Riskin.

Sidney Buchman

Harry Cohn's biographer, Bob Thomas, has called Sidney Buchman "the one film maker Cohn trusted above all others."[4] Unlike Cohn, Buchman had gone to college, and even went on to do graduate work at Oxford. After working as an assistant stage director at the Old Vic, Buchman had two of his plays produced on Broadway in 1930–31. They were not hits, and Buchman went to work as a screenwriter for Paramount. His first work was writing dialogue for a Fu Manchu serial *Daughter of the Dragon*, which naturally led him to writing on De Mille's production *The Sign of the Cross*.

After leaving Paramount in 1934, Buchman's agent got him a job at Columbia, where he remained until 1951. His first important film for Columbia was *Theodora Goes Wild* in 1936, and on it he had to fight against Cohn's ideas on how Columbia films should be structured. The story concerns a small-town girl who returns from the big city with a baby. Buchman deliberately made the beginning of the film rather mundane to increase the impact of her arrival home with the baby. Cohn objected, stating his rule that Columbia pictures should start off fast. Buchman argued and persuaded Cohn to try it Buchman's way. The scene worked, as did the rest of the film.[5] The following year Buchman, without credit, contributed dialogue to another classic Columbia comedy *The Awful Truth*, and in 1938 cowrote with Donald Ogden Stewart an adaptation of Philip Barry's 1928 play *Holiday*.

From his first year at Columbia, Buchman had worked with Columbia's most successful director, Frank Capra. One of Buchman's first assignments was to rewrite some dialogue in *Broadway Bill*. Buchman also helped Capra and Robert Riskin try to whip *Lost Horizon* into shape, since Riskin's script was too long and Capra kept adding to the film while it was in production.[6]

Buchman's most complete and successful collaboration with Capra was with the 1939 "unofficial sequel" to the 1936 film *Mr. Deeds Goes to Town*, *Mr. Smith Goes to Washington*. Robert Riskin, Capra's chief screenwriting collaborator, had left the lot to work for Samuel Goldwyn. Buchman accompanied Capra to Washington, D.C., to research the story. Among other places they visited was the National Press Club, which was perhaps useful for Buchman, since he was one of the few screenwriters of the period who had *not* been a newspaperman. Capra recalls, "For an hour or more Sidney and I soaked up the details of the tradition-rich club and its members. Buchman's ear was cocked for any bits of characteristic dialogue, which he jotted down, while I zeroed in on visual particulars."[7]

Capra also seems to imply in his memoirs that he collaborated with Buchman on the script,[8] but it appears Buchman went off to Palm Springs and wrote at least the first 100 pages of the script completely alone. He sent them to Capra, who was pleased, and then Buchman completed a first draft of 350 pages, which was subsequently cut to 200.[9]

Buchman's script for *Mr. Smith* is one of the richest and most detailed in terms of characterization of any of the scripts for Capra's films. Generally the villains in Capra's films are conventional big shots, usually played by Edward Arnold. Arnold is here as Boss Taylor, but Taylor is given less screen time than Senator Payne, Smith's colleague in the Senate. Payne was a close friend of Smith's father and is idolized by Smith. Buchman shows us how Payne comes to realize how corrupt he has become, which is essential for his final suicide attempt to work dramatically.

Mr. Smith is also marked by Buchman's skill at dialogue for nearly all of the 186 (by Capra's count) speaking parts. His dialogue is so good that Capra can, as he does in a long drunk scene, simply place the camera in front of the two actors and record the scene in one take. It helps to have Jean Arthur and Thomas Mitchell reading the dialogue, too.

Buchman followed *Mr. Smith* in 1941 with *Here Comes Mr. Jordan*, one of the few successful screen fantasies, and the following year wrote the lively and intelligent *Talk of the Town*. In 1945 his script on the life of Chopin, *A Song to Remember*, which he had prepared some years earlier as a potential Capra film, was produced, and the following year he worked without credit on the writing and production of *The Jolson Story*, then wrote and produced the sequel *Jolson Sings Again*. While several other writers worked on the first Jolson film, it was Buchman who found the key by defining the story as "a love affair. The lover is applause. Jolson's wife could handle another woman, but she was no match against the applause."[10]

Robert Riskin

At the age of thirteen Robert Riskin left school and went to work for a textile mill. The men running the mill produced some films for Famous Players-Lasky, and since they knew Riskin wrote stories, they asked his opinion of the films. He told them the films were terrible, and soon he was making films for them, writing, producing, and directing one-reel comedies in Florida. When he turned eighteen, World War I was on and he volunteered for duty with the Navy. [11]

In the twenties Riskin wrote several plays, which were produced by his brother Everett, who later became a producer at Columbia. His play *Bless You, Sister* became the basis for Frank Capra's 1931 film *The Miracle Woman*. Riskin did not write the screenplay, but did meet Capra, and Capra asked Riskin to help on the dialogue for *Platinum Blonde* that same year. Riskin's dialogue is lively, but the film suffers from the miscasting of Jean Harlow as a high-society girl. It would be another year before John Lee Mahin would write *Red Dust* for Harlow.

In 1932 Riskin wrote *American Madness* for Capra and managed to make the manager of a bank sympathetic in the middle of the depression. Riskin's bank manager actually cares about his customers, so much they can be persuaded not to take their money out of the bank when it appears to be failing.

In 1934 Riskin and Capra turned out their Academy Award winning collaboration, *It Happened One Night*, against the advice of nearly everybody, who told them the story was old hat and that bus pictures were dead. What Riskin found in the Samuel Hopkins Adams short story "Night Bus" was the potential for a lively and charming film. The basic structure of the story and the script are similar, but there have been some major changes. The heiress in the film is running away from a marriage forced on her, not because her father won't let her marry the man of her choice, as in the story. The man she meets on the bus, Peter Warne, who had no particular occupation in the story, is a reporter in the film. While the business of Peter putting up the walls of Jericho between them at the motel is in the story, including its use at the end, many of the more memorable scenes from the film are not. All the detail about undressing, including what comes off first, is an invention for the film. While it is mentioned in the story that they hitchhike at one point, the wonderful hitchhiking montage is not even suggested. [12]

It Happened One Night is very much an escapist comedy, but Capra wished to go beyond that, and Riskin obliged with their next film, *Broadway Bill*, and more notably in *Mr. Deeds Goes to Town*. In *Mr. Deeds* a young man from a small town inherits a fortune and then has to deal with the big-city slickers who would like to relieve him of the burden of all that wealth. What Riskin does in the script (and Capra in the direction) is provide a nearly perfect balance between the comedy elements (Deeds playing his tuba) and the social comment (the insanity hearing). Riskin's dialogue is as good as screen dialogue gets, with a rhythm that's as playable and funny as the meaning of the gags. Listen to the flow and pacing of Walter Catlett's speech in the nightclub. Do not read it; listen to it.

Riskin got the unenviable task of adapting James Hilton's *Lost Horizon* for Capra, and helped turn a rather humorless novel into a warm film. In 1938 Riskin adapted the Kaufman and Hart play *You Can't Take It With You* for Capra, shifting it from a celebration of a single wacky family into a populist comedy. Riskin reunited with Capra only once more, for *Meet John Doe*, a 1941 Warner Brothers release.

It is too much to say that Riskin was responsible for Capra's success. Capra was a gifted director, particularly in his work with performers, and that talent is seen in his films before he worked with Riskin. What Riskin did was develop the material, provide the frame, that Capra could use to show his talents on. It is not surprising that the most famous Riskin-Capra story, which was spread by Riskin's brother Everett, but denied by Riskin himself,[13] goes like this:

In the midthirties Riskin began to get fed up with the critics praising the films he wrote for Capra as demonstrations of "the Capra touch." One day Riskin walked into Capra's office, threw a pile of blank pages down on his desk, and said, "All right, let's see you give the Capra touch to that." Capra graciously notes that "Bob was too much of a gentleman to come up with that corny scene."[14]

15

Other Studios, Other Writing

Other major studios made contributions to screenwriting in the studio period as well. Studio story departments also had an influence on the screenwriting process, and B pictures and animation called for special screenwriting talents.

Universal

As at Paramount, there was no single producer or production head at Universal who dominated the screenwriting process. Unlike Paramount, there does not even appear to be a succession of influential producers or executives. Which is perhaps why many first-rate screenwriters passed through Universal on their way to other studios.

Bess Meredyth wrote the serial *The Trey O'Hearts* for Universal in 1914 before going on to a long career at MGM and Fox. Grace Cunard, who starred in serials for Universal, wrote a 1914 three-reeler *The Bride of Mystery* for herself, and did the stories for two of her subsequent films.[1] Before Jeanie Macpherson wrote for De Mille, she wrote for Universal. When the print of a western she wrote was destroyed, she was also given the opportunity to direct the remade version, which brought about her introduction to De Mille, since they were shooting on the same locations.[2]

In the early thirties, Universal had Preston Sturges under contract briefly before he went to Paramount. In 1932 Sturges did a script for *The Invisible Man*, but his was no more successful than the eight previous attempts by others and was not used. In 1934 Sturges adapted Ferenc Molnar's play *The Good Fairy*. The heroine, named Lu in the play, became Luisa Ginglebusher in Sturges's script. Although the film was a hit, it was only later at Paramount that Sturges was to develop his comic vision completely.[3]

There was one screenwriter whose romantic sensibility and ability to handle the fantastic seemed at home at Universal, and that was John Balderston. In 1926, with J. C. Squire, he wrote the successful play *Berkeley Square*, based on Henry James's *The Sense of the Past*, about a young American who trades places with the ghost of his ancestor. The play was filmed in 1933, with Balderston collaborating on the screenplay with Sonya Levien.

In 1927 Balderston rewrote Hamilton Deane's play of Bram Stoker's *Dracula*, which starred Bela Lugosi on Broadway, and which was the basis for the 1931 Universal film. Balderston went to Hollywood in 1931 and worked on the screenplay for *Frankenstein*. Although the final screenplay was credited to Garrett Fort and Francis Faragoh, Balderston appears to have done the adaptation and structural work that under later credit arbitration rules of the Screen Writers Guild would probably have earned him a credit on the film.[4]

In 1932 Balderston wrote *The Mummy*, and in 1935 wrote *The Bride of Frankenstein* with William Hurlburt. There is some dispute as to whether it was Balderston or the director James Whale who made more of an effort to get closer to the tone of Mary Shelley's original story in the sequel than the first film had.[5] Since it was Balderston who created the mentor of Dr. Frankenstein in Dr. Pretorius and through him raised the questions of good and evil that are part of Shelley's story, the case can be made for Balderston.

Balderston went on to write for other studios as well, bringing his romantic style to such films as the 1937 version of *The Prisoner of Zenda*, and he occasionally returned to the horror and suspense genres with such films as *Mad Love* (1935) and *Gaslight* (1944), but it is for his Universal films that he is noted.

RKO

Because of the great variety of investors in RKO, both in the beginning in 1928 and over its life span, there was constant haggling over the finances of the studio. Changes in the job of production head were constant. Ron Haver has written, "This revolving door policy approach to studio authority gave the RKO films their distinctive eclecticism."[6]

Eclecticism is hardly the word for it. The first head of production, from 1929 to 1931, was William LeBaron. To take advantage of sound, the new studio's first big film was an adaptation of Ziegfeld's Broadway hit, *Rio Rita*. Rather than follow the pattern of the other studios in the earliest days of sound, LeBaron did not hire a Broadway-trained writer to adapt the show. Instead he selected Luther Reed, whom he had known at Cosmopolitan, to write *and* direct the film.[7] It was a smash hit, grossing $2.25 million. LeBaron's next big picture for RKO, *Cimarron*, won the 1931 Academy Award not only for Best Picture, but also for Best Screenplay Adaptation, by Howard Estabrook. Unfortunately, it also lost $565,000.[8] LeBaron's other films also did not do well, since they tended to reflect his Broadway-trained taste. Both the stories and the comedy writing of his RKO films seemed to critics and public alike as less than inspired. He did not yet have the writers he would several years later at Paramount.

LeBaron's replacement was a young, energetic producer named David O. Selznick, who took charge of the studio in October 1931. Selznick brought in writers Gene Fowler, Jane Murfin, and Rowland Brown, who wrote one of RKO's more striking films of the period, *What Price Hollywood?* (1932), generally considered as a "first version" of *A Star Is Born*. Selznick also hired Zoe Akins, who wrote the Katharine Hepburn film *Christopher Strong*. Selznick also brought Ben Hecht and Dudley Nichols to RKO for the first time, although neither has credited screenplays under Selznick's reign.

Selznick left in 1933 and was replaced first by Merian Cooper, the producer of *King Kong*, and then from 1934 to 1936 as production head (and from 1936 to 1939 as producer) by Pandro Berman, who had worked under both LeBaron and Selznick. Berman was the producer of most of the Astaire-Rogers musicals at RKO, as well as *Stage Door* and *The Hunchback of Notre Dame*. He was replaced by George J. Schaefer, a former head of sales for Paramount. It was Schaefer who brought in independent production units to RKO, including Orson Welles's Mercury Theatre.

In 1947 the newest in the long line of production heads at RKO was Dore Schary. Schary had been a screenwriter at MGM in the thirties, and had won an Academy Award for Original Story for his 1938 film *Boy's Town*. Schary was a producer for David O. Selznick, and through that arrangement his films were released through RKO. Schary was considered an intellectual in Hollywood, and he wanted to do more intelligent and realistic films. Before his appointment to head of production, he had produced *Till the End of Time*, a strong look at returning World War II veterans.

One of the first productions he supervised at RKO was a combination of the "message" pictures Schary wanted to do, and the type of film that RKO became noted for during Schary's regime, the film noir. Adrian Scott, an RKO producer, read a novel by Richard Brooks (himself later a screenwriter) called *The Brick Foxhole*, about a bigoted Marine who kills a homosexual. Scott wanted to do a film about anti-Semitism, and made the victim Jewish. It was this element that struck Schary, since Schary had gone into army camps and lectured on anti-Semitism during the war. Schary was aware the script had been turned down by the previous administration.[9]

Adrian Scott was working on another picture with the screenwriter he picked for the 1947 film, which was retitled *Crossfire*. The writer, John Paxton, figured the story could be done in the mystery format:

> The clue I got for a way to do the film, at least, made it possible for me to do it was: murders in stories have always been committed for specific gain—for the jade necklace—for the "Maltese Falcon"—or for jealousy. But what was baffling

was here I had an abstract motive which was hate, he kills a perfect stranger, and that the run-of-the-mill cop would do all the routine things, and because he wasn't looking for it, it would be right under his nose, and when he finally realized it the case was solved. It was this pattern . . .

Well, as soon as I discovered the cliché format I wrote the damned thing in five weeks. It was the fastest picture I ever wrote.[10]

Paxton also wrote other films for RKO that can be considered film noir. Prior to *Crossfire*, he wrote *Murder My Sweet*, *Cornered*, and *Crack-up*, all of which are less message pictures and more conventional films noir.

Charles Schnee and Daniel Mainwaring each wrote a classic film noir for RKO in addition to writing several for other studios. Schnee's was *They Live by Night* (1949), an adaptation of Edward Anderson's novel *Thieves Like Us*. The story of a Bonnie-and-Clyde-like couple, it was the first directorial effort of Nicholas Ray, who had worked on the treatment adapting the novel. Schnee also wrote *I Walk Alone* (1947) and *Scene of the Crime* (1949), the first for Paramount, the second for MGM.

Mainwaring's film noir was *Out of the Past* (1947), based on his own novel *Build My Gallows High*. (For this and other films Mainwaring used the pseudonym Geoffrey Holmes.) The plot is extremely complex, particularly in the second half of the film, and the director, Jacques Tourneur, does not make it as clear as he could who knows what at what point in the story. Mainwaring also wrote *The Big Steal* (1949), also for RKO, *The Phenix City Story* (1955), and *Invasion of the Body Snatchers* (1956).

Story Departments

Like early silent companies, the major studios each had a story department that evaluated material. Each studio's story department was headed by a story editor and employed several readers (later called story analysts). In addition to the routine reading of screenplays, novels, and plays submitted to the studio, the story department handled other chores, such as the reading and translation of material not written in English, preparing synopses of material told to studio producers, legal comparisons of scripts and stories to avoid involving the studio in lawsuits, story research, analysis of scripts from other studios, opinions on early drafts of scripts done at the studio, keeping classification files of material submitted to the studio, as well as records of what writers had previously submitted to the studio.[11]

William Dozier, story editor at Paramount in the forties, wrote that 5,067 pieces of material were covered by both the New York and Hollywood story departments of the studio in 1942, while the following year 3,811 pieces were covered.[12] In one collection of papers from the career of a story analyst at

Twentieth Century-Fox,[13] one can see the enormous variety of material submitted to a major studio. In addition to the expected reports on original screenplays, published and galleys of soon-to-be-published novels, stage plays, and short stories, there are a libretto for an opera, an outline and a personal scrapbook on a subject, articles both published and unpublished on historical subjects, a script for a TV musical show, court records of a trial (submitted by one of the lawyers of the case), a factual story privately published, and unproduced radio, television, and stage plays. Dore Schary notes that a story department's preparing of synopses is absolutely essential, since it enables executives and producers to keep up with the amount of story material available, and a good synopsis can be particularly helpful because the storyline is often clearer in summary than in the original work.[14] Sidney Buchman was certainly aware of the value of the story department; it was Columbia's story department that had prepared the synopsis of *The Gentleman from Montana* that Frank Capra read. Buchman turned the story into *Mr. Smith Goes to Washington.*[15]

The story department was of course useful as well for producers who could not take the time to read. George Byron Sage, a story analyst at Fox, once wrote for a producer a synopsis of the Book of Ruth in the *Bible.*

B Pictures

After the introduction of the double bill in the early thirties, minor studios specialized in making B pictures: films with low budgets, short production schedules, and cheap talent. Since the second film on a double bill was rented for only a flat fee, it made no sense to spend much money on them. If they could be brought in at a reasonable price, the fees guaranteed their profitability. Rather than see the minor studios make all the money from B pictures, many major studios developed their own B-picture units.

A typical B-picture unit was Brynie Foy's at Warner Brothers. Foy was not only notorious, but prided himself on his notoriety, for taking A pictures and turning out B-picture versions of them. Nunnally Johnson describes the way he worked:

> He'd go and see *The Good Earth.* The next morning he'd call a writer in and say, "Take a look at this picture, *The Good Earth,* and see if we can't make it in Kansas." Suddenly the next thing you knew, there'd be something, *Sunbonnet Kate,* and it was *The Good Earth,* but it all took place in Kansas. But he was very happy to admit it. He certainly never made any bones about it.[16]

Foy once boasted that he had remade the film *Tiger Shark* five times.[17]

Foy's unit was useful for the studio:

> They'd hire writers like Erskine Caldwell and others with fancy names. Hire them, then fire them after nine months. And with three months to go on their contracts, they'd be sent to me. I'd give them *Mandalay* to work on. They all loved that title, it inspired them.
>
> Then one day Jack [Warner] called and asked, "Do you have a script down there called *Mandalay?*" I said, "I sure do," and he blew up and said, "Well, you've got three hundred thousand dollars in it." I said, "That's right. I sure do. That's for all those fancy writers you fired. They've all done one [version of the script]. I've got five hundred scripts on *Mandalay.* No sense letting them ruin something I might use.[18]

Before he was at RKO Dore Schary agreed to take over MGM's B-picture unit in 1940. He made an effort to upgrade the product (although the unit had been responsible for the Andy Hardy films, which had been very high grossers). Schary felt he could use the low budget program to make more substantial films. He remembers:

> Our apparent success brought in high-salaried writers who volunteered to write scripts in tune with our budgets since they knew I had established a policy of choosing screenwriters who were capable of doing a script from start to finish and guaranteeing them that their work would not be watered down by a squadron of rewrite men.[19]

The first hit from Schary's unit was *Joe Smith, American*, with only one writer, Allen Rivkin, credited. On *Pilot No. 5*, the only writer was David Hertz. On *Journey for Margaret*, there were only two writers, Hertz and William Ludwig, and on the unit's biggest hit, *Lassie Come Home*, Hugo Butler was the only writer. By the time Schary left MGM, many of the B pictures were making more than the A pictures at MGM.

Working for B-picture units or at the studios that made primarily B pictures was not pleasant. George Seaton went from MGM to Republic Pictures. The first words of his Republic producer Phil Goldstone to the writers were, "Fellows, we've got to make this picture economically."[20] They were given three weeks to do the script. The studio called one Wednesday night to tell them the film was canceled, then called them on Friday to say it was back on the schedule, thus avoiding paying the writers for Thanksgiving.[21] Physically, writing at Republic was not pleasurable. Seaton says it was "a cesspool! We had a little room which also served as a dressing room and you had horse smell all over the place, they were doing so many westerns."[22]

Seaton found writing B pictures at Columbia not much better. He was assigned what had been the Three Stooges' dressing room: "It was the crummiest place you've ever seen . . . a lot of graffiti on the walls and the smell of greasepaint."[23] Their producer at Columbia, Sid Rogell, kept after them for two hours, trying to get them to come up with an idea. They asked for some additional time, and Rogell replied, "You worked at Metro, but it's a whole different thing here. We've got to get stories fast." Rogell called in another writer, Fred Niblo, Jr., who came up with an idea in twenty minutes.[24]

Edward Anhalt, later a top screenwriter, wrote B pictures in the forties:

> We would go into the back lot and find some sets that an 'A' picture had finished with. Then we'd write a story to fit some of the standing sets. I can't imagine now how we wrote stories that way, but we did. We'd take four weeks to write a screenplay and then it would take eleven or twelve days to shoot it, and they just kept grinding them out. They cost $35–$40 thousand to make.[25]

Dore Schary also wrote B pictures for Columbia in the early thirties. He was the cowriter of a picture called *Fury of the Jungle* and "to my chagrin and a sharp reappraisal of my value to the enterprise, I discovered that small monkey we had written into our script was getting more per day than I was per week."[26]

Screenwriting for Animation

The earliest animated films were made up as the artists drew them. Dick Huemer, later a story man for Walt Disney, went to work in 1916 at the Raoul Barre studio. He recounts how the short cartoons were created:

> There was no story—we'd say "Let's have a picture about a building, it'll add up in the end." Each guy sat at his desk with a pile of paper and did his animation, and when it was finished he handed it over and they would put it together. Enter left, exit right—that's what it amounted to. No definite plot line. Never. We were having fun. We'd laugh at each other's stuff, but when it ran in the theatre—plop! Nothing. . . . Because we hadn't considered what the impact of what we were drawing would be.[27]

Walt Disney changed that. Even as early as his first sound cartoon in 1928, *Steamboat Willie,* there was a detailed script, which included the description of the action on the left side of the page and rough sketches on the right.[28] By 1931 Disney had even begun a story department, putting in it those animators who had particular gifts for story construction.[29] The story department was soon followed by the development of storyboards by Webb Smith, a former newspaper cartoonist. Smith made rough sketches of the action of a cartoon, which he pinned up on the walls. Disney first objected to the pinholes in the walls, but then ordered corkboard to be used to pin the sketches to.[30] The stories were then constructed in sketches and eventually transferred to the script format Disney used, which by the midthirties had the sketch on the top of the page with the text underneath.[31] Disney also developed a system of story conferences similar to those Thalberg and Zanuck conducted. Richard Schickel describes the conferences and Disney's role in them:

> His story conferences were models of democratic give-and-take, and every-one who ever sat in on one seems to agree that it was as an editor and critic of stories that he had his finest creative hours. He had a fine sense of pacing, a gift for stretching and embroidering a basic gag or situation that some have com-pared to that of the great silent comedians, and above all, an infectious enthusiasm for ideas, even bad ones, that kept the ideas bouncing until, somehow, the plot or situation or character was sharpened to a satisfactory but not necessarily preordained point.[32]

It was Walt Disney's sense of story that enabled him and his company to move into full-length animated films. Series of gags are acceptable in short films, but features required a strong story, which Disney and his story people labored over. On their first animated feature in 1937, *Snow White and the Seven Dwarfs*, there were story conferences almost every day.[33] One of the major reasons for the decline in the quality of the animated features from the Disney studio after Disney's death in 1966 was the lack of anyone else in the studio with Disney's story sense.

There was less concern for story in the cartoons from Warner Brothers, and more concern for individual gags, particularly verbal ones. The Disney cartoons depend more on sight gags, while the Warners characters talk a blue streak. In this the Warners cartoon characters probably follow in the footsteps of their creators. Michael Maltese describes how the story department at Warners worked:

> . . . When a director, like Tex Avery, or Friz Freleng, or Frank Tashlin, needed a story they'd go into this pool and see who had a story for them. These kids would all bat their heads together and come out with the ideas, and they'd all talk at once, and the directors would jot down notes, and then the guys would draw up sketches and we'd pin up the sketches on these boards on the wall. If, say, the Monahan bunch was being used by Freleng, then Avery was given a story by Hardaway and Miller and Millar. And then when they were through, they in turn would do a picture for Friz, and the other bunch would do one for Avery or Tashlin.[34]

When Maltese left Warner Brothers and went to MGM, he was reunited with Tex Avery, but Fred Quimby, the humorless supervisor of cartoons at MGM, instructed him, "Well, look if you're going to work with Avery, have this understood: We will not stand for any of that Warner Brothers rowdyism in our cartoons!"[35] So Avery made them less rowdy but more suggestive, particularly his ones with Little Red Riding Hood and the Wolf. Avery also found himself working with a story man who went on to more conventional literary pursuits, Heck Allen, who wrote western stories and novels under the names Will Henry and Clay Fisher. Avery calls him "the best gag man I ever worked with."[36]

Avery found that often the more time spent on the story, the weaker the cartoon.

If I had a record, you could go back to the weakest pictures we made there [at MGM, where there was a footage quota the animation department had to meet], and you'd find that perhaps five weeks were spent on story. And six weeks is the limit. You'll find one where the story's completed in two weeks, most of the time you'll find that's a good cartoon. Because it comes easy, it moves right out.[37]

16

Independent Screenwriters

There were, even during the heyday of the major studios, several important screenwriters who managed to have successful careers without being tied by contract to a single studio.

Ben Hecht

Ben Hecht was the archetype of the reporter turned screenwriter. Or at least he made himself out to be, which was typical of Hecht's sense of self-promotion. Hecht was a reporter on two Chicago newspapers, and he later transmuted those experiences into the best of the many stage plays he wrote, *The Front Page*. *The Front Page*, both as a play (first produced in 1928), and in its subsequent film versions (in 1930, 1940, and 1974), established the character of the scoop-chasing reporter, a character used extensively by the screenwriters of the thirties and later.

After Hecht came to Hollywood in reply to Herman Mankiewicz's telegram, his first notable screenwriting work was in constructing the story for *Underworld* (1927). Mankiewicz instructed Hecht on how virtuous the hero and heroine had to be in films of the time, and so Hecht decided to do away with them and just do a film about the villains, basing his characters on people he had known, or at least heard about, in his Chicago days. He remembered, "As a newspaperman I had learned that nice people—the audience—loved criminals, doted on reading about their love problems as well as their sadism."[1] Hecht's eighteen-page story was turned into a screenplay by Robert N. Lee, and the director assigned was Josef von Sternberg. Hecht's story and Lee's script was a tough, realistic tale, but Sternberg directed it in a more expressionistic manner. This did not bother Hecht so much as the sentimental touches Sternberg added. After the main character robbed a bank, he stopped to give money to a blind beggar before he made his getaway. Hecht was so appalled at this he sent a telegram to Sternberg saying, "You poor ham take my name off the film."[2] This did not stop Hecht from collecting an Oscar for Best Original Story for the film.

Hecht's most substantial and enduring films tended to be those he wrote for the major directors of the period. Hecht wrote all or part of six films Howard

Hawks directed all or part of, beginning with *Scarface* (1932), and continuing with *Twentieth Century* (a 1934 adaptation of their own play by Hecht and his most important collaborator, Charles MacArthur), *Viva Villa!* (1934), *Barbary Coast* (1935), *His Girl Friday* (the 1940 adaptation of *The Front Page*, which Hecht worked on without credit), and *Monkey Business* (1952). Doug Fetherling, who has examined the screenwriting of Hecht in great detail, describes the advantages of the professional relationship between Hawks and Hecht to both men:

> Hawks taught Hecht a great deal about how to put both power and subtlety into films, knowledge Hecht employed when he became a director himself. Hecht in turn encouraged Hawks to develop the quality most notably absent in the films he made with other people: a sense of humor. Coming from Hecht it was a backhanded, epigrammatic and rapid-fire sense of humor, but it added a great deal to their relationship. It nearly succeeded for a time in making Hawks a more European, less American director.[3]

Hecht also worked on five different projects with Alfred Hitchcock. The first was *Foreign Correspondent* (1940), on which Hecht was merely one of eight writers. In 1945 Hecht wrote the script for *Spellbound* about a relationship between a woman psychiatrist and a patient, helping overcome Ingrid Bergman's objection to playing the lead: "I don't believe the love story. The heroine is an intellectual woman, and an intellectual woman simply cannot fall in love so deeply."[4] His next film for Hitchcock, the following year, was *Notorious*, one of the best films of both men. The cynicism Hecht gives the characters and their reactions to the situations they find themselves in is presented lightly and slickly enough so the audience does not have time to dwell on the unsavory aspects of the film's people with whom the audience is involved. Hecht sets up some classic Hitchcock sequences, such as the theft of the key and the search in the wine cellar. Hecht and Hitchcock bring off a striking closing scene, which is all suspense, without any big physical action to finish the film. They also manage to shift the sympathy from the hero and heroine to the nominal villain of the film for just a brief moment at the very end of the film. Hecht is also reported to have worked, without credit, on the director's *Lifeboat* and *Rope.*

Ben Hecht worked on many screenplays for which he did not receive screen credit. On the surface, Hecht seemed rather cheerfully cynical about credits, as he was about much of Hollywood and the screenwriting experience in general. At the same time Hecht filmographies of later years list many films where his credit is dubious at best. From at least as early as 1971, for example, *Roxie Hart* (1942) keeps showing up in Hecht filmographies. The screenplay is officially credited to Nunnally Johnson, who was also the producer of the film. Johnson and Hecht were close friends for many years, but in addition to the fact that Johnson denied that Hecht had anything to do with the script[5] there is no evidence in the scripts that Hecht was involved.

Hecht's most famous claimed uncredited work was *Gone With the Wind*. In his memoirs, Hecht tells a wonderful tale[6] of being approached one Sunday morning by David O. Selznick and Victor Fleming, the producer and director of that film, and being asked to rewrite the script after shooting had been under way for some three weeks. Since Hecht had not read the book, Selznick and Fleming told him the story, and Hecht says he wrote the first half of the film in seven days, working from what he called a "first 'treatment,' discarded three years before,"[7] which had been written by Sidney Howard.

Sidney Howard did write a treatment, or adaptation, in 1937, two years before Hecht worked on the film, but it was hardly discarded, since it was the basis of the screenplay Howard wrote, which was subsequently revised by at least sixteen other writers, including F. Scott Fitzgerald, Val Lewton, Edwin Justus Mayer, Donald Ogden Stewart, and more extensively Oliver H. P. Garrett, whose revisions had to be revised back to Howard's original script.[8] Very little of Hecht's work remains in the film, the most notable being the introductory titles describing in romantic and sentimental terms the South before the war.[9]

Perhaps the cynical Ben Hecht was in truth just as sentimental about his work as a screenwriter.

Jules Furthman

Pauline Kael, writing in 1967, claims that Jules Furthman "has written about half of the most entertaining movies to come out of Hollywood" (to which she added, "Ben Hecht wrote most of the other half ").[10] Even if one might want to spread the wealth around a little more evenly, Furthman's body of work is still impressive, and at least partially responsible for the best films in the careers of two critically acclaimed directors, Josef von Sternberg and Howard Hawks.

Because he was often ill as a young boy in Chicago, Furthman read widely from an early age. He began writing and selling magazine stories in his twenties. His first screen credits are for stories for several 1915 films for Universal, and his scenario credits begin in 1917.[11]

From 1918 to 1920 Furthman wrote for American/Pathe, Famous Players, and Fox under the name Steven Fox, most likely because Furthman sounded too Germanic during World War I. In 1920 he went back to his real name and until 1923 wrote exclusively for Fox. His films at Fox are primarily western and adventure pictures, with titles like *The Texan, The Iron Rider, The Big Punch, Colorado Pluck,* and *North of Hudson Bay.*

In the later twenties Furthman found a berth at Paramount, where he wrote *Hotel Imperial* and *The Way of All Flesh.* It is rumored that Furthman worked on *Underworld,* although it is his brother Charles who received credit for the adaptation of Ben Hecht's story. Furthman did write three more twenties gangster films for Sternberg, *The Dragnet, The Docks of New York,* and *Thunderbolt. The Docks of New York* introduces a character that would often recur in Furthman's scripts, both for Sternberg and Hawks: the good-bad girl, in this case a cynical prostitute whose faith in humanity is restored by her marriage to a shipwright.

In the early thirties Furthman wrote three of the major films Marlene Dietrich starred in under Sternberg's direction. The first, *Morocco,* was actually released in the United States before *The Blue Angel,* the film Sternberg made in Germany in which he presented Dietrich for the first time. The second Furthman-Sternberg-Dietrich collaboration was *Shanghai Express,* the most complexly plotted of the three, and the third was *Blonde Venus.* Richard Koszarski has pointed out that the Furthman-Sternberg-Dietrich collaborations are much more coherent than the Sternberg-Dietrich films written by other writers. About the first two films of the collaboration, Koszarski writes:

> There is not a frame in either film which one could cut without making the whole incomprehensible (cutting the others [those not written by Furthman] would only make them seem less perfect). The tensions in *Morocco* succeed because the tightness of the script creates a sense of concentration which is so gloriously missing in [the non-Furthman films]. *The Shanghai Express* also bears these marks of perfect completion; far from being a *"Grand Hotel* on wheels," as some have written, it is a structure in which each part plays an indispensable role. There is no meandering, only the strict delineation of a journey from points A to B, detailing the moral and emotional progress of the characters as well as the physical progress of the Express. Each of the characters on the train is indispensable to the Dietrich-Clive Brook story, and each is utilized to the fullest. (Furthman must have enjoyed working on this Harry Hervey story, because twenty years later his name appears again in connection with the fourth film version, William Dieterle's *Peking Express* [1952]. . . .)[12]

Josef von Sternberg returned the favor by not mentioning Furthman at all in his autobiography.

In 1932 Furthman left Paramount and went to work for Thalberg at MGM. Many of the forty projects Furthman worked on MGM were eventually produced, but he got screen credit on only three: *Bombshell,* a lively collaboration with John Lee Mahin that starred Jean Harlow; *China Seas,* a romantic adventure in the vein of *Shanghai Express* except on a ship instead of a train; and *Mutiny on the Bounty*. Furthman had the good sense to be one of the last writers on the latter rather than one of the first, which assured him a screen credit, as was the custom of the time.

In 1936 Furthman first worked with Howard Hawks on *Come and Get It!*, and three years later he wrote *Only Angels Have Wings*, supposedly based on Hawks's own tales of his flying experiences. What Furthman delivered is an adventure picture that goes beyond the action to examine the underlying attitudes of the men, and the women, involved in the dangerous business of flying the mail over the Andes. Furthman has constructed characters and scenes that enable the audience to see how the characters *feel* about the work they do, without them having to talk directly about their feelings. Hawks has the actors play it in the usual Hawksian easygoing, masculine manner, but Furthman's script provides the depth that other Hawks films often do not have.

In 1945 Furthman (and William Faulkner) adapted Hemingway's *To Have and Have Not* for Hawks, and the following year the same two writers, along with Leigh Brackett, tried to figure out the plot of Raymond Chandler's *The Big Sleep*. They failed (as did Chandler when they asked him about a plot detail), but embellished the story they did use with vivid dialogue and equally vivid scenes. In their last collaboration, *Rio Bravo* (1959), Hawks and Furthman did not bother with even attempting a plot. The shaggy-dog looseness of the film appealed to many. It was Furthman's last credit.

Dudley Nichols

The most critically acclaimed and highly respected (particularly by other writers) screenwriter of the thirties and forties was Dudley Nichols. The acclaim and the respect came because of Nichols's attempts to bring intelligence and literacy to the screen. As Paul Jensen has noted, however:

> Coming at a time when movies were notoriously confectionary, Nichols's limited struggles to impose substance on the anti-intellectual Hollywood product and to circumvent the more obvious absurdities of censorship do deserve admiration. In our own infinitely liberal climate [Jensen was writing in 1970], however, his small victories and larger capitulations (both conscious and not) seem examples of old-fashioned superficiality. And the fact that the motion picture Establishment virtually deified him warns that perhaps Nichols was less courageous than he, and everyone else, thought—his courage flowed in traditional channels which left the powers-that-be feeling tolerably comfortable. [13]

After service as a young man in the Navy, Nichols became a trial reporter, which may explain the presence of trial sequences in many of his films. He also covered the New York theater scene, and his filmography shows a number of adaptations of plays.

In the late twenties Nichols became a screenwriter at Fox. On his first film he was paired off with the man who had directed the one film he most vividly remembered, *The Iron Horse.*[14] The director was John Ford, and the film they did together, a submarine story called *Men Without Women,* was the first of fourteen scripts Nichols would do with Ford.

The earliest Nichols-Ford films are not particularly distinguished, although the two Nichols wrote with Lamar Trotti to star Will Rogers, *Judge Priest* and *Steamboat Round the Bend* have their charms, most of which seem to come from the lines Rogers wrote for himself.

The picture that made both Ford and Nichols's reputations was the 1935 adaptation of Liam O'Flaherty's novel *The Informer.* One can still see why the script and film had an impact at the time. The story of Gypo Nolan's informing on his friend is not the simple melodrama of the time, and the characters are sharply drawn. Nichols provides, as he often does, vivid roles for the actors to play. Unfortunately, Nichols's flaws as a screenwriter are now more noticeable than they were in 1935. While Nichols is writing for the camera, much of his visual detail is very obvious symbolism, such as the wanted poster of Frankie that seems to follow Gypo all over the city.

The other classic collaboration between Nichols and Ford also shows Nichols's weaknesses as a screenwriter. *Stagecoach* is based on the short story "Stage to Lordsburg" by Ernest Haycox. Nichols has elaborated on the characters from the story, but he has turned them all into clichés, with no particular depth. It is only because Ford bullied the actors into believing their characters that they play at all. Nichols's sense of story structure was one of the weakest of the major screenwriters, and *Stagecoach* demonstrates this. Nichols compounds the structural problem of Haycox's story. Both story and script tell two stories, one about the Indian uprising, which includes the attack on the stagecoach, and a second story about the outlaw (Malpais Bill in the story and The Ringo Kid in the script) seeking revenge. Haycox keeps them more or less in balance, but Nichols emphasizes the Indian story at the beginning, then drops it after the attack on the stagecoach, which is more of a major scene in the script than in the story. The Ringo Kid story begins well into the film and continues for twenty minutes after the end of the Indian attack.[15] The script does provide some flashy scenes for the actors and several striking Fordian visuals in Monument Valley.

Nichols's script for the 1940 Ford film *The Long Voyage Home* is a better script. It is based on four one-act plays by Eugene O'Neill about life on board a freighter. In combining the plays, Nichols spread out the action, and the material itself provided stronger and deeper characterization than in *Stage-coach.*

Nichols wrote for other directors as well, including *Bringing Up Baby* and *Air Force* for Howard Hawks, *Swamp Water* and *This Land Is Mine* for Jean Renoir, and *Man Hunt* and *Scarlet Street* for Fritz Lang. In the fifties, Nichols's scripts became less "important" in terms of subject matter, and several of them made more entertaining films than his more serious work. *Rawhide* is an interesting reversal on *Stagecoach*, in that the small cast of characters are held hostage at a stagecoach stop by an outlaw who can be seen as a less-benign version of The Ringo Kid. *Prince Valiant* is passable as scripts for comic-book movies go, especially in comparison with later comic-book film scripts, and *The Tin Star* is an excellent western. Nichols's last filmed script, *Heller in Pink Tights* in 1960, is a delightful film about an acting troupe in the old west. A line of Woody Allen's can be paraphrased to say that Nichols's *later* funny ones are better.

Herman Mankiewicz and Orson Welles

When Herman Mankiewicz was at Paramount, he was protected by B. P. Schulberg. When Schulberg left Paramount, so did Mankiewicz. Mankiewicz then went to MGM where his new protector was producer Bernie Hyman. Mankiewicz's credits at MGM, when he did manage to get them for his work, were generally on films of no great interest. He also managed to insult most of the people he worked with, especially the producers. In 1939 MGM let him go, and he was reduced to writing radio scripts.

He was writing for the West Coast edition of the *Mercury Theatre of the Air,* a radio anthology series begun in 1938 in New York, using the actors of the Mercury Theatre. The producer, director, star, and occasional writer of the programs was a young man named Orson Welles. George J. Schaefer, the new head of production at RKO, had invited Welles and his group to come out to Hollywood to make films. While trying to figure out what film to make, the group continued its radio program from Hollywood.

There is some dispute about who first came up with the idea of doing a film that was a thinly disguised story of publisher William Randolph Hearst and his affair with actress Marion Davies.[16] The preponderance of evidence suggests Mankiewicz, and it is certainly Mankiewicz who did the first drafts of the script. To get him away from the lures of Hollywood, Mankiewicz was sent off to Victorville, in the Mojave Desert, to write, along with a secretary, Rita Alexander, and John Houseman, the producer for Mercury. While it is possible that Mankiewicz was creating entirely on his own, it is likely that there had been discussions with Welles before he left. In any case, the two drafts Mankiewicz completed at Victorville were written by him, and they lay out the basic structure of the film that became *Citizen Kane*. The first draft was 250 pages long, and the second one 325 pages. After the second draft, Mankiewicz went to MGM for another assignment, and the revisions, which included considerable cutting, were made by Welles, working as a combination writer/editor in the way he had done with the scripts written by other writers for the radio programs. While Mankiewicz had the energy and the early enthusiasm to whip out a lengthy first draft, he did not necessarily have the dedication to do the fine-tuning any script required. Welles, on the other hand, did not necessarily have the patience to do all the creative work required on a first draft, but was brilliant as an editor/rewrite man. As a screenwriting collaboration, they were well matched.

The first and second drafts had been written in April and May of 1940, and Mankiewicz returned to work on the script in June and July of that year. Welles had done what were the third and fourth drafts of the script, and now with both of them working there were three more drafts. The seventh draft, dated July 16, was the shooting script.[17]

It had been Welles's habit on the radio program to take the credit as writer as well as director, and there are indications he intended to do so with the film. When it became apparent that there would be both legal and publicity problems if he denied Mankiewicz credit, Welles had the credits made with both their names, and with Mankiewicz's first. The new Screen Writers Guild objected, on grounds that a producer, which Welles technically was, could not take credit on a script unless he had written it entirely himself. Welles, with Mankiewicz's support, appealed, and the dual credit was allowed to stand. Both men accepted the Academy Award the script won.[18]

Welles's next script, *The Magnificent Ambersons*, was written without any collaborator. Welles worked out notes on how the Booth Tarkington novel was to be adapted, and script supervisor Amalia Kent put the notes and the novel into screenplay form.[19] With the exception of some long dialogue scenes taken directly from the novel, which were subsequently cut from the film, the screenplay is an excellent job of screenwriting.[20] It does have the same flaw as the film, which is it does not actually show George getting his "comeuppance." Since so much has been made about this possibility, an audience naturally wants to see it, not just read a newspaper clipping about it.

There is another slight problem with the script, and that is that it does not show Eugene at the hospital. Instead we get a description of the scene as a voice-over by Eugene as he writes a letter to Isabel about it. Much has been made over the years of how badly the film was cut in the shortening process and how badly the additional scenes were shot, but the final scene as written is rather flat, and the film's scene of Eugene at the hospital is much more dramatically interesting. In addition, there is very little of the material cut from the first draft that is essential to the film, although there are of course scenes one longs to have seen. The film of *The Magnificent Ambersons*, as it now stands, is not nearly the desecration legend would have it, and even in its truncated form, it is a demonstration of the quality of the screenwriting work of Orson Welles.

17

Writer-Producers

In spite of everything, the screenwriters in the studios were not a happy lot, and everything is not too strong a word. Most screenwriters made more money than they had made (and in many cases ever imagined) in their lives. They were part of a glamorous new business, creating a new art form as they went. They had many friends, old and new, in the same line of work. And the climate in Los Angeles was not bad, either.

A warm sun can count for only so much, however. In the silent days the writers and everybody else thought of themselves as part of the process of making films. Everybody did everything on the early films. A bit of this team spirit still existed in the major studio days, but now there was a division of labor among the collaborators.

Screenwriters were more and more limited to being involved in merely the first step in the creation of films. They would develop the ideas and have an overall concept for the film, but they had very little control over the final film. The head of the studio, the producer of the film, other writers, the director, the stars, the editor, and others all made their "contributions" to the film, and many of those contributions took away from the original writer's concept. Screenwriters figured out ways to improve their status within the system. The screenwriters could work within the system and become producers and/or directors. They could develop a union for screenwriters. Or they could go outside the system to try to change it by joining the Communist party. Some writers took one of these paths, some took several, but very few took all of them.

Within the studio system, the most obvious way to increase one's power and control over the filmmaking process was to become a producer. The heads of the studios saw themselves as producers and therefore the most important figures in the making of the films. When Dore Schary asked to direct a film, Louis B. Mayer wanted to know why Schary wanted to direct rather than produce. Schary writes, "Mayer preferred producers—to him they were the captains of the armada, and the writers, actors, directors merely members of the crew."[1] When Joseph Mankiewicz asked Mayer for the same thing, Mayer insisted Mankiewicz would have to be a producer first, saying, "You have to learn to crawl before you can walk," which Mankiewicz thereafter described as the best description of a producer's posture he ever heard.[2]

123

Since the studio heads thought of producing as more prestigious than screenwriting, it was the obvious way for them to reward the screenwriters whose intelligence they admired. It was also easier and safer, from the studio's perspective, to reward good screenwriters by making them producers than by upgrading the conditions of all screenwriters. If the studio gave power to screenwriters, its own power would be diminished. Better then to promote the screenwriters with producer potential.

There were historical and artistic reasons for the studios promoting screenwriters to producers as well. In silent films, the writers' involvement in the writing of titles often led the writers into the supervision of, or at least involvement in, the editing of the films. Writers were able to see the film as a whole and with titles help make sense out of what the director had shot. Since the function of a producer is to supervise the making of a film, from the writing through the editing, one of the qualities a producer should have is a sense of the overall structure of the film. Writers develop that sense while working on screenplays. Writers often have more of a feel for the film's structure than the director. Very often a director will become so involved in the specifics of shooting the day's work that he cannot keep in balance the relationship of that work to the whole film. A writer has himself and the paper; a director has a cast, a crew, sets, locations, props, and the expense of a production constantly in mind. It takes extraordinary concentration for a director to hold the entirety of a film in mind.

In addition, a director may shoot material he loves that may not fit into the film. A writer is used to editing his own material and is less likely to be unwilling to give up material that does not fit in the film. Part of this may be that the writer's work is cheaper (words on paper) and he does not necessarily get as attached to the material as a director can to pieces of film that have taken hours or even days to shoot. One of the reasons a screenwriter might then wish to become a producer is to be able to supervise the editing of the film and cut out the more extreme extrapolations of the director.

Control of editing was not the only reason writers agreed to become producers. Given the studio structure, producers had not only more prestige, but more power within the studio hierarchy. As a producer a screenwriter was in a better position to fight for bringing more interesting material to the screen. The screenwriter-producer could protect his own material by not hiring any other writers to work on it. He could also protect other writers' work as well, although there was always the possibility he would want to rewrite it to his satisfaction.

Joseph L. Mankiewicz

Screenwriters such as Frank Woods and C. Gardner Sullivan became producers in silent films. In the early sound days, there was Herman Mankiewicz. Herman's younger brother Joseph became one of the first screenwriters at MGM to move into producing. Joseph Mankiewicz came to Hollywood as a result of another of his brother's famous telegrams. This one, in 1929, read: FOR CHRIST'S SAKE, COME OUT TO HOLLYWOOD.[3] The younger Mankiewicz started as a titlewriter for Paramount, then wrote films in the early days of sound. In 1933 he went to MGM, and in 1935 he became a producer.

His first film as a producer was an overgrown B western *Three Godfathers*, but his next film was the 1936 antilynching film *Fury*. Mayer and the other executives at MGM felt the story was too depressing for an MGM film, but allowed Mankiewicz to make it. The idea for *Fury* had come from Norman Krasna, and Mankiewicz developed it. Mankiewicz also pushed for Fritz Lang to direct the film, then later had to cut a sequence Lang shot of ghosts chasing the leading character down the street. The sequence had provoked laughter in an American preview audience.[4]

Mankiewicz produced several Joan Crawford vehicles, and in 1938 was appointed to MGM's executive committee as well as the supervisor for the studio's junior writers. In 1938 he also produced *Three Comrades*, which was the only screen credit F. Scott Fitzgerald received. As Mankiewicz noted later, "If I go down at all in literary history, in a footnote, it will be as the swine who rewrote F. Scott Fitzgerald."[5] Fitzgerald had written dialogue that the star of the film, Margaret Sullivan, found unsayable, and she complained to Mankiewicz. His rewriting provoked a famous, pleading letter from Fitzgerald[6] in which he asked, "Oh, Joe, can't producers ever be wrong? I'm a good writer, honest." Some years later Mankiewicz said:

> I hired Scott for *Three Comrades* because I admired his work. More than any other writer, I thought that he could capture the European flavor and the flavor of the twenties and early thirties that *Three Comrades* required. I also thought that he would know and understand the girl.
> I didn't count on Scott for dialogue. There could be no greater disservice done him than to have actors read his novels aloud as if they were plays. . . . Dialogue spoken from the stage enters through the ear rather than the mind. It has an immediate emotional impact. Scott's dialogue lacked bite, color, rhythm.[7]

Fitzgerald was not the only writer to complain about Mankiewicz's tampering with their work. Edwin Knopf said, "It is both Joe's strength and his weakness that he thought that he could rewrite anyone."[8]

Mankiewicz saw both sides of the issue. When he was working as a writer-producer under senior producer Sam Katz, he wrote memos to Katz, one as a writer, the other as producer. In the producer memo, he complained he could never get hold of Joe Mankiewicz the writer, and in the writer memo he said,

"Let me tell you that Mr. Mankiewicz doesn't read what I give him, and when he does, he fails to comprehend it. He is just this side of an illiterate, and I'm writing my ass off."9

The Fox Writer-Producers

All three of the first-line screenwriters at Twentieth Century-Fox eventually became producers, primarily of their own screenplays. When asked how he became a producer in 1952 on *Way of the Gaucho*, Philip Dunne replied, "The way everything happened at that studio. Zanuck said, 'You're a producer.' It was in my contract right along. He said, 'You want to produce this picture?' I said, 'Sure.' I thought it was fun."10 Part of the reason Zanuck suggested it for this picture was that it was shot in Argentina, and given Dunne's lifelong interest in politics, Zanuck said, "You like to play politics. You have a big chance now with [Juan] Perón."11 Having the writer in the country as producer was also helpful, because when the unit arrived in Argentina, Dunne discovered the book the script was based on was inaccurate about Argentine life. He had to rewrite the film while it was in production.12

Lamar Trotti became a producer in a similar way. He was on location in 1942 keeping an eye on his script for *Thunder Birds* when a wire arrived from Zanuck telling him he was now the producer of the film.13 Trotti then alternated producing his own scripts and writing scripts for Zanuck's productions.

Nunnally Johnson became a producer earlier than Dunne and Trotti. When Twentieth Century merged with Fox in 1935, Zanuck needed more associate producers to supervise production. Johnson recalls:

> I suppose I took it because he asked me to and if he'd asked me to jump off a bridge I'd have done it. I mean I had such a regard for him and of course being a producer sounded as if I had more control. I didn't really have a great deal more control, because Darryl at that time was [in charge of everything].14

In addition to producing his own scripts, Johnson was supposed to supervise other writers. He found he could not do it, "That was a complete fiasco because I cannot tell people how to write."15 He found it was easier to rewrite the scripts than to try to tell someone else how to do it. Zanuck and Johnson finally decided that Johnson would only produce his own scripts.

Warner Brothers and Jerry Wald

Many of the screenwriters at Warner Brothers became producers: Robert Lord, Seton Miller, and Robert Buckner. Buckner was a Vriginian noted for his western scripts, particularly *Dodge City* (1939), *Virginia City* (1940), and *Santa Fe Trail* (1940). Buckner became a producer in 1942 for his script of *Yankee Doodle Dandy,* the biography of George M. Cohan. It was up to Buckner to deal with the demands Cohan made on what could or could not be used in the film.[16] In the forties Buckner not only produced his own scripts but those by other writers for *Gentleman Jim, Mission to Moscow,* and *Life with Father.* In 1948 he went to work for Universal, where he produced only his own scripts.

The most interesting producer to emerge from the writers at Warners was Jerry Wald. He received his first screen credit as a writer in 1934, and it was Wald who used the Epstein twins as cowriters on his earliest films to help promote himself.[17] Jerry Wald was also rumored to be one, if not the major, inspiration for the Sammy Glick character in Budd Schulberg's novel *What Makes Sammy Run?* In the early forties, he gave up writing and began producing. He constantly used a variety of writers; on the development of *Mildred Pierce* he had seven at various stages.[18]

Wald left Warners in the early fifties, going first to Columbia and then Fox, where he produced *Peyton Place* and *Sons and Lovers.* Philip Dunne, who directed Edward Anhalt's script for Wald's 1958 production of *In Love and War,* recalls:

> Jerry was Jerry Wald. There was nobody quite like him. He was an omnivorous reader and he lost none of it. He would get to the office early in the morning and . . . he'd copy out pages of Proust and try to introduce it into the dialogue. This amazing, agile, fertile mind was working all the time. . . . Jerry's big problem was he could never leave the script alone. . . . As a result, I was up on location in Monterey, and Jerry was rewriting the opening, which we weren't going to shoot for four weeks. . . . I was up there shooting the ending of the picture without a written scene to shoot, so I had to write the ending on the set. . . . The day after I shot the scene, a 15-page scene arrived which was supposed to be the ending. I had to call up and say, "Look, I shot the ending yesterday."[19]

Paramount and Columbia

At Paramount, Herman Mankiewicz was followed as a producer by Billy Wilder's writing partner Charles Brackett in the early forties. Brackett had in effect served as producer in his collaboration with Wilder. He provided the sounding board for Wilder's imaginative plot twists and turns.[20] On their ninth script, *Five Graves to Cairo* (1943), Brackett became the producer, a position he held until Wilder broke up the partnership after *Sunset Boulevard*

in 1950. Brackett settled at Fox in the fifties, where he wrote and produced *Niagara, Titanic,* then produced *The King and I,* and *Ten North Frederick.*
At Columbia Sidney Buchman produced as well as wrote, and Virginia Van Upp followed in his path. A former child actress, she turned to writing films in the thirties. In 1944 she wrote *Cover Girl,* which helped establish Rita Hayworth as a star. Hayworth and Harry Cohn were impressed enough with her work that when Van Upp developed *Gilda* Hayworth wanted her to produce it, and Harry Cohn concurred. Hayworth later had second thoughts, saying it was Van Upp's fault Hayworth had such a miserable private life. Hayworth told her, "Every man I've known has fallen in love with Gilda and wakened with me."[21] Van Upp also helped recut *Lady from Shanghai* after its first disastrous premiere. She worked with Orson Welles reorganizing the script and deciding what additional material had to be shot.[22]

Studio Heads

For all the reasons screenwriters made good producers, writers also made good heads of production at the studios. There were Zanuck, Schulberg, and LeBaron. Buchman and Van Upp were at different times Harry Cohn's chief executive producer. Dore Schary headed the B-picture unit at MGM, then overall production at RKO, and he returned to MGM in June 1948 as head of production for the entire studio, a job he held until 1956.

For a brief period in 1935 at Paramount the head of production was Ernst Lubitsch, a director. For all the supposed importance of the director in the making of films, Lubitsch was the only director who was ever head of production at a major studio between 1920 and 1950.

18

Writer-Directors

From the early days of the movies, writers were also directors. Stanner Taylor was the first Biograph writer to move into directing, and when he was unsuccessful at it, he was followed by another writer, D. W. Griffith. Mack Sennett was a writer before he directed, and Thomas Ince wrote and directed. Gene Gauntier was a writer as well as actress before she directed. Chaplin and Keaton were writers as well as actors and directors.

The division of labor at the major studios reduced the number of writer-directors, and the introduction of sound divided the labor even further, since there was now more involvement on the part of the screenwriters in writing dialogue. The early thirties saw only a few writer-directors within the studio system. One of the earliest and most interesting was the by now virtually forgotten Rowland Brown. Brown was a former juvenile delinquent whose experiences with criminals and jails gave him firsthand knowledge of the underworld he wrote about when he started writing for films.[1]

Brown became a screenwriter in 1928 and three years later he directed his first film, a gangster picture called *Quick Millions,* starring a then-unknown Spencer Tracy. The following year he wrote and directed *Hell's Highway,* and in 1933 he made *Blood Money,* a tough little film about a bail bondsman who deals with cops, crooks, a slumming society girl, and a madame played with great ferocity by Judith Anderson. According to his later collaborator on the script for *Johnny Apollo,* Philip Dunne, Brown was a "strange, poetic, hard-boiled, very interesting, big bear of a man, rather incoherent, but with a tremendously fertile mind. The best things in the picture are his, I can say without equivocation."[2] Dunne thinks Brown did not continue as a director because

> he never got along with anybody, which was a terrible working habit because a good part of the job was being able to get along with people. . . . He had the seeds of his own destruction in himself. He would get into a situation where he would bust off the picture and walk out or be thrown out. And he'd go to drinking.[3]

After his three films in the early thirties, all for different studios, Brown returned to writing and never directed again.

In 1934 two other screenwriters, Ben Hecht and Charles MacArthur, turned to directing. They talked Paramount into letting them make films in New York at the old Astoria studios on Long Island. In the next two years Hecht and MacArthur were to write, produce, and direct four films. Without a producer to keep their wilder flights of fancy under control, the material they selected and wrote was not particularly appealing to a mass audience, or indeed to many critics. Their direction did not help. They did have the assistance of their "associate director," cinematographer Lee Garmes, who laid out the camera angles and whatever camera movements might be needed. In describing their third film *Soak the Rich*, Geoff Brown describes most of the directorial problems of the Hecht-MacArthur films:

> The performances are generally too glum (particularly that of New York model Mary Taylor playing Belinda), the staging always too slack. In their two previous films, Hecht and MacArthur's direction is persistently clumsy, with ill-judged changes in camera set-ups, the actors perpetually standing in clumps, spouting monotone, surrounded by obtrusively empty sets—but the 'style' seems perversely suited to the bleak, frigid atmosphere of *Crime Without Passion* and *The Scoundrel*. Here, with the crazy dialogue and slapstick spurts of action . . . the inadequacies loom dangerously large.[4]

The films were not successful at the box office, and Hecht and MacArthur returned to writing scripts for other directors, although Hecht did direct three more films. *Angels Over Broadway* (1940), *Specter of the Rose* (1946), and *Actors and Sin* (1952), but Hecht's unevenness in directing actors is apparent in all three.

In 1937 Robert Riskin persuaded Harry Cohn to let him direct a film. The picture was the third of four vehicles for opera singer Grace Moore at Columbia, *When You're in Love*. It was not a particular success and Riskin never directed again. Capra suggests why Riskin was not particularly suited to directing:

> He had all the required talents of a filmmaker. What he lacked was not talent but a native drive—the ability "to get things done under stress." The bedlam of film production got to him. Evidently he was his sharpest and most creative when writing alone in the quiet of his thoughts.[5]

Given these screenwriters' lack of success at directing, it is surprising the studios even considered letting any other writers try it. The screenwriter who made the successful transition that opened the floodgates for others was Preston Sturges.

Preston Sturges, the Screenwriter-Director

From the early thirties, Sturges was trying to maintain control over his scripts. On *The Power and the Glory*, his contract specified having the film shot as written. In 1933 Sturges wrote the first draft of what became *The Great McGinty* with the hope that he could direct it, but the box-office failure of *The Power and the Glory* made the studios lose interest in Sturges directing. Sturges went to Paramount and his experiences there made him more determined than ever to direct his own scripts. He was not happy with the directors he worked with, partly of course because he thought he could do a better job and partly because he simply did not think they got as much out of his scripts as they should have.

He seemed to have a particular grudge, as did other writers at Paramount, against Mitchell Leisen. A former costume and set designer for De Mille, Leisen began directing for Paramount in 1932 and was considered one of the studio's top directors of the thirties.[6] Unfortunately, the writers at Paramount hated him, since he seemed more concerned with the look of the film than the script and the dialogue. Billy Wilder's biographer Maurice Zolotow writes of him:

> Leisen was as narcissistic as any actor or actress. He changed clothes—at the studio—three or four times a day. He preened himself. He was a compulsive tie-knot tightener and hair comber. He wore startling colored slacks and embroidered Ecuadorian blouses and lurid sandals. Or he might appear in an elegant pongee suit and a panama hat.[7]

No wonder the Paramount writers like Sturges and Wilder, who specialized in deflating pomposity, despised Leisen. And wanted to direct instead of him.

By 1939 Sturges was ready to leave Paramount if William LeBaron, the head of production, would not allow him to direct. Sturges had written enough successful films for the studio that he knew, and LeBaron knew too, he could get a deal with another studio that might be willing to let him start directing low-budget films. LeBaron was reluctant to let Sturges direct. First of all, Sturges was more valuable as a writer, turning out scripts for the staff directors. Second, letting such a top writer as Sturges direct would set a precedent. LeBaron knew he would be besieged with other writers, including those with less talent and potential than Sturges, wanting to direct. Third, letting the writer direct gave him a more complete control over the film: a writer could be replaced and a director could be replaced and even a producer could be replaced, but it would be more difficult to replace someone in all three positions and still have the film be reasonably coherent.

Sturges made LeBaron the offer he could not refuse. Sturges would sell his script for *The Great McGinty* to Paramount for one dollar *if* he was allowed to direct. From a business point of view it made sense to LeBaron, although he was not convinced a dollar was large enough to make the deal legal. They settled on ten dollars.[8]

Sturges succeeded where the screenwriters-turned-directors before him failed. *The Great McGinty* was only the first of the string of hits that Sturges wrote and directed in the early forties. Unlike Roland Brown, he got along with the people he worked with (most of the time). Unlike Hecht and MacArthur, he wrote scripts that amused the mass audience and he knew how to direct actors. Unlike Riskin, he loved the activity on the set. He used the intensity of the filmmaking process to increase the pacing and the energy of his films. The Sturges films of the early forties got louder and faster, if not necessarily funnier.

Unfortunately LeBaron left Paramount in 1941, and Sturges had to deal with Buddy DeSylva. DeSylva left Sturges alone until he had a flop, and then began to insist on cuts and changes in Sturges's films. In 1943 Sturges left Paramount, unfortunately leaving not only DeSylva's interference, but the entire support team he had built up at the studio in the previous three years. Sturges simply did not make pictures as good away from Paramount as he had there. There is an ironic footnote: Mitchell Leisen also saw his career diminish with the decline of the studio system, since he was no longer working with writers of the caliber of Sturges.

The Flood

There were many other screenwriters in Hollywood who thought, either longingly or angrily or both, of becoming directors. John Huston's agent, Paul Kohner, took note of Huston's interest and arranged Huston's contract with Warner Brothers so that if the studio picked up Huston's option as a screenwriter he would be allowed to direct.[9] Huston's choice for his first directorial effort in 1941 was Dashiell Hammett's *The Maltese Falcon*, which surprised his supervisors, Henry Blanke and Hal Wallis. Warners had made the story into a film twice before and it had flopped both times. Huston however stuck to the book. He also prepared his direction carefully, making sketches of each camera setup and going over them with William Wyler. Huston rehearsed the actors and most of the time they fell into the patterns his sketches called for. Sometimes when they did not, he changed the pattern. Huston claims that "during the filming not one line of dialogue was changed. One short scene was dropped when I realized I could substitute a telephone call for it without loss to the story."[10] Huston is not entirely accurate. The opening scene in Spade's office is condensed and clarified from the screenplay to the film, and there is considerable condensation from the final script, which runs 147 pages, to the film, which runs 100 minutes. The final scene of the screenplay, an unneeded summing up of the plot back in Spade's office, has been dropped. This is why the final shot in the film, of Spade carrying the falcon down the stairs is so bland: it was not intended as the final shot of the film. Huston's direction, particularly his camera placement, is very simple, but very effective. With that cast and that script, it did not have to be anything else. [11]

The year 1941 also saw Orson Welles's debut as writer and director, but Welles was, as always, a special case. His contract with RKO, calling for him to write, direct, and star in films was signed at approximately the same time Sturges made his deal to direct *The Great McGinty*. Welles's spectacular impact as cowriter and director of *Citizen Kane* probably helped the transition of screenwriters into directors, although the controversy over *Kane* and the lack of commercial success of *The Magnificent Ambersons* might have hindered the transition if it had not been for the success of Huston and the other screenwriters-turned-directors at this time.

In 1942 Billy Wilder got the opportunity to direct. Like Sturges he had long held an animosity towards Mitchell Leisen. When Wilder's biographer Maurice Zolotow quoted some of Leisen's comments about how Wilder was a "madman" and how Wilder's partner Charles Brackett helped calm him down, Wilder replied:

> Leisen spent more time with Edith Head worrying about the pleats on a skirt than he did with us on the script. He didn't argue over scenes. He didn't know shit about construction. And he didn't care. All he did was he fucked up the script and our scripts were damn near perfection, let me tell you. Leisen was too goddam fey. I don't knock fairies. Let him be a fairy. Leisen's problem was that he was a stupid fairy. He didn't have the brains to see that if Charlie and me, if we put in a line, we had a goddam reason for putting in that line and not a different line, and you don't just go and cut a line or a piece of action to please some actress, at least without putting another line or action in its place. I ask you, is that so difficult to understand? And Charlie hated him as much as I did. Because if we gave in to him, there would be holes in the script which he shot. Charles never was a peacemaker. That's bullshit. It was [producer] Arthur Hornblow who refereed our fights. [12]

After several fights with Leisen on *Hold Back the Dawn*, Wilder became determined to direct. Wilder later thought the Paramount front office agreed to let him direct thinking that he would fail and go back to writing. [13] The script was *The Major and the Minor* and Wilder talked Ginger Rogers and Ray Milland into starring in it. Both agreed to do it because they thought it was a good script. Milland did not think Wilder was serious when he told him he was going to direct, but when he got the script, "I liked the story. It didn't bother me that it was Billy's first picture. Hell, in those days you finished one picture on Friday and started a new one on Monday."[14]

Wilder was physically ill with diarrhea before he started shooting and he went to discuss with Ernst Lubitsch what to do about it. Lubitsch replied, "I have directed fifty pictures and I'm still crapping in my pants on the first day."[15] Lubitsch brought several of the German directors then in Hollywood, including Wyler, William Dieterle and Michael Curtiz, to Wilder's set the first day. Preston Sturges showed up as well. Zolotow says, "As a result of all these geniuses on the set, the first day of shooting was a shambles. Billy did not get a single foot of usable film."[16] Wilder then learned to discuss his setups with his editor, Doane Harrison, who had begun as an editor for Mack Sennett.[17]

In 1943 Delmar Daves, who had screenwriting credits from 1929 including *The Petrified Forest* and *Love Affair*, began directing with *Destination Tokyo*. In 1945 George Seaton persuaded Zanuck to let him direct at Twentieth Century-Fox. Seaton had a bad experience with his script for the 1943 film *The Eve of St. Mark*. He had been unable to talk to the director, John Stahl, before the film was shot. When they met at the preview of the film, Seaton told Stahl that it was not his script up there. Stahl said, and Seaton agreed, that Stahl had not changed a word, but the emphasis was different than Seaton had intended. Seaton explained what he had in mind. Stahl replied, "Oh my God. It would have been so much better if we'd only had a chance to talk this over before I started shooting." Stahl told him the next day he should direct.[18]

Zanuck wanted Seaton to start with a low-budget film, as Huston had with *The Maltese Falcon*, but Seaton did not want to be typecast as a B-picture director, so he asked to do the Betty Grable musical *Billy Rose's Diamond Horseshoe*. Zanuck replied, "Oh my heavens, that's going to cost a million eight [$1,800,000]. I can't let you, an inexperienced director, take a budget of that size."

Seaton said, "Let me make a deal with you. Have somebody stand by and if the first rushes are not to your liking, replace me." Zanuck agreed.[19] The film was shot in three-strip Technicolor, which meant that it took three days to get the rushes back, so Seaton knew he had three days to make good. Instead of beginning with a small scene, he started with a scene in the Diamond Horseshoe with Grable dancing amid four hundred extras. Seaton asked the cinematographer, Ernest Palmer, to select the best angle to show it all off. Seaton recalled, "Now my theory was, with all that happening, Betty Grable kicking her legs and singing and all those showgirls, nobody would know whether it was good direction or not." Three days later Zanuck saw the rushes and told Seaton, "You're a hell of a director. Go ahead, kid, keep going."[20]

Joseph L. Mankiewicz managed to offend Louis B. Mayer enough in 1943 so that Mankiewicz's contract was transferred to Twentieth Century-Fox. Mankiewicz and his agent arranged for the Fox contract to include the option to direct, which Mankiewicz did for the first time in 1945 with *Dragonwyck*. Mankiewicz did the screenplay, which was originally to be directed by Lubitsch. Lubitsch had a heart attack on his previous film, however, and Mankiewicz took over the direction with Lubitsch remaining as the producer. The two men had known each other at Paramount in the thirties, but did not get along on this production. Lubitsch was constantly second-guessing Mankiewicz about camera placement, and Lubitsch eventually took his own name off the film's credits.[21]

In 1947 Robert Rossen, whose screenwriting credits went back ten years, began directing. In 1950 Richard Brooks moved into directing. In 1953 Nunnally Johnson started directing. In 1954 Philip Dunne directed for the first time. In 1955 Blake Edwards began directing. By the midfifties, the move from screenwriter to director was commonplace, and American films were enriched by the narrative skill, the literate wit, the concern for character these writers brought to their direction. It is difficult to imagine any better-written or -directed films than some of those done by the writer-directors mentioned in this chapter: *Sullivan's Travels, The Treasure of the Sierra Madre, Some Like It Hot, Miracle on Thirty-Fourth Street, All About Eve, All the King's Men, In Cold Blood,* and *The Pink Panther.*

Not every screenwriter who turned director was successful at it. Dudley Nichols directed three undistinguished films and then returned to writing. Philip Dunne recalls that another writer "got on the set and couldn't open his mouth. He was paralyzed. They had to take him off. He just didn't know what to say. He stood there and went blank. This has happened with other writers who tried to direct."[22] Robert Riskin had his followers as well as Preston Sturges his.

19

The Guild

While many screenwriters looked to increase their power within the system by becoming producers or directors or both, others looked to collective action: a screenwriters union. This was not a new idea. The first club for screenwriters was formed in 1912 in New York by Epes Winthrop Sargent, with branches in Boston, Chicago, and New Orleans. Other groups followed.

In 1914 the Photoplay Authors' League was formed in Los Angeles. Its original members included Clarence Badger, Anita Loos, Thomas Ince, D. W. Griffith, and its first president Frank Woods. The League, like the other organizations, was more a social club than a conventional labor union, but it did begin to bring writers' problems to producers' attention. The League only lasted until 1916, when it was disbanded to prepare for the establishment in 1920 of the first Screen Writers Guild.[1] The objectives of the Guild were "protection of its members against unfair treatment," and "securing better treatment for its members,"[2] but the Guild was primarily a gathering place for writers.

In 1927, at the suggestion of Louis B. Mayer, the Academy of Motion Picture Arts and Sciences was formed. The academy's five branches included one for writers. One of the founding members of the Academy was Frank Woods, who served four years as the first executive secretary of the Academy. The Writers' Branch of the Academy took over from the original SWG the allocation of screenwriting credits.

In the earliest movies, there were no credits at all, then credits were assigned arbitrarily by the studio or the producer. Very arbitrarily. Often a producer would give himself a credit on the screenplay, although he had not done much writing. Directors would take credit as well. Producers would assign credits to their friends and relatives. Very often writers who had done substantial work in the early drafts of the script were overlooked for writers who simply did a final polish on the script. The arbitrary assigning of credits became a demonstration of the producer's or the studio's power.

Contributing to the problem was the nature of filmmaking itself. The writer's work, particularly at the studios, is at the beginning of the filmmaking process and those early decisions made by him (and the producer) are crucial to setting the structure and tone of the film. Then a variety of other decisions are made, but on the basis of the script. As the process continues, the early decisions are taken for granted and less importance is placed on them, particularly by the director, than on the decisions made later. Therefore, to a director and even to a producer, the latest contribution of a screenwriter, made closer to or in the middle of the making of the film, may seem at the time of credit allocation to be the most important. If credit allocation is left to producers and directors, it is likely that the later writers on a project will get the credit. Which is exactly what happened both before and while the Academy handled the credit system.

Mayer's idea was that the Academy would be dominated by the studios. The Academy was, in effect, a company union. The most vivid writer's reaction to this has been attributed to Dorothy Parker: "Looking to the Academy for representation was like trying to get laid in your mother's house. Somebody was always in the parlor, watching."[3]

In January 1933 the Academy called for all contracts to be eliminated as they expired, and in March approved the idea of pay cuts for those not protected by a union. Earlier Fox tried to cut wages, but the International Alliance of Theatrical Stage Employees (IATSE), the union for the technicians, voted against it and was able to enforce its vote on the studios.[4]

Even before the announcement of the March pay cuts, writers, impressed by IATSE's actions, met to organize. Ten screenwriters met in the back room of Stanley Rose's Bookshop and wrote up a four-page proposal. The proposal included a statement on the necessity of an organization powerful enough to force the producers to act on its demands, a suggested connection to the Dramatists Guild of America in New York (which would, along with a powerful West Coast Guild, make it possible to shut off the source of story material to the studios), a proposed system of royalties payments to screenwriters, and a demand that writers should be the ones to determine writing credits. The proposal may have included a demand that writers rather than producers have control over their material.[5] The proposal was mimeographed and passed to other writers. The next meeting was scheduled for the following week and each one of the ten was to bring one other writer. Instead of twenty, however, over fifty writers showed up at the Knickerbocker Hotel in Hollywood on February 10.

This meeting was "militant," in Lester Cole's words, but not politically militant. Cole was not then a Communist and he knew that none of the other ten from the first meeting were either.[6] Howard Green, president of the old Screen Writers Guild, warned against political militancy and said the new Guild's concern should be purely "economic."[7] Green's concern foreshadowed the split that would soon overtake the new Guild, but the writers were at the moment more involved in the economic issues. Also speaking at the meeting were three Broadway playwrights-turned-screenwriters who talked about the Dramatists' Guild fight in New York in 1919. The Guild struck and came away with a contract that called for approval in any alterations in their plays and equal rights with producers in the sale of rights.[8]

On April 6, 1933, the first official meeting of the new Screen Writers Guild was held. (The old SWG was officially dissolved in 1937.)[9] By mid-April 200 writers had resigned from the Academy and joined the new Guild, and within the year there were 640 members.[10] John Howard Lawson was elected the first president of the Guild. There was, however, a rather large gap between establishing the Guild and getting the studios to accept it.

The writing of the National Recovery Administration's rules for labor-management negotiations in late 1933 favored management, and in fact made it possible for the studios to ignore the guilds (the actors formed the Screen Actors Guild in July). When the NRA was declared unconstitutional in May 1935, the management of the studios continued their recalcitrance.[11]

All of the studios resisted the Screen Writers Guild, but MGM was most violently against it. Mayer objected to the guild, and Thalberg was, if anything, more vehement. Thalberg said, "Those writers are living like kings. Why on earth would they want to join a union, like coal miners and plumbers?"[12] George Oppenheimer thought that

> Thalberg was also actively opposed to the Guild, not so much because of an antilabor bias, but because of his patriarchal attitude toward all who worked for him. He wanted to be the one to dispense favors, and any organization that deprived him of his patronage was his enemy.[13]

In a meeting with the writers, Thalberg threatened to close the studio if they voted for the Guild. The coldness of his manner as he talked shocked those who had worked for him for years.[14]

There were those writers who agreed with Thalberg. The ideal of the Guild was a solid front, but there was never complete unity among screenwriters. The split in the members of the Guild formed in 1933 can be described as between the Right and the Left factions. The Right consisted of those who thought it unseemly for writers to belong to a union and had faith that management would treat them well. These writers generally joined the union over purely economic issues, particularly pay for younger and inexperienced writers. The writers of the Right were usually older and established writers. Many had been in movies since the silent days, when the spirit of cooperation truly existed among those who worked on a film. Mayer and Thalberg tried, with some success, to promote that family feeling at their studio (as did the heads of the other studios). There were also younger writers who felt this way. John Lee Mahin and James Kevin McGuinness, both writers at MGM and both active on the Right, had backgrounds in advertising and journalism and like writers on the Left came to Hollywood from the East. The writers on the Right felt a militant union was a betrayal of the industry that had given them so much.

The writers of the Left tended to be the younger writers from New York. The industry they came into was already stratified and they saw that their position, particularly in comparison with the members of the Dramatists' Guild, was weak. They were both more militant and more overtly political than the writers of the Right. While the writers of the Right worked and often socialized with the producers and executives, the writers of the Left were more involved in political and union organizing.

The dispute between the factions of the Guild continued throughout 1934 and 1935. The Left was more active within the Guild, while the Right arose to stop activities that were in their minds too extreme. One of those was the proposal that the Guild should align itself with the other writers' unions: the Authors' League, the Dramatists' Guild, the Newspaper Guild, and the Radio Writers Guild. This would give the SWG enough power to force the studios to recognize them as the legitimate bargaining agent for writers, but the Right felt that such a connection would in fact lower the status of the writers, since it was a loss of autonomy.[15] The Right was also concerned with what it saw as the guild's move politically leftward. The militancy of the guild leadership was to the Right a sign of Communist influence within the Guild. There were leaders of the Guild, such as Samuel Ornitz, who were members of the Communist Party,[16] but their activities at the time centered more on organizing the guild and getting it accepted as the bargaining agent for the writers. There were also many leaders of the guild who were not, then or ever, members of the Party.

Throughout the spring of 1936 the studios put pressure on the guild and its members, and the Right tried to get the proposals for amalgamation with other guilds watered down. In May the Guild voted for the principle of amalgamation, 193 to 25, and also voted for an article in the guild bylaws that would keep members from signing contracts extending beyond May 1938.[17] In June 1936 several conservative members of the guild broke away from it and formed a rival union, the Screen Playwrights.

In a published 1979 interview, John Lee Mahin, one of the founders of the Screen Playwrights, insisted the organization was the writers' idea,[18] but in a 1968 interview with Estelle Changas for the UCLA Oral History of the Motion Pictures Project, Mahin stated that he and the other writers approached Thalberg first to recognize the SWG. When Thalberg refused, he also suggested they form another union, which Mahin identifies as the Screen Playwrights.[19]

The Screen Playwrights certainly received encouragement and support from MGM. They were allowed to use the studio's facilities for their organizational work, and the contract they signed in 1937 was similar to an agreement prepared with Thalberg before his death in September 1936.[20] The Screen Playwrights did not attract large numbers of writers, but the enrollment in the Screen Writers Guild did decline, from a combination on the part of producers of force (threats and firings) and generosity (long-term contracts and promotion to producer for writers who resigned from the Guild).

The new 1935 National Labor Relations Act (the Wagner Act) was held constitutional by the Supreme Court in April 1937. Two months later the SWG filed a petition with the National Labor Relations Board to become the bargaining agent for writers. The NLRB decreed in June 1938 that an election would be held among writers employed at the studios. The SWG won by a vote of 267 to 57, and it was certified in August 1938 as the bargaining agent for writers.[21]

There still remained, however, the slight problem of negotiations over a contract. The management continued to stall bargaining sessions with the SWG. Philip Dunne, who was on the first bargaining committee for the SWG, remembers:

> Finally we had what was supposed to be a bargaining session, but which was really a shouting match, because Zanuck was the chairman of the producers' negotiating committee and people just shouted. It wasn't collective bargaining. They had movie cameras and everything. Eventually they settled down. We finally negotiated a contract.[22]

One former executive secretary of the guild has been quoted as saying, "The 1941 contract was terrible. It tied the Guild in a knot."[23] Compared to what many Guild writers had hoped for, he was right. The contract did not provide for writers to retain control over their own work. Given the nature of both the film industry and the filmmaking process, it is most unlikely that such control could ever be obtained through a collective bargaining procedure. Many Guild members saw this early and downplayed the drive within the Guild for control, not only because of the impossibility of getting it but also because of the anger such demands produced within the studio managements.

The 1941 agreement also had a no-strike clause for the length of the contract (seven years). In later negotiations this was eliminated, and the guild called strikes in 1959–60, 1973, 1981, and 1985. The 1941 contract did establish a minimum wage ($187.50 per week), which in subsequent negotiations has extended to specific minimums not only for weekly pay rates, but also minimums for both high- and low-budget films for screenplays, rewrites, and polishes.

The 1941 agreement also called for an 80 percent Guild shop at the beginning of the contract, going up to 85 percent after six months, then up to 90 percent in May 1945. This was to permit members of the Screen Playwrights not to have to join the Guild immediately. Most of them did, and by September 1944 the studios were 90 percent Guild shop.[24] John Lee Mahin rejoined the Guild in 1948.[25]

The Guild also won in the 1941 contract the right for the Guild to decide on the screenwriting credits for films. As Philip Dunne said in 1970, "We felt that this machinery should properly belong to the writers. Now of course the studios couldn't agree with you more. This takes a big headache off them and puts it on the Guild."[26] It may be a headache for the Guild, but it is an essential service to its members. A writer's reputation and his fee depend on his credits, and not only on having a credit on a successful film, but having any credit at all. In later years having a credit on a film determines whether a writer receives any percentage of the income of the increasingly substantial subsidiary markets, such as television and videocassette sales. A screenwriter's credits are as close as he gets, as a screenwriter, to power in the industry.

As developed by the Guild, the credit arbitration process works in the following way. A studio or producer will assign tentative writing credits for a film and those credits are submitted to the Guild and to any writers who have worked on the project. If there is no call for arbitration, the credits stand (however, if a producer lists himself as one of the writers, the credits automatically go to arbitration). Any writer on the film can call for arbitration. The studio submits the written material it has, such as treatments and script drafts, and writers can submit written material as well. The names of a panel of members of the Guild who have agreed to serve are presented to the writers and each writer is allowed to reject a "reasonable" number. Three Guild members then read the written material independently of each other, and without knowing the names of the writers involved. A decision is reached based only on the written material, not material in the film that does not appear in the written material. After the results are announced, any of the writers can ask for a review by the board and present their case. If the writers are not satisfied, they can appeal to the executive committee of the Guild. Generally the writer who was the first writer on the script gets the first or top credit. A second writer on an original screenplay has to have done 50 percent of the script used in the film to receive credit. Additional writers get credit on the screenplay if they have contributed a third of the script. Credits for the screenplay are limited to three writers or two teams of writers.[27]

In the eighties there have been some complaints by screenwriters about the system, but objections to the credit arbitration system have traditionally come from directors. A typical case was William Wyler's objection that Christopher Fry did not get credit on the screenplay for the 1959 film *Ben Hur*. Fry had

worked with Wyler on the set in Rome, and Wyler protested publicly that a
writer of Fry's stature should be given credit. The Guild responded that the
arbitration panel had based their work on the scripts presented and that Fry
had not objected to the lack of credit.[28]

The Guild began its life during the most "industrial" portion of the
American motion-picture business, when the major studios were organized
and run like factories. It has, however, continued to be a force in the period of
television and independent production. In 1954 the Screen Writers Guild
joined with the Radio Writers Guild and the Television Writers Group of the
Authors' League to form the new Writers Guild of America, with two
branches, one on the East Coast and one on the West Coast.[29] The Writers
Guild of America, West (WGAW) took over negotiations not only for television writers, but also for screenwriters on the issue of additional payment for
films sold to television. In the 1948 agreements, the guilds gave up any
additional payment for pre-1948 films sold to television, but reserved the right
to ask for payment for post-1948 films. Negotiations over payments did not
occur until 1959. Producers strongly resisted and the result, in 1959–60, was
one of the bitterest of WGAW strikes. The writers won both the principle and
the money. In the first eleven months of 1980 *alone*, members of the Guild
received $2,796,823 in residuals from the sale of films to television.[30]

In the 1973 negotiations, the WGAW had put into the contract payment
from the sales of videocassettes, although at the time cassettes were still in the
future. A dispute over whether the percentage would come from the producer
or the distributor's share became one of the issues of the 1985 negotiations,
but the unwillingness of the members of the guild to endure a prolonged
strike led the Guild to settle for a percentage of the producer's share, the lower
figure of the two.[31]

The strike, the strike vote, and the settlement in 1985 had all the internal
squabbling that has marked the history of the Guild. There were the usual
emotional meetings, the name-calling, and the general spectacle the writers
make of themselves from time to time. Frank Pierson, one of the negotiators
for the Guild, explains the internal disputes in the Guild in the 1985 strike:

> We had a large number of organized and vociferous critics whose noisy press
> campaign undermined our credibility. We had an Eastern guild restless and
> distrustful of our militancy. We had soap writers openly threatening to scab, and
> groups publicly announcing their intention to form another union. Manage-
> ment also perceived us as divided into screen vs. TV, hyphenate [someone who
> is both writer and director, actor or producer] vs. freelancer, East vs. West, rich
> vs. poor, daytime vs. prime-time.[32]

The ideal of the founders of the Guild was strength through unity. There has been strength but very little unity. Why do screenwriters seem unable to get along without fighting? Partly it is because writers are so individualistic. Partly it is their nature to feel themselves smarter than others, particularly producers, directors, and actors but also other writers. Partly it is because within the industry they have, as writers, in spite of all the good the Guild has accomplished, little power and control, so it is not surprising that they feel strongly about the Guild, since it is one area in which they can have control. Partly it may be that the Guild has been from the very beginning an impossible ideal in the real world of the movie business.

In addition to those divisions mentioned by Pierson, there was of course historically another major division that did as much damage to it as any of the others. The original split between the Right and the Left had serious consequences when the government began to investigate the influence in Hollywood of the Communist Party.

20

The Party

Part of the appeal of the Communist Party in the thirties was its promise to change the system, and for screenwriters that meant a change in the studio system. The Party's activities did change the system, but not in ways anyone foresaw. The changes were not necessarily for the better for screenwriting in the American film, and the cost for screenwriting, and particularly for screenwriters, was enormous.

Screenwriters joined the Party at different times. Samuel Ornitz had been a member of the Party in New York since the midtwenties.[1] John Howard Lawson had been involved with left-wing activities in New York in the twenties, but he did not join the Party until 1934, after two stints in Hollywood, the last in 1933 when he was the first president of the Screen Writers Guild. Left-wing writers did not come to Hollywood with the intent of fomenting political activity. They came for the jobs and the glamour.[2]

A combination of events drew screenwriters into the Communist Party. On the international scene, there was the rise of fascism in Italy and Germany, which in the isolationist early thirties in America, only the Communists seemed to be protesting against. The Communist government in Russia was at the time acclaimed by the intellectual left both as the wave of the future and as actually working. On the national scene the Communist Party's support of progressive causes, such as union organizing and equal justice for minorities, attracted those who wanted to find an outlet for their social activism.

The fight over the organization of the Screen Writers Guild pushed many into the Party. Lester Cole discovered when he was invited, after his activities in the Guild in 1934, to join a Marxist study group, that "the writers in attendance were known to me as hard workers for the Guild."[3]

The Communists' activities on behalf of the Guild were active demonstration of their announced support of the underdog, but the Party had other appeals to writers as well. Writers thought of themselves as intellectuals, and the self-proclaimed intellectual foundation of the Party appealed to the writers' image of themselves. Writers active in the Party were also working off whatever guilt they felt over earning large salaries.

The appeal of the Party was social as well. Dalton Trumbo joined the Party

144

in 1943 because he had worked with many of the people in it and considered them his friends.[4] The Party met a need to belong not entirely met by the "family" atmosphere at the studios.

It is also likely that writers seduced by the father figures running the studios could also be seduced by the people running the Party. John Howard Lawson, the father figure for many writers in the Party, was just as dogmatic as Mayer, Thalberg, and Zanuck. John Lee Mahin, a strong anti-Communist, saw the connection, "We simply felt we could deal better with Uncle Louis [Mayer] than with Uncle Joe [Stalin]."[5] The writers who joined the Party did not see its excesses. Albert Maltz remembers that the Russians hid the flaws in their system by doing "a magnificent propaganda job."[6]

The Communist Party was interested in Hollywood for the same reason everybody else was: the visibility and the glamour. The Party recruited other workers in the movies, but not with the degree of success it had with the writers, for reasons already mentioned.

A second reason the Party wanted writers was because of what it felt was their role in the creation of films. The erroneous assumption, perhaps based on the Party's experience with other writers, was that the writers had some control over their work. One reason writers were attracted to the Party was their feeling of lack of control over the end results of their work. The Party assumed it could get, if not propaganda, at least "socially correct" treatments of subjects into films via the screenwriters. The Hollywood branch was a little less doctrinaire than other branches, but it did try to "help" the writers. It set up a Writers' Clinic in which Party members, notably John Howard Lawson, gave criticism and advice on scripts, often in harsh terms. This criticism is one reason many writers left the Party.[7]

The Party's influence over the subject matter in films was small. While studio heads were willing to hire writers they knew were Communists, they were not about to allow them to put any obvious propaganda in their films. MGM and Fox softened potentially pro-Communist material in Dalton Trumbo's 1940 script for *We Who Are Young* and John Howard Lawson's 1939 script for *Four Sons*, respectively.[8] Richard Collins and Paul Jarrico worked on the screenplay for *Song of Russia*, and as a result of conferences with the studio, producer, and director had to cut pro-Russian material.[9] In addition to the studios keeping an eye on what was in their films, the Production Code Administration, the industry's self-censorship organization watched for potential propaganda as well. The administration noted that twenty pieces of material submitted to them between 1935 and 1941 as potential films had pro-Communist content in them, and one 1939 screenplay was not made by the studio that submitted it because the administration thought it was "obviously Communist-inspired."[10]

In addition, the collaborative nature of filmmaking worked against the inclusion of propaganda. Whatever the writer may have put in the script, the producer, director, and actors, not to mention other writers, could easily change. Even if the other members of the production team were sympathetic, dramatic values took precedence over political ones. On *Cornered*, the producer Adrian Scott, the director Edward Dmytryk, and the first writer John Wexley were all Party members, but Dmytryk and Scott were put off by the long propaganda speeches Wexley put into the script and brought in another writer, John Paxton. Wexley asked John Howard Lawson and Albert Maltz to discuss the matter with Scott and Dmytryk, which they did, but they also felt that the draft of the script by the other writer was not all that different from Wexley's. Wexley said later of the film, "It was superior to most 'B' melodramas and an alert viewing audience could fill in the gaps."[11]

The members of the Communist Party in Hollywood did make positive contributions to screenwriting. They were among the most active of the early fighters for the Screen Writers Guild. There were attempts, some aborted and some successful, to get serious subject matter into the films they worked on. The period of the most significant positive contribution of the Communists in Hollywood was, not surprisingly, World War II, when the goals of the American government, the motion-picture industry, and the Party were most similar. The Hollywood Writers Mobilization, organized by the Guild, provided writers for a variety of wartime efforts: pamphlets, speeches, and scripts for various propaganda efforts.

The left-wing writers also wrote screenplays for the Hollywood war films. Larry Ceplair and Steve Englund, who have examined the activities of the Hollywood Left in detail, write that while the Communist writers did not get much left-wing propaganda into their wartime scripts

> they nevertheless did manage to avoid overemphasizing or overdramatizing the role of the extraordinary individual (the war hero) and instead focused on the teamwork and suffering of the average soldiers. Scripts like those for *Sahara* (Lawson), *Thirty Seconds Over Tokyo* (Trumbo), *Objective Burma* [Alvah]Bessie and [Lester]Cole), or *Pride of the Marines* [Albert](Maltz) stressed the collective effort of the front-line troops, and they presented as authentic a picture of the reality of war as it was possible to do in Hollywood. Finally the [Hollywood] Ten's scripts avoided, for the most part, the more overt forms of jingoism and racism which marred many other Hollywood war films—e.g., references to "Japs," "yellow dogs," "Krauts," etc.[12]

Perhaps the Errol Flynn vehicle *Objective Burma* does not "overdramatize the individual hero," but it should also be noted that non-left-wing screenwriters wrote their share of nonclichéd scripts, such as Nunnally Johnson's

The Moon Is Down, George Seaton's *The Eve of St. Mark,* and Lamar Trotti's *Guadalcanal Diary.*

The Investigations

Because of President Roosevelt's enormous popularity, the political Right found it rather easier to attack the more extreme examples of his policies than the man himself. With the success of the conservatives in the 1938 nonpresidential elections, the Subcommittee of the House of Representatives on Un-American Activities (HUAC) under its chairman Martin Dies attacked the Federal Theatre Project (FTP) as a hotbed of Communist influence. The attack was by both investigation and press release. In 1939 Congress withdrew its support of the FTP. The Hollywood Left attacked Dies's attack on the FTP and by early 1940 Dies brought his committee to investigate Hollywood.

Based primarily on the testimony of former Communist John L. Leech, newspapers reported that several well-known industry figures were Communists, including such non-Communists as Humphrey Bogart, James Cagney, Fredric March, and many others. They were invited by Dies to testify in "executive session," to clear their names.[13]

Philip Dunne heard from a friend that Dies was about to name him as a Communist as well, and Dunne was determined to clear his name. He believed the government did not have the right to ask him about his political affiliations, but thought "the position was that one ignorant congressman was about to tell the world that I was something I was not and that I embraced doctrines that in truth I abhorred." A friend of his in Congress told him, "Martin's only after headlines anyway. He wants to try for the Senate and he doesn't particularly care what the headlines say, as long as they spell his name right."[14] Dunne met with Dies and got himself cleared, as did the others. They shook hands for the cameras Dies provided, and Dunne appeared on the front page of the *Los Angeles Times* for the first time, along with Bogart, March, and Cagney.

The studios generally took a neutral position on Dies's 1940 investigations. The studios were not so neutral the following year, when Jack Tenney, the chairman of the Joint Fact-Finding Committee on Un-American Activities of the California state legislature, announced his committee was going to investigate "Reds in movies." When word got out that studio executives had been asked to "contribute" money to the committee, the hearings collapsed. Tenney tried again six months later and again in 1943, but without success.[15]

The next national congressional attack came from three isolationist senators in 1941. Their objection was to the supposed "pro-war propaganda" in such films as *Confessions of a Nazi Spy, Sergeant York,* and *Dive Bomber.*

Since the challenge here was to the producers' control of the films, as opposed to the political beliefs of those working for them, the studios fought back. The head of the Motion Picture Producers Association, Will Hays, denounced the subcommittee, as did the studio executives, who felt that public sentiment was generally pro-Allied and against some of the extremely anti-Semitic remarks of members of the subcommittee. The producers hired former presidential candidate Wendell Willkie to represent them in front of the subcommittee in the September 1941 hearings. Those hearings were widely condemned in the press, and the attack collapsed. As Ceplair and Englund note:

> The industry's clear victory in Washington demonstrated that unified, organized, and aroused film producers and executives constituted a formidable force—far stronger than the guilds. This strength was used narrowly and rather selfishly, though, in defense of the product itself and their control over it; it was not used in defense of constitutional principles. When, six years later, the Thomas Committee came back to town combining the strategies of both Nye-Clark and Dies—attacking films in general and film artists in particular—the producers once again defended the former, while they prepared to sacrifice the latter.[16]

One of the reasons given by many historians of this period[17] as to why the studios cooperated with the HUAC investigations, particularly those in 1947, was that this was a method by which the studios could get revenge for the creation of the unions and guilds of the 1930s. It is important to understand why the 1947 hearings were different from the earlier attempts, which the studios resisted.

A major change was in public attitude. In 1941 the studios had used both the negative public reaction to the anti-Semitic comments and the positive feeling for the Allies to help defeat the subcommittee. By 1947 the investigators had sharpened their act and were not antagonizing public opinion. Indeed, with the sudden shift of Russia from ally to enemy after the end of the war, the anti-Communists found themselves riding on a tide of public feeling they mercilessly exploited.

The Hollywood Communists had done serious damage to their own cause. Even with the rumors coming out of Russia of the purge trials and other problems in the late thirties, it was then still possible, as Albert Maltz said, because of Soviet propaganda, to believe that joining the Communist Party was not only the right thing, but the moral thing. Bit by bit the Party had given away the moral high ground. One element of the Party's early appeal was its anti-fascist and anti-Nazi stand. In August 1939, however, the Russians and the Germans signed a nonaggression pact, and on instructions from

Moscow, Communist Parties around the world began defending the pact and attacking preparations for war. There was an equally quick reversal in June 1941 when the Germans invaded Russia and once again became the enemy. The Party tried to defend both reversals on moral rather than practical grounds and looked amoral in the process.

The Party's handling of Budd Schulberg's 1941 Hollywood novel *What Makes Sammy Run?* also helped to isolate the Party in Hollywood. Schulberg decided to leave the Party rather than submit to "self-discipline," which the Party thought he needed to write a more "progressive" novel. The first reaction from the Party to the novel was positive. Charles Glenn wrote a positive review in the Communist *Daily Worker*, but was then forced by the powers of the Hollywood branch to write a second review condemning the book. The Party's dislike of the novel was partly because of Schulberg's reluctance to let the Party "help" him write it, partly because the book did not give the Party as much credit in the founding of the Guild as it thought it should have, and partly because Schulberg exposed the anti-Semitism in the Left in the middle of the Hitler-Stalin pact.[18]

The Party also created a problem for itself with its insistence on secrecy. There were legitimate reasons for the Communist Party in the thirties to maintain a degree of secrecy, given the "Red Scares" of the twenties. The secrecy within the Party also appealed to several Hollywood writers who joined it, since it reinforced their view of themselves as "special." Unfortunately, this secrecy alienated those who might have been more inclined to support the Party members during the 1947 investigations and after.

During the war, the resistance to Communists grew, in spite of their war efforts, or perhaps because of them. The openness of the Communists' involvement in the war work may have seemed to the Hollywood Right that the Communists were coming out into the open and making a more obvious effort to take a position of power in the film business. In 1944 a number of the Hollywood Right formed the Motion Picture Alliance for the Preservation of American Ideals specifically to combat the influence of the Left in Hollywood. Among the screenwriters active in the alliance were former Screen Playwright members James McGuinness and Howard Emmett Rogers, and other writers such as Borden Chase, Casey Robinson, and Morrie Ryskind.[19] The alliance was the most vigorously anti-Communist group in Hollywood, outdoing even the studio-run Motion Picture Producers Association. The Producers Association had a variety of goals, but the alliance's goals were almost exclusively to rid the industry of Communists. To that end, the alliance, against the wishes of the producers, invited HUAC to resume its investigations.[20]

In 1945 HUAC announced it would investigate Hollywood, but no public hearings were held.[21] By early 1947 the Red-baiting of the alliance provoked

HUAC, now under the leadership of J. Parnell Thomas, to return to Hollywood. The committee began closed-door investigations in May 1947, talking primarily to "friendly" witnesses, i.e., those who cooperated with the committee. Many of the witnesses at these hearings were screenwriter members of the Motion Picture Alliance, including Howard Rogers, James McGuinness, and Rupert Hughes. [22]

On June 2, 1947, Eric Johnston, the new president of the Producers Association, met with the studio heads. He wanted their approval of three points: (1) the industry should insist on open and fair investigations by HUAC, (2) the industry should agree not to hire any Communists, and (3) former Secretary of State James Byrnes should be hired to represent the Producers Association in Washington. The studios agree to points 1 and 3, but not to number 2, since that threatened their control of the studios. [23]

On September 21, 1947, HUAC issued subpoenas to forty-three film-industry people calling for their testimony at hearings in Washington in October. [24] Nineteen of those called were members of the Left in Hollywood and became known as the Unfriendly Nineteen. Only ten of those actually testified and they became known as the Unfriendly Ten, or the Hollywood Ten. Of those Ten, only one, Edward Dmytryk, had never been a screenwriter.

During the summer and fall of 1947, the Nineteen and their lawyers worked out a strategy they hoped would keep them employed in the film industry, keep them out of jail, keep them from informing on others, and enable them to expose the committee. [25] Unfortunately, their insistence on the latter point virtually insured losing on the first two.

The Nineteen, before their appearance in Washington in October, were not without support. The producers had stood up for the right to hire whom they wanted in 1941 and again in June 1947. In October Eric Johnston told the lawyers for the Hollywood Nineteen that there would not be a blacklist. [26] The Screen Writers Guild did not want to take on HUAC directly, primarily because they wished to protect the Guild as an organization more than they wished to protect the screenwriters who had been subpoenaed. The Guild left the defense of the writers up to the individuals themselves. [27]

There were also those liberals who were willing to stand up not so much for the Nineteen themselves as for the principle that the First Amendment of the Constitution of the United States of America did not permit a government body to inquire into the political affiliations of its citizens. William Wyler, John Huston, and Philip Dunne formed a Committee for the First Amendment in September. This committee was designed to protest the HUAC investigations and to try to help head off the coming blacklist. [28] The committee organized a flight to Washington in October of not only themselves, but such stars as Humphrey Bogart, Lauren Bacall, Danny Kaye, and Gene Kelly.

The plan the Nineteen and their lawyers had was to have the Nineteen attempt to answer the questions the committee asked "in their own way." What this meant in actuality is that those Ten who actually testified seemed to be less interested in the Constitutional question than in making speeches. A year later, when Philip Dunne was to be called as a character witness for Dalton Trumbo in his trial for contempt of Congress, Dunne listened to the audio tape of Trumbo's testimony, which Trumbo's lawyer was planning on playing in court. Dunne thought that

> to play the tape for the jury would be disastrous. What came through was a loud and obstreperous witness obviously evading the questions posed to him by a kindly and fatherly Congressman Thomas. There was nothing kindly or fatherly about Chairman Thomas, but that was how he managed to sound on that particular tape. I am afraid that, throughout the dismal affair, the efforts of the Hollywood Ten in the fields of both legal defense and public relations were uniformly as disastrous.[29]

The legal defense, claiming first that the Ten *tried* to answer and then (when the case was on appeal) standing on the First Amendment, turned out to be the wrong approach when the Supreme Court in 1950 ruled against the Ten. The public-relations problem was even more immediate. The Ten managed to alienate whatever support they had in the film industry. They, and the Communist Party, played politics, played badly, and lost.

A month after the hearings in Washington, on November 24, the heads of the major motion-picture companies met at the Waldorf-Astoria Hotel in New York to discuss what to do. Eric Johnston told the executives that he saw only two choices: either keep employing the Ten and promise to keep subversive material off the screen, or refuse to employ the Ten. Johnston pointed out a number of signs that public opinion was turning against Hollywood, primarily as a result of the behavior of the Ten at the October hearings, and he recommended the second option. The producers and executives at the meeting who were most opposed to firing the Ten were those from Hollywood who had worked most closely with them: Dore Schary, Samuel Goldwyn, and Walter Wanger. It was, however, the New York heads of the corporations that carried the vote.[30] The group drafted the Waldorf Statement, which said that the Ten's "actions have been a disservice to their employers and have impaired their usefulness to the industry." The statement went on to note the studios would fire any of the Ten "until such time as he is acquitted or has purged himself of contempt and declares under oath that he is not a Communist," and would not hire any Communists. The studios expressed a desire to work with the guilds "to eliminate any subversives, to protect the innocent, and to safeguard free speech and a free screen wherever threatened."[31]

In spite of their attempting to pose as protectors of free speech, what the heads of the studios had done with the Waldorf Statement was to take the first step in creating the Blacklist. The Blacklist was designed as a public-relations effort by the major studios to protect themselves against the government and public opinion. The studios, however, were more vulnerable than they thought, because major changes developing in the motion-picture industry would help break up the studios' control of motion-picture production. The irony is that the Blacklist, because of those changes in the industry, also made possible the creation of the Black Market, which in turn helped in a small but important way to destroy the studio system.

Gene Gauntier: Kalem's ace screenwriter . . . among her other jobs. (Courtesy of the Academy of Motion Picture Arts and Sciences)

Frank Woods: first president of the Photoplay Authors' League, a founding member of the Academy of Motion Picture Arts and Sciences, and, incidentally, Griffith's cowriter on *The Birth of a Nation*. (Courtesy of the Academy of Motion Picture Arts and Sciences)

Thomas Ince: writer, director, producer, studio head, and the founder of the American narrative film tradition.

C. Gardner Sullivan: Ince's chief screenwriter. Wait a minute. Ince only worked in silent films, but that shirt, those blinds, that watch are all very much of the thirties—and evidence that silent screenwriters like Sullivan made the transition to sound films very nicely. (Courtesy of the Academy of Motion Picture Arts and Sciences)

Two writers from the thirties: Bartlett Cormack (left), writer of the 1931 version of *The Front Page*; and Sidney Buchman (right), writer of *Mr. Smith Goes to Washington*. (Courtesy of the Academy of Motion Picture Arts and Sciences)

Orson Welles: even younger than when he cowrote *Citizen Kane,* if that's possible.

Preston Sturges: the screenwriter (note script in hand) becomes a director (note camera above).

John Huston: from *Across the Pacific* to *Beat the Devil*. (Courtesy of the Academy of Motion Picture Arts and Sciences)

Two sets of Oscars, public and private: (Left) Billy Wilder picking up three for *The Apartment*, thus demonstrating the advantages of independent production. (Below) Dalton Trumbo—in short sleeves—finally getting his Oscar for *The Brave One*, twenty years after the fact, from Walter Mirisch, president of the Academy.

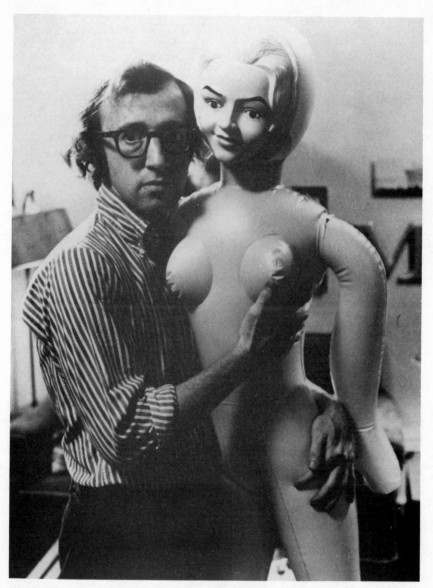

Woody Allen: the ultimate auteur and the body of his work.

Three screenwriters: Akira Kurosawa (left), author of *Throne of Blood*, which borrows from *Macbeth*; Francis Ford Coppola (middle), author of *The Conversation*, which borrows from *Blow-Up*; and George Lucas (right), author of *Star Wars*, which borrows from *The Hidden Fortress*.

John Sayles giving the Borowsky lecture at the Academy; writers' dress styles have changed a lot since Gene Gauntier and Frank Woods. (© Copyright Academy of Motion Picture Arts and Sciences)

Part 3
Independent Production
1950–80s

21

Decline of the Studios

After the boom years of World War II, the major-studio system was hit by a combination of forces that brought about its downfall. First, many countries around the world decided to freeze profits from the showing of American films, which meant the money could not be sent back to the United States. Second, the HUAC investigations hit the industry. Third, the antitrust suits that had been wending their way through the courts were finally settled in 1948, and not on favorable terms to the industry. Fourth, commercial television established itself in American life.

Frozen Profits and Overseas Production

The easiest answer to the problem of funds frozen overseas was for studios to make films in foreign countries to use up the currency. Philip Dunne's *Way of a Gaucho* was shot on location in Argentina. Nunnally Johnson wrote *Three Came Home* and *The Mudlark*, which were filmed in the Philippines and England, respectively. When director Lewis Milestone went to Australia to film *Kangaroo*, he discovered, like Dunne, that the novel that had been purchased for filming was inaccurate and that the script had to be rewritten.[1]

The Conservative Influence on Films

The impact of the HUAC investigations on screenwriters will be dealt with in considerable detail in the next chapter, but there was also the impact of the conservative drift in the country on the kinds of films made. In the immediate postwar period there were several films made on social issues, such as *Gentleman's Agreement* (anti-Semitism), *The Snake Pit* (conditions in mental hospitals), and *Pinky* (race relations), and *The Best Years of Our Lives* (problems facing returning veterans), but by the early fifties (when HUAC returned, armed with a favorable Supreme Court decision), studios had become a little more hesitant in making such potentially troublemaking films.

The studios did try to appease the Right by making anti-Communist movies. The movies made by and/or for the anti-Communists have almost no

155

sense of what Communism is. *Big Jim McLain*, a 1952 film, was cowritten by Richard English, who had produced a radio series about people who left the Party.[2] The Communists in the film are more interested in crime than politics. Even John Lee Mahin was appalled at Myles Connolly's rewrite of Mahin's *My Son John*,[3] which made the film pure, and bad, propaganda. The film seems to suggest that anybody who reads or thinks is a Communist, and probably perverted in other ways as well.

Scripts, and the movies made from them, got blander. Robert Riskin's last two produced screenplays, *Mister 880* and *Half Angel*, have none of the substance of his earlier work. There was also a trend in the fifties to remake previous successes. This may have come from a desire to say to the Right, "What could be a more American story than one that has already made money?" or it may have simply been the floundering on the part of an industry that was losing its bearings. Some of the remakes were commercially successful, such as MGM's *Quo Vadis* and De Mille's *The Ten Commandments*. MGM's *Ben Hur* was both an artistic and commercial success. MGM did remakes of *The Women* and *The Philadelphia Story* but without the literate wit of the originals. Perhaps the worst remake of the fifties was *You Can't Run Away from It*, with a screenplay by Claude Binyon that flattened out Robert Riskin's *It Happened One Night*.

Divorcement

In 1948 the United States Supreme Court ruled in the case of the *United States vs. Paramount Pictures*. Paramount was found in violation of the antitrust laws. The outcome was that the studios had to give up control of the theaters they owned. The divorcement of the production and distribution sides of the business from the theater side meant the companies could no longer control guaranteed markets for their films. There was then no longer a need for the studios to have all the talent under contract, since they did not have guaranteed work for them. This meant in turn that the studios would have to hire people individually to work on each film, or each group of films, which in turn shifted control of the production of films away from the old studio heads and into the hands of those talents with whom the studios wanted to work.

The power arrangements for screenwriters shifted. Instead of working for studios heads, they now found themselves working for independent producers, directors, actors, and sometimes even themselves. The changes brought about by the Paramount decision continue into the present. The pattern in American moviemaking since 1948 has been clearly moving away from studio control of production, and more recently, from studio control of distribution as well.

Decline of the Studios

This change in power relationships did not happen overnight. Indeed, the studio system of production exerted considerable influence throughout the fifties, both for better and worse. Dore Schary was head of production at MGM from 1948 to 1956, and the system of individual production units continued at MGM during and after Schary's tenure. Two of those units were run by Arthur Freed and John Houseman.

Even after Schary's arrival Arthur Freed reported directly to Mayer. Schary generally left Freed's unit alone unless he felt the script was terrible.[4] In 1951 Freed saw the French film *Gigi* and eventually decided to remake the film as a musical. Freed had a transcription of the French film made, and screenwriter Alan Jay Lerner used it as the basis for his first-draft script. The other executives at the studio saw this draft and asked Freed why he wanted to make a movie about a "whore." Lerner himself was not happy with this draft, but Lerner remembers, "Arthur . . . knew *that* screenplay was just a loose frame until the score was developed."[5] After the first sneak preview of the film, Lerner returned to the project to write additional scenes that were added to the film or substituted for scenes dropped.[6]

As *Gigi* neared completion in 1958, Freed purchased the rights to Jack Kerouac's novel of life among the beats in North Beach, *The Subterraneans*. Freed wanted to make a small-scale, black-and-white drama, but the MGM studio style (the film was finally made in color and CinemaScope), still practiced by those who had been there for years, worked against the writing of the story and the characters.[7]

In 1951 John Houseman joined MGM as a producer at the request of Dore Schary, with whom Houseman had worked at RKO. Houseman and Schary had similar tastes in films, at least in comparison with the other producers at MGM, but Houseman found it difficult to do small pictures at MGM. The studio was geared to making large, clean movies. Houseman discovered, for example, that the typing pool was run by "a severe, protective lady who would refuse typing if it threatened to corrupt her girls' morals. Of the synopsis of a risky [sic] new play she declared that she 'wouldn't let a girl type this sort of thing unless she'd been married at least twice.' "[8]

One of Houseman's first productions at MGM managed to combine the style of the studio with a tough, sardonic script. *The Bad and the Beautiful* began as a short story about a broadway producer submitted to the studio. Houseman thought of the possibility of translating it to Hollywood, and hired

Charles Schnee, with whom he had worked at RKO, to do the script. Schnee spent several weeks before actually writing the script simply transferring the details to the movie business. He was assisted in this by Houseman, who helped structure the main character personally on David O. Selznick and professionally on Val Lewton, who had produced a series of low-budget horror movies at RKO.[9]

Houseman found himself fighting off attempts by the studio to make him use the contract writers. For *Executive Suite*, an all-star-cast film about a fight among corporate executives to take over a furniture plant, Houseman was able to hire a young New York writer named Ernest Lehman, whose first screenplay it was. If the management at MGM was willing to do a film about business, they were unlikely to do one about labor. When Houseman proposed one, the members of the executive board of the company made it clear it was not an idea they liked.[10] The film was never made and Houseman eventually left MGM.

When Twentieth Century-Fox made an effort to get viewers away from television by introducing the wide-screen process CinemaScope in 1953, Darryl Zanuck found himself looking for material for the wide screen. He now had to encourage B-picture material like *Beneath the Twelve-Mile Reef* and historical spectacles like *Desirée*. While Fox had done historical films in the thirties, they generally had strong story lines. But Zanuck was so tired now that even when he did get a good script for a spectacle, such as Casey Robinson and Philip Dunne's script for *The Egyptian*, Zanuck's mistakes in casting destroyed the film. While doing pictures like that, Zanuck was also turning down scripts like Budd Schulberg's *On the Waterfront*. Schulberg recalls that Zanuck spent the meeting they had on the script talking about *Prince Valiant*.[11]

When Zanuck left the studio in 1956, he was replaced by Buddy Adler. Adler was not a story man. He did not read scripts well, if at all, and he certainly did not discuss them with the intelligence of Zanuck. Nunnally Johnson could have accepted this if Adler had someone with a good story sense reading the scripts for him, but Johnson was not impressed with the person who did Adler's reading either.[12]

Philip Dunne had problems with Adler as well. Adler insisted that the film adaptation of John O'Hara's novel *Ten North Frederick* should show that the main character's life was a happy one. Dunne pointed out the story was the opposite. Adler's reply was, "I don't like tragedies."[13] Adler let Dunne write and direct the picture, but on a limited budget with sets left over from other Fox films. When the picture was completed, Adler had a crucial line cut from the film. When Joe Chapin asks his wife if she has had affairs, she replies, "Yes, damn you, I have." Dunne and the producer of the film, Charles Brackett, had received agreement from the Production Code Office that "damn" could be used in the scene, but Adler was bothered by nervous titters in the audience at the sneak preview and had the "damn you" deleted.[14]

The Rise of the Independents

In 1951 Arthur Krim and Robert Benjamin, two lawyers experienced in the film business, took over the running of United Artists. Producer Stanley Kramer, who had released films under the old UA management was now at Columbia, but he owed the company one more film. It turned out to be *High Noon*, a large success for the company, as was their next film, *The African Queen*.[15]

Both films started a policy that would cause UA to become the most important studio of the fifties, and change the way other studios were run. Rather than put a large staff under contract the management at UA was able to get producers, directors, stars, and screenwriters to work for them by promising them a percentage of the profits of their films and, perhaps more importantly, creative freedom after the subject of the film and its budget were agreed upon. The filmmakers were, for nearly all practical purposes, independent of the kind of control that the studios had previously demanded.

The producer of *The African Queen* was Sam Spiegel, who had recently formed Horizon Pictures with a studio writer-director who was happy to be rid of studio control. The latter was John Huston, cowriter with James Agee and director of *The African Queen*. It was Huston who insisted Agee be his cowriter on the film. Huston wrote later:

> Jim was a willing collaborator. We quickly worked out a routine. We'd discuss a sequence, then block it out and write alternate scenes. Then we would exchange scenes and rework each other's material. This method was all right, except that Jim got too far ahead. I marveled at the volume of material he was turning out. Then I discovered that he was not going to bed at ten p.m., but working deep into the night.[16]

Agee ended up in the hospital and was unable to go on the African location of the film. Neither Huston nor C. S. Forester, who had written the novel, were happy with the two endings the novel had (one in the American edition, and one in the British). Huston and his friend Peter Viertel came up with the ending used in the film, in which Rosie and Charlie and the remains of the *African Queen* destroy the German ship.[17]

If Huston and Agee's script for the independently produced 1951 film could have easily been produced at a major studio, Huston and Truman Capote's script for the 1954 *Beat the Devil* shows both the advantages and disadvantages of independent production. Huston had Peter Viertel and Tony Veiller do the first draft. They both agreed the script was not very good and left the project. The picture was being shot on location in Italy, and Huston knew that Capote was in Rome. He asked him to come along and help out. Huston tried to figure out as many delaying tactics as he could while he and Capote redid the script.[18]

Beat the Devil is generally accepted as a parody of the classic Hollywood thriller. Huston's *Maltese Falcon* is the film often mentioned, but Huston's 1942 film *Across the Pacific* (the screenplay was by Richard MacCaulay) seems to be the real model. Both *Pacific* and *Devil* deal with a diverse group of people who spend a good portion of their respective lives on board ship, with a variety of intrigues going on. In *Pacific* the plot concerns a Japanese attack on the Panama Canal, which Humphrey Bogart manages to thwart in the nick of time. In *Devil*, the plot appears to deal with a plan to buy up land in East Africa.

In *Pacific* each scene bears some relation to the plot and is played seriously. In *Devil* nobody seems to understand the plot, and the scenes are played for comic values. The emphasis in the latter film is on the individual scenes, often with no sense of connection between them. In *Pacific* there is a running gag in which Bogart talks in different scenes about Mary Astor being green when she gets seasick, blue when she's out in the cold, and red when she is sunburned. This all comes together in a later scene when he talks about liking her because she's multicolored. In *Devil* Gina Lollobrigida is painting Edward Underdown and talks about how the colors of his face have changed from red and brown to white, at which point she realizes he is ill. It is a funny scene, but amusing in itself, rather than in using the cumulative humor of the scenes in *Pacific*. The shaggy-dog humor of *Devil* appeals to sophisticates, but the picture was not a popular success at the time. Its parodying of Hollywood genres looks forward to the film parodies of the sixties and seventies.

Billy Wilder was another screenwriter-director who took advantage of the rise in independent production. At Paramount in the forties and early fifties he often aggravated the management by wanting to do strong material. He left Paramount in the midfifties and made *Love in the Afternoon* for the Mirisch Brothers, three brothers who set up their own production company. The Mirisches moved Wilder to United Artists for *Some Like It Hot* in 1959. *Hot* deals with two male musicians who witness the St. Valentine's Day Massacre in Chicago in 1929, then to escape the gangsters chasing them dress up as women and join an all-girl's orchestra. One of the musicians falls in love with the lead singer, and the other one has a rich millionaire fall in love with him. It is impossible to imagine Wilder, or any other writer pitching such an idea to the head of any of the major studios of the thirties or forties. The management at United Artists, however, had faith in Wilder (and his cowriter, I. A. L. Diamond). The management was only concerned about getting stars to appear in the film.[19]

Wilder and Diamond's next film, *The Apartment* told the story of a young executive who rises to the top by letting more-senior executives use his nearby apartment as a trysting place. It was again the sort of material the major studios would not previously have touched. Partly this was a change in the times, but mostly it was because the majors were very conscious of their position as big corporations that depended on the goodwill of the public, whom they took great pains not to offend. The independent companies were willing to give the writers more freedom in terms of subject matter than the majors were.

The loosening of control by the major studios was a mixed blessing for screenwriters. Preston Sturges had difficulties after he left the studio system as did other writers like Johnson, Huston, and Wilder. *The Angel Wore Red, The Kremlin Letter,* and *Kiss Me Stupid* are not great films, but are the price we had to pay to get *The World of Henry Orient, The Man Who Would Be King,* and *Some Like It Hot.*

The best example of a screenwriter who had difficulty dealing with independence in the fifties is Joseph Mankiewicz. In 1953 Mankiewicz left Fox and signed with United Artists, where his first film was *The Barefoot Contessa,* a story he had thought of doing as a novel.[20] Zanuck had managed to control Mankiewicz's tendency towards talky screenplays, sometimes by cutting the script, sometimes by cutting the film. On *Contessa* there was nobody but Mankiewicz to do the cutting. As a result there are long dialogue scenes that repeat points already made, as well as scenes in which the characters analyze each other and themselves. The low point of the film is a speech by a South American millionaire on oil-depletion allowances. What that has to do with the story of a poor girl who becomes a movie star is known only to Mankiewicz. Mankiewicz's screenplay for the 1958 film *The Quiet American* is also excessively talky.

Exploitation Films!

When the studios ceased to own their own theaters, they stopped their production of B pictures, and the B-picture units at various companies eventually changed into television divisions. Many writers of the old B pictures found new work in filmed television series. For example six of the fifteen credited writers on *The Lone Ranger* series in the late forties and early fifties had B-picture writing credits in the forties or early fifties, including Albert Duffy, who had written serials from 1940 to 1948.[21]

The B picture itself began to change in the fifties as well. In 1954 James Nicholson and Samuel Arkoff began as producer/distributors in what became known as American-International Pictures. Their first releases were conventional B pictures, but they soon realized the market allowed them to make no more on a film than the flat rental fee charged to the bottom half of the double bill. If they could make two movies to show on the same bill, they could get the entire rental fee, which was usually a percentage of the gross.

They also realized that there was now a new market for the next generation of B pictures. If television was keeping adults and families at home, teenagers wanted to get out of the house. Nicholson and Arkoff decided to make films directly for the teenage market. That meant not the sort of films the majors would necessarily be interested in, since the attitude of the majors had always been to provide entertainment for the entire family.[22]

What Nicholson and Arkoff made were films that could be easily sold to an unsophisticated and volatile market. In other words, exploitation films: quick, cheap films that had enough elements to make effective advertisements, but films that did not make anybody think about them in any but the most superficial way. After all, how much thinking could a teenager on a date at the drive-in do? Or want to do, even if he or she could?

In fact, the AIP films, as had often happened with earlier exploitation films, were often written *after* the titles had been thought up. Nicholson says, "We do our planning backwards. We get what sounds like a title that will arouse interest, then a monster or a gimmick, then figure out what our advertising is going to consist of. Then we bring in a writer to provide a script to fit the title and concept."[23]

One of the most proficient writers for AIP was an ex-lyricist named Charles Griffith. He was approached by AIP's house director, Roger Corman, to write a western. Corman took him to a Randolph Scott western and told him to write the same thing, only to make the sheriff a girl. Griffith went out to the western set that was going to be used and figured out how to write the entire film so it could be done on one location. He also named the characters and places in his script with the names that were already painted on the false fronts so the company would not have to repaint the sets.[24]

In 1959 Griffith wrote *A Bucket of Blood*. He remembers, "When I was writing it I had to hide the fact that it was a comedy from Roger. Roger didn't want comedy or drama. He said. 'To do those you have to be good, and we can't be good so we'll do action.' "[25] Corman realized the script was a comedy and Griffith told him, "Roger. You're going to make it for thirty thousand dollars. How can you lose?" Corman replied, "All right. How do you shoot comedy?" Griffith answered, "Just shoot it straight."[26] Corman was so pleased he asked Griffith to rewrite the film, and the next version became *The Little Shop of Horrors.*[27]

AIP intended their films to be different from major-studio productions. In the fifties and sixties they were, but when the majors began to go after the adolescent market in the late seventies, they found themselves making big-budget versions of the AIP exploitation movies.

22

The Black Market

In April 1950 the Supreme Court of the United States refused to hear the cases of contempt of Congress against John Howard Lawson and Dalton Trumbo, thus confirming a circuit court of appeals ruling against the writers. By September 1950 the Hollywood Ten were in prison, and by spring 1951 screenwriters and others had begun to receive subpoenas for the second HUAC investigations of Hollywood.[1] The industry was by then simply trying to control the damage as best it could.

The committee itself became both more subtle and more ritualized. It was no longer enough for witnesses to admit they had been members of the Party. It now became a test of loyalty that witnesses identify those who had been members of the Party with them. There was no legislative need for names. The committee had, from undercover FBI and Los Angeles Police Department informants, virtually complete membership lists.[2] Witnesses were forced to go through what Victor Navasky has called "degradation ceremonies" to establish their loyalties: the only way to be cleared was to become an informer. Conversely, the only way to retain one's "purity" to the Left was to avoid becoming an informer. The situation was not as morally simple as either side would have it.

Screenwriters who testified did so for a variety of reasons. Many people were out of the Party and no longer felt any loyalty to it. Leo Townsend was put off by the anti-Semitism he found in the Party.[3] Isobel Lennart was pressured by family responsibilities, and felt that her work as a screenwriter sustained her.[4] Robert Rossen also faced the pressure of writing or not writing. His widow recalls, "It ended up with Bob doing what he did or dying by attrition—because Bob couldn't get a job writing, and in my book if he couldn't write, he couldn't live."[5] Townsend, Lennart, and Rossen got back into screenwriting, but not every writer who testified did. Sylvia Richards took a leave of absence, her film was assigned to another screenwriter, and she was never asked to work in the business again.[6] There was, it should be noted, an element of hypocrisy in the Communist Party's sudden moral stance against informing. Some years before the HUAC investigations, the Party had asked Phil Cohen, a therapist to whom the Hollywood branch of the Party sent many of its members, to "inform them of any anti-Party things that would come up in the course of therapy. I wouldn't do it."[7] On the other hand, when Party members came to Cohen to discuss whether they should testify, he often guided them toward testifying.[8]

Budd Schulberg

Budd Schulberg left the Party in 1939 over the question of his freedom to write as he wanted and his disenchantment with the Party continued to grow. He appeared before the committee on May 23, 1951. After Schulberg testified, he was approached by director Elia Kazan to write a screenplay for what would eventually become the 1954 film *On the Waterfront*, which has been interpreted by many as Kazan and Schulberg's defense for their both having testified before the committee. Schulberg's screenplay was not Kazan's first attempt to do a film about corruption in the longshoreman's union. In 1950 Kazan had worked with playwright Arthur Miller on a screenplay entitled "The Hook."

Miller's screenplay concerns thirty-two-year-old longshoreman Marty Ferrara. Marty is at first reluctant to fight the union leaders, but he eventually runs against and loses the election to Louis, the president of the union. Louis wants to make Marty a union delegate, but an old-timer on the docks encourages Marty to be his own man and fight corruption his own way.

Schulberg took very little from Miller's script. In an early Schulberg draft titled "The Golden Warriors,"[9] Joey Doyle is killed because he was running for office against the corrupt union bosses. In the final shooting script,[10] Schulberg has changed the motivation for the murder to Joey's possible testimony before the Crime Commission. In Miller's script, the central dramatic question is whether Marty is going to fight the union bosses. From the beginning drafts of Schulberg's script, the question is whether Terry Malloy, the ex-boxer and longshoreman, is going to testify against the union bosses at hearings run by the Crime Commission.

Schulberg's version is less episodic and more dramatically focused than Miller's. In "The Golden Warriors" draft, several scenes are used to establish Edie Doyle, Joey's sister, who arrives home from school after Joey's death. Father Barry's decision to become involved also takes several scenes in this draft. In the final draft, Joey's death, Edie's determination to find the killer, and Father Barry's decision are all part of the same scene. The famous "taxicab scene," which by legend was improvised by Marlon Brando and Rod Steiger, appears in "The Golden Warriors" draft[11] closer to its final form in the film than almost any other scene, but in the final draft borrows Terry's description of the fight with Wilson from an earlier scene in the early draft.[12]

What the focusing of the scenes does is to intensify the drama, which in turn makes us feel the pressures applied to Terry from both sides: from the Crime Commission investigators, Edie, and Father Barry to testify, and from Charley and the union bosses and members *not* to testify. The heart of the film, and what gives it its emotional power, is the understanding Kazan and Schulberg have of the costs of going through the experience of testifying against people they have known and worked with.

It is one of the richest ironies, in a period flooded with them, that the best screenplay to come out of the HUAC investigations was written by a screenwriter who had testified. The assumption so many on the Left made was that screenwriters were somehow both intellectually and morally superior to the rest of the people working in the movie business. Writers were not; and it was a shock to many, especially the writers themselves, to discover it. It should not have been a shock. Artists, and especially writers, by nature write about, talk about, testify about their lives. It is a sign of their concern with the moral issues involved that writers on both sides worried over the issues of testifying or not testifying and in Schulberg's case dealt so vividly with the emotional costs of testifying.

Writers who Left Hollywood

Howard Koch was one of the original Hollywood Nineteen. He was never a member of the Communist Party, but was probably suspect because he was the sole screenwriter on the 1943 film *Mission to Moscow*, a wartime pro-Soviet film President Roosevelt asked Warner Brothers to make. Jack Warner did not help matters any by testifying in the October 1947 hearings that he thought Koch was a communist because he kept trying to get Communist propaganda into the film. Warner later admitted he had made a mistake. Much later.[13]

Koch's subpoena continued until the early fifties. An agent offered to "arrange" Koch's testimony, which along with a $7,500 legal "fee" would get Koch off the hook. Koch refused, and when it was clear he would no longer be able to work in the industry, he moved, first to New York, and then to Europe.[14]

Koch found that American screenwriters were in demand in London. In order for the films he wrote to be sold in the American market, he found it necessary to write under the name Peter Howard. Koch and his wife, who used the name Anne Rodney, also wrote for British television. They were two of many American expatriate writers hired by American producer Hannah Weinstein for several television series she produced in England in the fifties. Other exiled screenwriters working for her included Ring Lardner, Jr., Ian McClellan Hunter, Philip Stevenson, and Fred Rinaldo. Her television series included *The Adventures of Robin Hood, The Adventures of Sir Lancelot,* and *The Pirates.* All were good enough to be sold to American network television which was in theory also obeying the Blacklist.[15]

Donald Ogden Stewart, who had been a member of the Party, was never actually subpoenaed. His studio, MGM, wanted him to volunteer to testify, but he refused.[16] Stewart went to England and worked on British films. He did uncredited work on *Summertime.*[17]

Carl Foreman left the Party in 1942. By 1951 he was a partner with independent producer Stanley Kramer. When Foreman was subpoenaed in September 1951, he was working on the screenplay for *High Noon,* a western about a marshal who tries unsuccessfully to get the people of his town to help deal with the release from prison of an outlaw. Foreman found the similarities to his own situation striking. He later said:

> There are scenes in the film that are taken from life. The scene in the church is a distillation of meetings I had with partners, associates and lawyers. And there's the scene with the man who offers to help (the marshal) and comes back with his gun and asks, "Where are the others?"
> (Gary) Cooper tells him there are no others.[18]

Cooper knew that Foreman was using the film as an allegory for his own experiences,[19] but Cooper was supportive of Foreman, even though his politics were considerably to the right of Foreman's.[20] The problem with allegory is that it can be interpreted several ways. When the film was released, Cooper was seen in the Midwest as a symbol of Eisenhower working against the Communist threat,[21] and probably the more devoted followers of Senator Joseph McCarthy saw Cooper as symbolic of their hero.

Kramer bought Foreman out of the company and Foreman went to England in 1952. Like others he worked on the Black Market.[22] In 1956 Foreman's lawyer, Sidney Cohn, worked out an arrangement with the committee whereby Foreman could testify about his own activities without naming names. Foreman testified in executive session, which gave rise to rumors that he had named names, but those who have seen his testimony say that he did not.[23] Unfortunately the technique Cohn used caused a backlash among the die-hard right-wingers and the committee was not able to use it again.

Other writers left the country. Adrian Scott went to England. Michael Wilson, Paul Jarrico, and Ben Barzman went to France. Albert Maltz, Hugo Butler, John Bright, Dalton Trumbo, Ring Lardner, Jr., and Ian McClellan Hunter all spent time in Mexico.[24] Several of these writers (Scott, Maltz, Trumbo, and Lardner) were members of the Hollywood Ten, and the rest were those who had refused to testify. According to the Waldorf Statement, they could not be hired by the major studios. But the Blacklist did not work out exactly as planned.

How the Blacklist Worked, Sort Of

In theory, the Waldorf Statement made things simple: people who refused to testify before the committee were refused employment in the movie industry. Even within the relatively rigid studio system, however, there was great flexibility. The emphasis was on the practical question of how to get something done. This is an amoral mentality that leads to negotiation, hustling, and compromise. The Right was stupidly rigid to expect the movie industry to follow a single pattern of behavior. There were simply too many people with too many motives, and only a few of those motives were political.

Take the question of answering whether one was a Communist or not. The Hollywood Ten provided a variety of answers, or nonanswers, to the committee. Later, loyalty oaths were demanded of studio personnel. George Seaton recalls Nunnally Johnson's response to this:

> Nunnally considered it degrading and childishly stupid, and demanded to confront his inquisitor face to face. So a studio executive asked him: "Are you now or have you ever been a member of the Communist Party?" Nunnally glanced furtively around the room and then in conspiratorial whisper replied: "We're not allowed to tell." They never bothered him again.[25]

A typical Johnson line: to the point, witty, and wonderfully ambiguous: does the "we" refer to the Party or to the United States Constitution?

Seaton himself was just as strong-willed when Y. Frank Freeman at Paramount insisted on loyalty oaths. Seaton wrote a letter to Freeman telling him he should not bother to send it, because he wouldn't sign it. Freeman never sent him the oath, and Seaton continued to work at Paramount.[26]

If there was a way to get on the Blacklist, there were ways to get off it, which helped undermine the rigidity of the Blacklist and eventually punched so many holes in it that it was ripe for collapse. Lawyers spent considerable time working out methods to get their clients off the Blacklist. In some cases this involved testimony, in others there were behind-the-scenes negotiations. One of the best-known lawyers in the field was Martin Gang, who represented at one time or another Dalton Trumbo and Sylvia Richards, as well as many actors and directors. Gang not only negotiated with the committee, but also with the studios and the local organizations that helped clear people.[27]

Sidney Buchman had Edward Bennett Williams as his lawyer. When Buchman was called to testify in 1951, he admitted to being a member of the

Party himself, but managed both to avoid naming names and to be fined only $150 for contempt. There were immediate rumors that Harry Cohn arranged a fix, but that has consistently been denied by Williams and Buchman's wife of the time.[28] Buchman did leave the country in 1953 to join other writers in exile.

In addition to the Blacklist, there was also a "graylist," made up of people who had not been called to testify, but who were "suspicious." They could be "cleared" by having someone acceptable vouch for them. One producer deliberately vouched for a writer he knew had been a member of the Party, since he knew the writer was no threat to Hollywood or the country.[29] Fay Kanin discovered she and her husband Michael were on the graylist when William Wyler told her about it. Two years later director Charles Vidor told the studio he was working for that he wanted to use the Kanins on a film. When the studio told him no, he told the studio that if it did not let him use them, he would tell the world about the graylist. The studio relented.[30]

The Screen Writers Guild did not fight the Blacklist as strongly as the Left would have liked, primarily because it was torn by dissension between the Right and Left factions. In 1951 the Guild tried to work with the committee, and even provided it with union records, not only membership lists, but minutes of meetings as well.[31] The Guild was fighting to show it was not the hotbed of Communists that charges from the Right had claimed.

In 1952 the Guild tried to force RKO to give blacklisted writer Paul Jarrico credit on *The Las Vegas Story*, but Howard Hughes, then the owner of the studio refused. Jarrico and the Guild filed suits to force Hughes, but Hughes won the case when it went to the Supreme Court.[32] The following year the Guild voted to modify the basic agreement so that producers could deny credits to blacklisted writers.[33]

One of the most powerful men in the area of "rehabilitation" was Roy Brewer, the head of the International Alliance of Theatrical Stage Employees (IATSE), the stagehands union. When an ex-Communist came to Brewer, Brewer would get him to go to the FBI and HUAC, and then Brewer would help him get work. Brewer also came to realize the system was not working in the way it was supposed to. In 1956 he told John Cogley:

> One of the by-products of this problem is that we made heroes out of guys who are not heroes, and enemies out of people who ought not to be enemies. People who have social consciences are penalized, and guys who never helped anybody are way out in front. It was only the people who were trying to help others who got involved. And they ought not to be punished for this.[34]

The Right, after winning the battles of the Waldorf Statement and various court rulings, was losing the war.

The Black Market

The independent producers who existed at the fringes of the business realized immediately that the Waldorf Statement was a gold mine for them: the day Dalton Trumbo returned from the Washington hearings in 1947, he received his first under-the-counter offer.[35] The Blacklist made available to independent producers a group of skilled screenwriters at a fraction of their normal rates. Trumbo, for example, had been making $3,000 a week at MGM, but for his first Black-Market job he got $3,700 for the entire script.[36] Trumbo described the situation in a September 1948 letter to a friend, "It simply requires that I work three times as fast for about one-fifth of my former price."[37]

Trumbo's first Black-Market script was *Gun Crazy*, a classic B picture, written for the King Brothers, then just getting established as B-picture producers. It was the beginning of a professional relationship that would continue for over ten years. Trumbo was not the only one who worked for the King Brothers. Michael Wilson, Robert L. Richards, John Howard Lawson, Lester Cole, and Ring Lardner, Jr., also wrote for them, Lardner as early as 1949. Wilson did a screenplay entitled *Britain's Two-Headed Spy*, which was sold to the King Brothers. Trumbo consulted on the story, and the film was eventually made under the title *The Two-Headed Spy* in 1959, with Wilson using his "James O'Donnell" pseudonym.[38]

On *Gun Crazy*, Trumbo and the Kings agreed that his name should not appear on the film, and he began the practice that became common in the black market: another real writer was used as what was called a front for Trumbo and given the credit for the film, in this case Millard Kaufman.[39] The left-wing writers were friends, and some of those who fronted for Trumbo were later blacklisted themselves. Hugo Butler was the front and did the subsequent drafts on *The Prowler*,[40] and Ian McClellan Hunter's last credit before he was blacklisted was *Roman Holiday*, for which Trumbo wrote the original screenplay. Hunter rewrote it, and John Deighton did additional rewriting.[41] When Butler was working on *The Big Night*, he was blacklisted and replaced by Ring Lardner, Jr.[42] Most such arrangements were kept secret at the time, for obvious reasons, and many more remain secret to this day.

Trumbo and the other black-market writers also used fictitious or semifictitious names. Among the names Trumbo used were C. F. Demaine, Ben Perry, Sally Stubblefield, Silvaja Chandra, Sam Jackson, and the best known of the lot, Robert Rich.[43] Carl Foreman used Derek Frye. Hugo Butler used H. D. Addis and Hugo Mozzo.[44]

Another producer who used blacklisted writers from the early days was Sam Spiegel. Spiegel's production *The Prowler* was Dalton Trumbo's last screenplay before going to prison in 1950. Trumbo also played the voice of the unseen husband–disc jockey in the film.[45] Spiegel also produced *On the Waterfront*, but he did not give up on blacklisted screenwriters. After *Waterfront*, the first drafts of *The Bridge on the River Kwai* were written by Carl Foreman, and the later drafts and the on-the-set rewriting were by Michael Wilson.[46] Each writer later claimed to have written 80 percent of the screenplay.[47] The screenplay was officially credited to the French author of the novel the film was based on, Pierre Boulle. (When the screenplay won an Academy Award, Boulle accepted it with the only two English words he knew, "Thank you.") Wilson worked, again uncredited, on another Spiegel film, *Lawrence of Arabia*. He was one of several writers, but the final credit was given only to Robert Bolt.

Producers were not the only people helping blacklisted screenwriters get work. While most agents tried to persuade their clients to talk to the committee, two agents in particular helped blacklisted screenwriters get black-market jobs. George Willner, of the Goldstone-Willner Agency, became Trumbo's black-market agent in 1948. Willner helped Trumbo collect his money from *Gun Crazy* and got him *The Prowler*. Willner was subsequently blacklisted himself and forced to sell his $750,000 interest in his agency for $25,000.[48] He worked for a while selling textiles, then a decade later became an agent again. He then discovered "there was so much guilt around that there was no script I wouldn't sell, no matter how high the price."[49]

The other primary agent for blacklisted writers was Ingo Preminger, the brother of director Otto Preminger. Preminger the agent handled Hugo Butler, Michael Wilson, and Ned Young and Hal Smith, the team that wrote *The Defiant Ones*.[50] Preminger also handled Dalton Trumbo, including Trumbo's deal to write the screenplay for Otto Preminger's *Exodus*. Trumbo took great delight at the idea of the brothers haggling over his fee.[51] Later as a producer Ingo Preminger hired former blacklisted screenwriter Ring Lardner, Jr., to write *M*A*S*H*.

Breaking the Blacklist

The decision by the Screen Writers Guild in 1953 to allow producers to deny credit to blacklisted screenwriters brought an upturn in the Black Market. Before 1953 major companies and/or independent producers who released films through the majors had been reluctant to hire black-market writers since there was always the threat the blacklisted screenwriters would sue for credit. After 1953 the producers could point to the guild rule for at least semilegal justification for not giving writers credit.

The first "big" picture that took advantage of this change was the 1956 release *Friendly Persuasion*. A script, based on stories written by Jessamyn West, was written for Frank Capra in 1946 by Michael Wilson. Capra sold the project, including the script, to William Wyler. Allied Artists was interested in making the film but held off as long as there was a possibility that they would have to give Wilson, by then blacklisted, credit. The script was rewritten by Robert Wyler and Jessamyn West, and William Wyler suggested a three-way credit. The guild's arbitration process gave sole credit to Wilson, but Allied Artists refused to give him the credit. The studio released the film with no writing credit at all.[52]

The year 1956 was also the year of *The Brave One*, a King Brothers production written by Dalton Trumbo under a name that became almost as famous as his own, Robert Rich. The "official" credits for the film list the story by Robert Rich, with a screenplay by Harry Franklin and Merrill G. White. All were pseudonyms for Trumbo.[53] Robert Rich was nominated for an Academy Award for Best Motion Picture Story.

It was an interesting series of nominations for 1956. *Friendly Persuasion* was nominated for Best Picture as well as a nomination for Best Screenplay (Adapted). The latter nomination was ruled ineligible by a change in the Academy rules that permitted no blacklisted writer to win the Oscar,[54] but Robert Rich was not blacklisted. Rich was not only nominated, but won. Jesse Lasky, Jr., a vice president of the guild, was asked to accept the award. Lasky thought the name sounded familiar, and so he accepted the award on behalf of his "good friend." The next day it was discovered there was no Robert Rich.

The news media began to look into the story. The rumor that Rich was Trumbo began to circulate and reporters came to talk to him about it. He denied nothing, and he also sent them to talk to other blacklisted writers. Trumbo recalls:

> It went on and on and on. I just wanted the press to understand what an extensive thing this movie black market was. And in the midst of this, I suddenly realized that all the journalists—or most of them—were sympathetic to me, and how eager they were to have the blacklist exploded. There had been a certain change in atmosphere, and then it became possible.[55]

The following year the screenplay for *The Bridge on the River Kwai* won the Oscar for Best Screenplay (Adapted), and the year after that, 1958, Stanley Kramer produced *The Defiant Ones*. The screenplay was credited to two writers Nathan E. Douglas and Harold Jacob Smith. When Kramer bought the screenplay in 1957, he did not know that Douglas was a pseudonym for a blacklisted actor-turned-writer, Nedrick Young. When he found out, Kramer decided to go ahead with the picture, but on the condition that Young keep a low profile.[56] In late 1958 the *New York Times* revealed that Douglas was Young. In December 1958, George Seaton and Valentine Davies, representing the Academy,[57] met with Young and Smith and agreed to work to get the disqualifying rule changed on condition that Young and Smith did nothing to embarrass the Academy. The board of directors changed the rule, and the writers won the award for *The Defiant Ones*.[58]

Working behind the scenes was Dalton Trumbo. He was writing letters to other blacklisted screenwriters, talking to reporters and sympathetic members of the Academy, and in general helping orchestrate what he saw as the end of the blacklist, or at least the beginning of the end.[59] In January 1959 Trumbo wrote to Albert Maltz:

> The story [in particular the story of Robert Rich] will be told without rancor, without attacks on anyone, with good humor, *and with no digs at the Academy or its leaders*. (This, I think, is the tone for everyone who has anything to say from the blacklistees' side—restraint, cooperation with pleasant professional relations, etc., etc. Nobody's a martyr, nobody's mad, history hurt everybody, all made mistakes, and la-de-da-da-do.) The reason I make a point of this is that there can never be an *official* end to the blacklist—this is as close as we presently shall come. Therefore we must *pretend* this is the end (which it damned near is), and pose not as angry martyrs, as the persecuted, but as good *winners*. In this guise we assume our victory at last, and carry no grudges forward into the future.[60]

The other side realized it had lost. In a television broadcast on January 9, 1959, actor Ward Bond, the president of the Motion Picture Alliance for the Preservation of American Ideals, made a statement:

> They're all working now, all these fifth amendment communists and I don't think that anything I say about it will make much difference. There's no point at issue. We've just lost the fight and it's as simple as that. I think the fight may be resumed some day in the future. I don't know. It's going to take a tremendous change in public opinion, and I don't see how it's going to come about with the courts acting the way they have.[61]

The Blacklist was not over, in spite of what Bond thought. More remained to be done, but, writing to Michael Wilson in February 1959, Trumbo noted that the extremes of the Right and Left had died, and more importantly, "There is no longer a centralized control of the industry tight enough to enforce the blacklist."[62] By the late fifties, an increasing number of films were being made by independent producers, who were willing to take the chance of using blacklisted screenwriters. Furthermore, independent productions using scripts by blacklisted screenwriters had considerable success. United Artists,

one of the most successful studios of the fifties, not only provided a home for
independent producers, but was virtually alone in letting its producers know-
ingly hire screenwriters on the Black Market. [63]

After *The Defiant Ones*, there still remained the major studios to crack.
Not surprisingly, it was Dalton Trumbo who managed it. Kirk Douglas's
company, Bryna, had hired blacklisted writers before, [64] and Trumbo had
worked for Douglas before as well. When the company needed a quick
rewrite on *Spartacus*, which it was making for Universal, Trumbo obliged.
Word began to get out that Trumbo was the writer. By late 1959 Universal had
not decided whether Trumbo would get screen credit or not.

Trumbo meanwhile had moved onto another job, a rewrite of the script for
Exodus for Otto Preminger. While Trumbo was working on it, Preminger met
with Arthur Krim, one of the heads of United Artists, which was releasing
Exodus, and discussed the possibility of giving Trumbo screen credit. Krim
agreed, and Preminger, with his usual gift for self-promotion, let the *New
York Times* know. [65]

At the beginning of 1960 the Writers Guild went out on strike, and one of
the issues was the revision of the 1953 amendment that prohibited blacklisted
writers from getting screen credit. When the strike was settled in June of
1960, the amendment was revoked. In mid-August Douglas announced that
Trumbo was the writer of *Spartacus*, and more importantly Universal said he
would have the writing credit on the film. [66]

The American Legion, which had been consistently watchful of Communists and Communist influence in the movie business, established pickets
when *Spartacus* was released in the fall of 1960. It did no good. The picture,
in spite of mixed reviews, was a hit, helped perhaps by President-elect John F.
Kennedy's attendance with his brother Robert in Washington, D.C., where
they had to cross picket lines set up by the Catholic War Veterans to see the
film. [67] *Exodus* was also a hit. Money, which always talks in Hollywood, had
spoken.

After the Blacklist

Dalton Trumbo was back at work in Hollywood. Unfortunately his post-
Blacklist films tend to be "projects" more than films: *The Sandpiper, Hawaii,
The Fixer*, and *Papillon*. In 1971 he directed his own script from his novel
Johnny Got His Gun, but it is very flatly written and poorly directed.

Some blacklisted writers still had difficulties getting credits under their own
names, as happened with Michael Wilson on *Lawrence of Arabia*. Lester
Cole wrote the screenplay for producer Carl Foreman for *Born Free* under the
name Gerald L. C. Copley because the studio did not want to put Cole's

name on the film. When the film was a success, Cole suddenly found he was "hot" in Hollywood, but only for animal stories.[68]

Ring Lardner, Jr., had his first credit in 1965 on *The Cincinnati Kid*, then won an Oscar for his screenplay for *M*A*S*H*. Waldo Salt won an Oscar for *Midnight Cowboy* and another for *Coming Home*.

Some screenwriters of course did not come back. The loss of them, and of the years of the writers who did manage to come back later, was Hollywood's as much as theirs.

23

Projects

Within the old studio system, the "casting" of a film, including the writers, was a simple process. At Fox Zanuck had a card file on his desk. All he had to do was pull out a selection of cards, one for each person under contract, and the cast and crew of the film were complete. One reason Zanuck left as head of production in 1956 was that he found himself spending only 10 percent of his time involved in the actual production of films, and 90 percent dealing with agents and negotiations for talent no longer under contract.[1] Each film became a "project," which was made up of the right elements, one of which was a good property.

In the fifties and sixties a best-selling book or a hit Broadway play was considered a good property. There was higher status for those screenwriters who wrote adaptations, as during the days of the major studios. Some such projects did turn out to be impressive and successful films, while many others seemed pretentious and overslick, thus helping pave the way for the changes that came to the industry in the late sixties and early seventies.

John Michael Hayes

John Michael Hayes wrote for radio in the thirties, and after World War II he wrote network radio programs such as *My Favorite Husband, Amos 'n' Andy, The Whistler, Johnny Dollar, Richard Diamond,* and *Sam Spade.*[2] Hayes started writing for the movies in the early fifties. He had his first great success with the first picture he wrote for Alfred Hitchcock, *Rear Window.* He wrote three more for Hitchcock: *To Catch a Thief, The Trouble with Harry,* and *The Man Who Knew Too Much.*

Hayes split with Hitchcock when Hitchcock tried to get Hayes to let another writer share the credit on *The Man Who Knew Too Much,*[3] and Hayes went looking for another small-town story to do. His agent pitched him to producer Jerry Wald for the adaptation of what was a scandalous best-seller, *Peyton Place.* It was generally thought at the time that it would be impossible to make it into a movie because of the language and what was, for the fifties, *raw* sex. Hayes read the book several times but did not think he could do it.

176

He could not figure out what point of view to take with the material. After six weeks of staring at the book, he saw how to do it. The emphasis in Hayes's version is on the coming of age of the teenage Allison MacKenzie, with each episode seen through her eyes. Hayes changed some characterizations in the novel completely. Norman Page is a teenage mother's boy throughout the book, but Hayes only has him that way at first. Norman is given a wonderfully delicate scene near the beginning with Allison, and then returns at the end of the film. He has joined the army and in the tradition of the time, it has made a man out of him. Hayes also changed the view of the town to a more balanced one. While there is still rape, incest, and illegitimacy, as well as small-town hypocrisy, there are also some positive values of small-town life. The general critical and public reaction to the 1957 film was that it was better than the book, which it was.

Hayes adapted the Harold Robbins novel *The Carpetbaggers* for a 1964 film. The film was a large-scale entertainment and probably the best of the adaptations of Harold Robbins's novels, but it did not have the substance of Hayes's script for *Peyton Place*. In *The Carpetbaggers* Carroll Baker played a character loosely based on Jean Harlow, and Hayes found himself writing a film about Harlow for her. Joseph E. Levine, who was also the producer of *The Carpetbaggers*, rushed production of *Harlow*. Since the script, by another writer, was nowhere near ready, Baker insisted on bringing Hayes in. Levine would only pay Hayes's normal rate with nothing extra for doing the screenplay virtually as it was being filmed. Baker came up with the money herself, and Hayes found himself writing pages only three or four days ahead of shooting.[4] The picture was not a success, in any way.

After the late sixties there was very little market for the kind of expensive, literate, often very witty adaptations Hayes was so good at. He continued to write screenplays, as well as serve as an executive at Avco Pictures, but the screenplays were not filmed.

Ernest Lehman

Before becoming a screenwriter, Ernest Lehman worked for a public-relations agency handling motion picture and theater accounts. This show-business world became the basis for several stories he sold to magazines. One of the stories, "Sweet Smell of Success," attracted the attention of Paramount, which brought him out to Hollywood. The studio did not buy the story, but Burt Lancaster's company did. Lehman did the first drafts on the script and Clifford Odets did the last drafts.[5]

Lehman worked with Billy Wilder on *Sabrina*, filmed in 1954. He and Wilder wrote whenever Wilder was not directing. Lehman fell ill and the doctor ordered him not to work, but Wilder sneaked over to his house at night. In addition, Humphrey Bogart took a dislike to Lehman and once ordered him off the set. None of the strain shows in the charming film.[6]

Lehman was a great believer in research. For *North by Northwest* he followed Cary Grant's trail in the film, starting at the United Nations (which gave him the idea of having someone killed in the Delegates' Lounge, called the Public Lounge in the film), and going through the booking process for drunk driving in Glen Cove, Long Island. He started to climb Mount Rushmore to see what was on the top, but instead sent a camera up with a forest ranger. Unfortunately the top of Mount Rushmore is nothing but rock, so a more useful top was created in the studio.[7] For *West Side Story* Lehman and the film's director Robert Wise toured the gang areas on the east side of New York, where they talked to gang leaders and police.[8]

Perhaps Lehman's most useful research was a trip to Salzberg for *The Sound of Music*. On stage the "Do Re Mi" number takes place in the baron's house. While in Salzberg Lehman had taken pictures of various locations, and he broke the song down in the script into lines that could be done at those locations. The result was a scene that not only showed the relationship of Maria and the children changing over a period of time, but also managed to show the locale in a way that kept it from being just a scenic interlude.[9]

Even twenty years after the release of the film, Edward Albee, the author of the play *Who's Afraid of Virginia Woolf?*, was still complaining about Lehman's adaptation.[10] There was more to Lehman's adaptation than just having the four characters go to a roadhouse for part of the film. Mostly he cut material and condensed speeches to make the material work as a film. At least part of the problem was the language in the original play, which was considered too strong to be done on film. Lehman brought the language within the acceptable standards for the industry. Enough of Albee's rawness was left so that Jack Warner, the head of the studio, arranged for theaters not to admit persons under the age of eighteen. This method worked effectively for this 1966 film, and led to the establishment of the Rating Code two years later.

Lehman was also the producer of *Virginia Woolf* and he followed that film by writing and producing *Hello Dolly*. Lehman considers it the least satisfactory of the four musicals he wrote, and thinks the problem was inherent in the material itself, since the character of Dolly, while in theory the star part, is not on screen that much.[11]

Hello Dolly was one of several large-budget musicals the studios produced after the success of *The Sound of Music*, and collectively they lost millions of dollars, effectively ending the studio production of big musicals. Lehman later turned to writing novels, including *The French Atlantic Affair*. When the novel was filmed for television, Lehman was only too happy to turn the job over to another writer, saying, "God, it was neat to be on the other side of the fence. Some other screenwriter had to sweat and say, 'Oh, my God, this is ridiculous. How am I going to make a movie out of this?' "[12]

Edward Anhalt

Before he became a professional screenwriter in the late forties, Edward Anhalt studied propaganda techniques on a fellowship at Princeton, wrote and directed 16-mm documentary films of his own, was a cinematographer on the classic 1939 documentary *The City*, worked for the OSS in World War II, and with his wife Edna wrote stories for the pulp magazines of the forties. He also worked for CBS in the late thirties and early forties, where he was the television cameraman on the first television production of a stage play. He would come back to television later.[13]

In the early forties the Anhalts began selling stories to the movies. The Anhalts moved into major-studio filmmaking with a story they wrote called *Panic in the Streets*. The story was a thirteen-page treatment they had written in eight hours, but several studios were in the bidding for it the next day, and it sold for seventy-five thousand dollars, a high price for an original in the late forties.[14] The film won the Academy Award for Best Original Story in 1950.

In 1952 the Anhalts started working on bigger budgeted films. The Anhalts split up professionally and personally in the late fifties, and Edward Anhalt did the 1958 film *The Young Lions* alone, if you do not count the eight writers who had done thirteen drafts before him. A major problem in adapting Irwin Shaw's lengthy World War II novel was that one of the three major characters, Christian, was a Nazi who remained loyal to the Party throughout the novel. Anhalt had Christian develop a growing disillusionment with Hitler in the course of the film.

The Young Lions also meant that Anhalt had to deal with the actor who played Christian, Marlon Brando. Anhalt says:

> Marlon Brando had a lot of problems about *The Young Lions*, a lot of internal questions that were never satisfactorily answered to him in the screenplay, and he would say, "I just can't do this." Particularly, there was one love scene, I remember, that he and I sat around, and somehow by playing the part (he'd play himself and I'd play the girl), we somehow got the scene out. That kind of thing. I've done that with actors.[15]

The 1958 film was one of the best of Anhalt's career and a great box-office success.

In the early sixties Anhalt brought his skills as an adapter to Hal Wallis, who by then had an independent production unit at Paramount. The first films Anhalt did for Wallis were not particularly distinguished: "I had to write two

Elvis Presley pictures in order to get him to let me write *Becket*."[16] His work
on adapting Jean Anouilh's play consisted of toning down the excessively
theatrical dialogue and taking out the more theatrical touches.

In 1974 and 1975 Anhalt did two adaptations, John Osborne's *Luther* and
Robert Shaw's *The Man in the Glass Booth*, for Ely Landau's American Film
Theatre series. Anhalt did more adapting than the other writers did for this
group of filmed plays.

In 1974 Anhalt returned to television to adapt Leon Uris's novel *QB VII*.
This was the first of what came to be known as a miniseries: a several-hour
film, often telecast over several days or even weeks. It was no longer necessary
for an adapter to eliminate material that would not fit into a two-hour
theatrical film. Novels that in the past would have been done as theatrical
films now found a home on television. Edward Anhalt continued to write for
theatrical films, but he also found himself doing more television work,
including television film adaptations such as *Contract on Cherry Street* in
1977 and *The Day Christ Died* in 1980, both of which had running times of
150 minutes.

William Goldman

If the arrival of the television miniseries made changes in the kind of
"projects" producers of theatrical films were interested in, William Goldman's
original screenplay for *Butch Cassidy and the Sundance Kid* had an even
greater impact. Actually the impact came more from Goldman's agent Evarts
Ziegler's deal for the script than from the script itself. The script was sold in
November 1967 for $400,000.[17]

William Goldman had by then been writing novels since 1956, and he had
two screenplay credits, the last being *Harper*, an adaptation of a Ross Mac-
donald novel. When Paul Newman agreed to star in the film, producer Elliot
Kastner told Goldman, "You just jumped past all the shit." Goldman later
agreed, "I was no longer a *putz* novelist from New York. Now I was a *putz*
novelist who had written a Paul Newman picture."[18]

Goldman first read about the outlaws Butch Cassidy and the Sundance Kid
in the late fifties, and he started picking up whatever information he could
about them, which was not much. In 1963 he discussed the material with
producer Lawrence Turman. Goldman thought Turman was "tremendously
helpful in trying to figure out a story line."[19] In 1966 he wrote a first draft of
171 pages in four weeks. Turman submitted this draft to Twentieth Century-
Fox, where it was not greeted with great enthusiasm. The reader's report, by
George Byron Sage, said:

This script is still in a very rough form. There really isn't a formal plot. . . . There is no firmly established theme. . . . Goldman's two leading characters and their mutual mistress have some good scenes, even though . . . the action is thoroughly disorganized. . . . This carelessly written script does little or nothing to sell the basic concepts. . . . Nevertheless, if the author is willing to put a lot more work in it, it has the prospect of being worth additional consideration. (One can hope that Goldman will also learn more about the basic technique of the business of screenplay writing in the process of such work. It's clear he *feels* many of the scenes himself but he doesn't know how to put them down on paper—and what he puts down demands more reading patience than most people can give him.)[20]

This was not the draft that brought the $400,000. Goldman reworked the screenplay and in October 1967 the script was again submitted to Fox in a form close to the final film. Condensed or cut out are such scenes from the earlier draft as a more detailed stay in New York where the trio meet Sundance's parents and a scene on the boat to Bolivia where Butch loses their money to a card shark.[21]

Sage's comment on the earlier draft that "there really isn't a formal plot" is also true of the final draft and the film. In the first half of the film Butch and the Kid are chased around the West by the Superposse, and in the second half they are chased around Bolivia by a not-so-super posse. Unlike the tradition of the classic Fox films, this is not a strong narrative line. What helps hold the film together is a tone that Goldman sets in the dialogue that makes us see the clichés of the Old West in a new light. Goldman realized, after complaints by some studio executives, that audiences might have trouble with two heroes who in effect run away from the action. So when Butch first brings up the idea of going to Bolivia, he compares it to going to California. Butch tells the Kid, "When I say Bolivia, you think California."

What also helps hold the film together is the relationship between Butch and the Kid, which we seen in a variety of contexts in the film. This also helps explain why the screenplay sold for so much money. Goldman had written parts for two stars. He had already written *Harper* for Paul Newman, and there were rumors that most of the male stars of the time were interested in this project. In fact, Goldman and others had trouble persuading the studio to take a chance with Robert Redford because he was not yet the star the picture would make him.

The money that went to Goldman for this script said that an original screenplay, which had very little status previously, could be a major element in a project. It was now socially acceptable to make a project from an original screenplay. Many of the major films that came after *Butch Cassidy and the Sundance Kid* were not adaptations but original screenplays, and the prices paid for original screenplays has continued to escalate.

Goldman continued to write original screenplays, such as *The Great Waldo Pepper*, but most of his subsequent work has been on adaptations, many from his own novels. One of his best screenplays was *A Bridge Too Far*, an adaptation of Cornelius Ryan's nonfiction account of the battle of Arnhem. The film was not well received critically in this country, and it did not do the business expected of it domestically, although it was highly praised and highly attended overseas. Goldman managed to keep the action clear, which was not as easy as it sounds, since the action was often unclear to the participants in the battle. There was no way Goldman could cut to a situation room to have two of the film's high-priced stars explain the current situation to the audience.

Paddy Chayefsky

Paddy Chayefsky is an example of a screenwriter whose career shows the influence of the change from adapted screenplays to original screenplays. Chayefsky made his reputation as a writer of original dramas in the early days of live television with such teleplays as "Marty" and "The Catered Affair." In 1955 he wrote the screenplay adaptation of *Marty*. In 1957 he adapted his television play "The Bachelor Party" into a film, which he followed a year later with an original screenplay for *The Goddess*. In *Marty* and *The Bachelor Party*, Chayefsky showed a particularly good sense for realistic but vivid dialogue. With *The Goddess* his screenwriting began to get overly literate.

In 1964 he wrote a sharp, funny film from William Bradford Huie's novel *The Americanization of Emily*, and in 1969 he was credited with the adaptation of the stage musical *Paint Your Wagon*, one of the biggest of the post–*Sound of Music* flops. He also was one of several uncredited writers on the adaptation of Alistair MacLean's novel *Ice Station Zebra*. He was unsuited for both *Wagon* and *Zebra*, since neither called for his particular skills at dialogue and characterization.

In 1971 Chayefsky returned to writing original screenplays with *Hospital*. It was, as Chayefsky himself later said, "deformed," adding, "In *Hospital* I had a detective story, a love story, a drama, a satire: I had all kinds of genres bouncing in the air at one time."[22] Part of the problem is that the satire is by far the most interesting part of the film, and the detective-story elements undercut it. Still, the satirical elements give the film considerable freshness, as does the attempt at bouncing genres. Chayefsky followed *Hospital* with another original screenplay, *Network*, in which he felt he managed to combine the variety of elements better than he had in the earlier film.[23] Both *Hospital* and *Network* have a richness of character and intelligence about them that make them the most appealing of Chayefsky's films.

One reason Chayefsky had the success he did in getting original screenplays produced in the seventies is that he turned over production to Howard Gottfried. Chayefsky had produced *The Goddess* and the production had been troubled.[24] Gottfried knew story and Chayefsky found him just as abrasive as he, Chayefsky, was.[25] Chayefsky and Gottfried were taking advantage of the change in the film business that in the decade or so after 1967 saw a number of first-rate original screenplays produced: *Bonnie and Clyde* in 1967, *Butch Cassidy and the Sundance Kid* in 1969, *Five Easy Pieces* in 1970, *The Candidate* in 1972, *Smile* in 1975, *Lifeguard* in 1976, *Citizens Band* in 1977, and many others. Not only was there, after *Butch Cassidy*, a certain status attached to original screenplays, but it was economically feasible and administratively possible for the major distribution companies, which is what the major studios had become, to finance small- to medium-budget pictures of quality.

Steve Tesich

One of those later small films was the 1979 film *Breaking Away*, written by Steve Tesich. Tesich was writing plays for Off-Broadway when film director Peter Yates suggested they work together on a film. Tesich had written two screenplays. One was called "The Eagle of Naptown" (an Indiana nickname for Indianapolis) about a boy obsessed with bicycle riding. While attending Indiana University he rides, as Tesich had, for his fraternity team in the Little 500 bicycle race held every year at the university. The other screenplay was called "The Cutters" about a group of local boys in Bloomington who resent the local Indiana University. Yates said later:

> I would have been happy to do either of them, but one lacked a certain spine, the other a certain atmosphere, and we just couldn't get them off the ground. Paramount had the sole rights to one of them—and they made Steve buy it back. The combination [of the two scripts] simply worked. The bicycle stuff gave a visual center to the cutters' plight that it didn't originally have.[26]

Tesich followed up with two more originals, an offbeat thriller called *Eyewitness* and one of the more interesting examinations of the upheaval of the sixties, *Four Friends*, a commercial failure that has a devoted cult of admirers. Tesich then got into project filmmaking with a charming adaptation of John Irving's basically unfilmable novel, *The World According to Garp*. Tesich did an excellent job turning out a script that captured the major themes of the novel while leaving out, from necessity, much of the density and texture of the book. Tesich returned to original screenplays and bicycle racing in *American Flyers*, but in the same year, 1985, he did a flat-footed and textureless adaptation of the nonfiction book *Eleni*.

Negotiations

One result of the change from studio production to independent production was the increased importance of the whole process of negotiation in getting a film made. In 1967 a producer at Fox told John Gregory Dunne, "The deal, that's all this business is about. Who's available when, when you can get him, start date, stop date, percentages—the deal, it's the only thing that matters."[27] As mentioned above, a large part of the impact of *Butch Cassidy and the Sundance Kid* on the industry was the enormous price Evarts Ziegler got for his client. Agents became even more crucial for screenwriters than they had been before, and this has led to complaints, not entirely unjustified, that agents are running the film business.

The screenwriter also finds himself spending more time at meetings than writing. One screenwriter who works steadily in the industry says that he spends 75 percent of his time in meetings and only 25 percent writing.[28] Even when a writer is writing, particularly a first draft, he is still negotiating. William Goldman points out that the first draft, or drafts, of the script are

> what either gets the movie off the ground or not. In a crazy sense you can almost say there are two entirely different versions of any screenplay. There's the stuff written before the movie is a go project, and there is what's written when the movie is actually going to be shot. And sometimes they have very little to do with each other. The purpose of the earlier version is to make it happen. The purpose of the later version or versions is to be as supportive to your director as you can.[29]

Development

Screenplays have always been developed, that is changed (hopefully for the better), as the material has either been adapted or the early drafts of screenplays revised. We have seen examples of it with *Casablanca* and *Breaking Away*, among others. In most of those cases, the process was generally a positive one. John Huston observed in 1983:

> In the old days, writers were on salary, and they wanted to stay on the script as long as possible. So the script got better and better. Now writers want to finish one job and get paid for it, and get on to the next. In the old days, the hacks

wanted to be good writers. Now the good writers are constantly being tempted by the next deal.[30]

By the eighties, the process of development became so complex that writers spent most of their time either taking meetings to pitch an idea or script or doing rewrites on their own or someone else's script. By the mideighties, the major companies combined were investing between thirty and fifty million dollars a year in the development process.[31] Most of the scripts in development were not made. Warner Brothers, nicknamed the Black Hole of development, had 250 projects in development in 1986, but only released 20 films. Paramount had 100 in development, but released only 13, 11 of which were produced "in-house," i.e., through the development process. Fox had 100 in development, released 16, of which only 4 were developed in-house.[32]

While some writers do not object to the development process (they make most of their money on development deals, regardless of whether the film is made or not), most do. They find continual interference from the studio because there are so many layers of executives to deal with. The major distribution companies have become so top-heavy with executives it is difficult to get anything creative done. The companies like the process because, as Beverly Walker writes, "The development system is run by the major studios, one of the few areas of the film industry they can almost totally control."[33] It is a system designed so the executives can say no. As screenwriter and former professional baseball player Ron Shelton says, "My director and I feel that until we've been turned down at least once by every studio in town, we're not even warmed up."[34]

Peter Bart, who left a newspaper job in 1967 to become an executive at Paramount, looked back nostalgically twenty years later:

> A visit to the studios circa 1967 would be an eye-opener to the film executive of 1987. For one thing, the executive staffs were minuscule by today's standards—no corridors lined with vice presidents and "presidents of production," no development committees reigning over "pitches," etc. At Paramount, a mere handful of staff people presided over a film program of more than twenty films.
>
> The reason offbeat films like *Harold and Maude* or *Paper Moon* or *Medium Cool* were approved at Paramount in that period was that no one bothered to stop them. If you had a film you believed in, other executives would say, "Go do it—just don't tell me about it until it's done."[35]

24

European Influences

The late fifties and early sixties were a time of great stylistic upheaval in European films. The European filmmakers assumed an audience interested as much in filmmaking style as story, unlike the mass audience that was interested primarily in story. There was an audience, to a large degree of young people, who had grown up with the movies and who had seen television take over the storytelling function of films. That audience included a number of American filmmakers and would-be filmmakers.

Bonnie and Clyde

In 1964 David Newman and Robert Benton were working for *Esquire Magazine*. They talked a lot about movies, since

> we were riding the crest of the new wave that had swept in on our minds, and the talk was Truffaut, Godard, De Broca, Bergman, Kurosawa, Antonioni, Fellini and all the other names that fell like a litany in 1964. . . . Our minds most recently blown by *Breathless*, we addressed ourselves more and more, during working hours and drinking hours, to the idea of actually doing something about it. And the first idea, the very first one, was a movie about two Texas desperadoes named Bonnie Parker and Clyde Barrow.[1]

Newman and Benton wrote a seventy-page treatment of the story. Their direct influences were Hitchcock, a retrospective of whose films they had recently seen, and Truffaut, particularly the combination of comedy and violence in *Shoot the Piano Player* and the sense of connection between past and present in *Jules and Jim*. They managed to get the treatment to Truffaut.

When Truffaut arrived in New York a month later, he discussed the treatment with them, but he was to direct another film, so he felt he could not do this one. Newman and Benton went to Texas, Benton's home state, to do research. They wrote the screenplay and sent it to Truffaut. Truffaut passed the script on to Godard.

> Godard was, if anything, the only film-maker in the world who excited us as much as Truffaut at that moment in time. We had seen and endlessly discussed

all his films, which had been coming out at the rate of every other month, it seemed. Each one a revelation, each one a re-definition of the limits of cinema, each one cause for reconsidering every idea about movies we had ever had, each one a major work.[2]

Godard's wanting to shoot the film three weeks after he read the script bothered potential producers, as did his suggestion he could shoot it in Tokyo. The project died.

Eighteen months later, Truffaut suggested to Warren Beatty that he look at the script. Beatty wanted not only to act in it, but produce it as well. He brought director Arthur Penn onto the project. Penn and the writers went over the script. The director liked the combination of violence and humor but he and Beatty had problems with an element the writers had borrowed from *Jules and Jim*. In their first drafts, the relationship between Bonnie, Clyde, and one of the gang, C.W. Moss, was a complicated ménage à trois. Penn amd Beatty realized this would probably turn off an audience, who would then be able to dismiss anything else the characters did as the work of perverts. The character of C. W. was described in the original screenplay as a "1931 version of a rock 'n' roll hood; blond, surly, not very bright."[3] The part was later cast with Michael J. Pollard and changed into comedy relief.

Newman and Benton found that Penn was particularly concerned about the "profile" of the film. In other words, the structure. They worked on it, but Penn was still not satisfied. Beatty suggested Penn talk to his friend Robert Towne, then beginning not only as a screenwriter but also as a script doctor. Towne helped Penn move the scenes around so that the visit to Bonnie's mother, which was earlier in the script, now comes after the bandits kidnap a young couple, one of whom turns out to be an undertaker. The changes show Bonnie's increasing awareness that they are doomed.[4]

In their note to Truffaut on the first treatment, Newman and Benton said of their heroes:

> If Bonnie and Clyde were here today, they would be hip. Their values have become assimilated in much of our culture—not robbing banks and killing people, of course, but their style, their sexuality, their bravado, their delicacy, their cultivated arrogance, their narcissistic insecurity, their curious ambition have relevance to the way we live now.[5]

It was precisely because Newman and Benton caught those qualities that the film was an enormous hit in 1967. Young people particularly felt increasingly alienated from middle-class America and found Newman and Benton's Bonnie and Clyde characters they could identify with. The rough combination of comedy and violence, which offended many mainstream reviewers such as

Bosley Crowther in the *New York Times*, hit a responsive cord in young Americans. What Newman and Benton had successfully learned from the French nouvelle vague films was how to manage several shifts of tone within a single film.

The Graduate

If Newman, Benton, Towne, and Penn were most influenced by the French filmmakers, the makers of *The Graduate*, the other big 1967 hit with young audiences, were more influenced by the Italians. The 1963 novel by Charles Webb was purchased by Lawrence Turman and then turned down by every major studio. Turman approached Mike Nichols to direct the film, but Nichols had at that point directed only on Broadway and not in films, and even with Nichols attached the project was turned down again by the majors. Turman had William Hanley and Calder Willingham both write drafts of the script, but Nichols was not happy with them and asked Turman to hire Buck Henry to write the film. Nichols says:

> I knew that Buck was extraordinary and funny and incredibly intelligent underneath all that kidding around. So we hired him. He never read anything but the novel. He never read the earlier scripts. He wrote an excellent, very long first draft. And then he and I spent literally six months working five, six hours a day. Now, three of those hours were spent goofing off and screwing around and making up horrifying stage directions for what Benjamin might be doing while he was driving along, playing with himself.[6]

The picture was released through a smaller company called Embassy.

When Nichols began to direct films, he prepared by watching Fellini's 8½ "for the tenth time."[7] Nichols, with Henry's help, developed a flow to the film that matches Fellini's. Montage sequences in American films tended before *The Graduate* to be primarily action sequences or propaganda pieces, but Nichols had something else in mind:

> I took advantage of Buck to really figure out ways of shooting things. Like that whole montage—out of the pool, into Mrs. Robinson's bed, back and forth, ending up leaping out of the water, landing on Mrs. Robinson—Buck and I did together over days and days and days.[8]

Both Henry and Nichols had worked in improvisational comedy before writing and directing, and the rhythm of the scenes in *The Graduate* shows that influence. Not that the scenes were improvised, but Nichols trusted the material enough to slow down the pace to observe the behavior. The dialogue and the thrust of the scenes are satirical, but the rhythm of the playing is different from traditional American comedy rhythms. The result is a Preston Sturges script played at an Antonioni pace. The result is funny, but appreciated more by younger audiences than older ones.

The wit of Nichols and Henry is that they applied the techniques for showing alienation not to adults, as the Italians had, but to the young people as the French had. *Bonnie and Clyde* and *The Graduate* defined a new genre of intelligent films for the young, and the fact that *The Graduate*, a little movie no major studio wanted, became the third-highest-grossing film up to then meant the youth movement was on.

Easy Rider

The episodic nature of the 1969 film *Easy Rider*, combined with the feeling of freedom the film suggests in its road scenes, as well as the general lack of intelligent dialogue between its two leading characters, certainly make it seem improvised. It wasn't. Laszlo Kovacs, the brilliant cinematographer of the film, remembers:

> It was totally planned. On top of that, a lot of people said we didn't even have a script. We had a very specifically written script by Terry Southern, Dennis Hopper, and Peter Fonda. It was an actual shooting script. All the scenes were carefully followed, especially the dialogue sequences after the Jack Nicholson character joins them. It wasn't just a bunch of stoned guys sitting around a campfire improvising that. It was charged that we lucked out, that we just turned on the camera and suddenly we captured the actors at the right moments. We did get lucky, but our luck was that people were receptive to it at the time of its release.[9]

In spite of its sense of freedom, *Easy Rider* is carefully structured. Each sequence makes a point about the characters. There is also movement in the film, not only of the motorcycles on the road, but in our growing understanding of these characters and their condition.

Five Easy Pieces

Easy Rider made Jack Nicholson a star, and he asked a friend of his to write a script for him. The friend was Carol Eastman, who writes under the name Adrien Joyce. An actress and dancer, she wrote a low-budget western Nicholson appeared in called *The Shooting*. The new script was to be directed by Bob Rafelson, who only asked that the character be a concert pianist.[10] Joyce based the main character, Bobby Dupea, partly on Nicholson, partly on a brother of hers who drifted around the country, and partly on Ted Kennedy, since part of the focus of the story was on how the youngest child in a competitive family survives (or does not survive; in the first drafts of the script, Bobby is killed when his car goes over a bridge into the water, an echo of Chappaquiddick).

The final segment of the film, in which Bobby returns to his family and begins to sort out his feelings about them (most touchingly in a scene with his father), is very moving and connected strongly with younger audiences going through their own engagements and/or disengagements with their parents.

The Second Youth Market

The enormous popular success of *Bonnie and Clyde*, *The Graduate*, and *Easy Rider* brought forth another group of films aimed at what would later be called the youth market. Unlike the earlier AIP films, the films of the second youth market, like *Five Easy Pieces*, tended to overestimate the intelligence of their audience rather than underestimate it. Because these films, like the European films that influenced them, seemed to break new cinematic ground by loosening up the conventional narrative patterns, the assumption made by both the studios and the filmmakers was that young audiences wanted movies that did not tell stories so much as "redefine cinema."

One result of this assumption was that an enormous amount of incoherent material was submitted to the studios. The papers of Fox story reader George Byron Sage show that the year 1969 was a particularly bad year. Sage commented again and again on material that not only did not tell a story, but did not seem to make any point at all. At least in the forties when nonstory material was submitted to the studio it made some sense.[11]

Not only did such material get submitted to the studios, some of it was made. The studios tried to find films they felt would appeal to an audience they did not understand. Some films of the period, such as *Getting Straight* and *The Strawberry Statement* (both released in 1970) made valid observations about life in America among the young, but more films were like the pointless *Magic Garden of Stanley Sweetheart* and the incoherent *Cover Me Babe* (both also released in 1970, although the release of the latter was severely limited).

As early as 1970 there were already beginnings of a backlash against the freewheeling aspects of the youth movement. In early 1970 *Airport* was written and directed by an old studio hand, George Seaton. Seaton's writing was certainly not at its best and there was nothing cinematically inventive in either the writing or direction; it was simply the story that carried the film.

Equally retrograde in terms of redefining the cinema was *Love Story*, also released in 1970. True, it was a film about two young people, and there was a romantic montage in the snow, but the appeal of the film was in its characters, its wise-guy–girl dialogue, and its story. *Airport*, released in early 1970, was the top-grossing film of that year, while *Love Story*, released in December, was the top-grossing film of 1971.[12]

The period from 1967 to 1977 was one of great artistic vitality for American films because the industry was in a balanced state. There was the influx of new writers (and directors) determined to loosen up the way American films were made. These new filmmakers brought back a freshness and quickness to American films not seen since the late thirties. The American film gained from this new freedom of style, but it also lost some of the skill at narrative filmmaking. Some, but not all.

The writers who could combine the newer styles with the older skills had continued success as the freshness of the sixties was applied to narrative films in the early seventies. Newman and Benton followed *Bonnie and Clyde* with *What's Up, Doc?*, and worked on the first *Superman* film. As early as 1972 Benton was directing as well, and he wrote and directed *The Late Show*, *Kramer vs. Kramer*, and *Places in the Heart*. Buck Henry did an excellent adaptation of *Catch-22* that Nichols smothered in an overproduced film, then Henry also worked on *What's Up, Doc?* and was codirector with Warren Beatty on *Heaven Can Wait*. Not every young writer had that kind of success. Dennis Hopper's career as a writer and director is checkered at best, and after a mediocre screenplay called *The Fortune*, also for Jack Nicholson, Adrien Joyce has had no additional credits since 1975.

This period of creative balance can be said to have begun to end in May 1977. May 25. About five in the afternoon. (Don't worry. That will be explained. In the next chapter, of course.)

The auteur theory

If the filmmaking styles of the French nouvelle vague had a generally positive effect on American films, the theoretical approach of the same filmmakers in their earlier days as critics had a decidedly negative effect. In the January 1954 edition of *Cahiers du Cinema*, François Truffaut put forth what he described as the *Politique des auteurs*, which became more commonly known in this country as the auteur theory. The word *auteur* literally means author, but, following the European tradition of the director having almost total control over his film, the term was applied to directors as authors. The auteur theory was that the director was the creator of the film.

The *Cahiers* critics applied their theory to American directors as well, but the critics were over six thousand miles away from where American films were made and were wrong about how American films were made. Furthermore, because of the youth of the French critics and because English was not their first language, they admired directors who worked in visual genres, such as action pictures, westerns, and thrillers. There was less interest in directors who were writers as well, since this smacked too much of the French "Tradition of Quality" that *Cahiers* objected to.

If it had not been for the success of the nouvelle vague films, it is likely that the auteur theory would have died a natural death. However, the theory was picked up and promoted by American critic Andrew Sarris (who was only three thousand miles away from where the films were made). Sarris and others established the auteur theory in America just as film studies were getting established in American universities. The auteur approach helped persuade nonfilm academics that film study was a respectable line of work and therefore film departments and courses could be considered legitimate academic endeavors.

For the critics and historians, the auteur theory became a way to justify films they had grown up with. Like the French, their admired directors tended to be those of the entertainment genres. The auteur critics rejected what the previous generation of critics had liked: filmmakers who brought some substance to their films. Those included directors who were writers as well. In Sarris's witty 1968 categorizing of directors, the "Less than Meets the Eye" group includes John Huston, Joseph L. Mankiewicz, and Billy Wilder.[13]

The acceptance of the auteur theory had disastrous consequences for screenwriting in American films. The general use of the theory gave film fans and film students a completely inaccurate view of American film history and the role of screenwriters in it. The belief in the theory by directors, their agents, their press agents, producers, executives, and others made a change in what was desirable or even acceptable in screenwriting for American films.

Hitchcock and His Writers

Alfred Hitchcock was the auteurists' darling. Not only was he a brilliant director with an impressive body of films, but he was also a terrific subject for an auteurist interview. While talking about his films, Hitchcock tended to forget the contributions of most of the other people who worked on them, particularly the writers. Hitchcock and his auteurist admirers talked and wrote at great length about how the movies Hitchcock made were "pure cinema" as opposed to "photographs of people talking." What Hitchcock and the auteurists never acknowledged was how essential screenwriters were to creating his films. Indeed, because of the complexity of plotting of thrillers, Hitchcock was perhaps more dependent on writers than any other director.

To see the importance of a good screenplay for a Hitchcock film, it is only necessary to compare a great Hitchcock film with a poor one. For the former, consider *Rear Window*, for the latter *Vertigo*. *Rear Window*, written by John Michael Hayes, was based on a short story by Cornell Woolrich. Hayes and Hitchcock expanded on both the characters and the plot of the story, changing the details of the murder and the hiding of the body to make the story more filmable. Hitchcock did what he generally did with the writers working with him: discussed in detail how information was to be shown visually in the film.[14] What Hayes did was come up with the characterization and the dialogue that play off beautifully against the visuals. In the famous opening scene, the details of L. B. Jeffries's apartment are shown in a pan around the room. The pan gives us many visual details, but the exact connections between the details are not established until the scene that follows. Jeffries is talking to his boss on the telephone and Hayes's seemingly casual dialogue ties together the details.

Rear Window consists of alternating scenes in which there is no dialogue (or at least none that we can hear) and scenes that are all dialogue. What is surprising is how much time is spent on dialogue scenes in which the characters try to figure out the murder. It is a measure of Hayes's skill at dialogue that the film does not seem talky. Hayes does provide for the standard Hitchcock tours de force, such as the scene in which Jeffries and the nurse watch Lisa go into Thorwald's apartment, but these scenes work on the screen because they have been so carefully set up in plot terms.

Vertigo also begins with a visual scene in which we see a friend of Scottie Ferguson fall to his death. In the next scene, as in *Rear Window*, the dialogue explains that the fall has caused Scottie to be afraid of heights. And explains it again. And again. The dialogue (the script is by Alec Coppel and Samuel Taylor) is sorely in need of Hayes's skill. Coppel and Taylor also fail to make the characters interesting. Scottie becomes obsessed with a woman he is hired to follow, but the obsession is shown merely by his driving interminably around San Francisco while he follows her. There is virtually no characterization given to the woman, unlike the sharp and witty characters Hayes wrote for Grace Kelly and Thelma Ritter in *Rear Window*.

The question those who have read auteurist criticism of *Vertigo* undoubtedly will ask is: if this picture is so bad, why do the auteurists think it is one of Hitchcock's best? It is not his best *unless* you examine a film *strictly* from an auteurist point of view: does the film show off the personality of the director? In a sense, *Vertigo* does. It shows Hitchcock's obsession with the cool blondes he kept trying to turn into Grace Kelly. Does it do it in an interesting and entertaining way? No. Why? Because the script is simply not up to it.

Hitchcock of course was not the only director to be given this treatment. Auteurist critics tend to admire the later John Ford films, which were made independently and often have scripts that are close to incoherent on a narrative level, but give Ford many opportunities to show off Monument Valley and his love of drunken farce. Auteurist critics tend to elevate Orson Welles's wonderful shaggy-dog story, *Touch of Evil*, into a great film, but it is only if you look at it as a showcase for Welles's talents as a director.

Sorcerer

Directors *loved* the auteur theory. It confirmed what they already knew: anything good on a picture came from the director, anything bad came from someone else, usually the producer, but often the screenwriter. Since the auteur theory became so widely accepted, American films have seen the increased use of writers hired to write scripts that show off the director's skill. Or at least his personality.

One of the more flagrant examples of this is a 1977 film *Sorcerer*, written by Walon Green and directed by William Friedkin. Friedkin was coming off the success of *The French Connection*, written by Ernest Tidyman, and *The Exorcist*, written and produced by William Peter Blatty. There were rumors of conflict between Friedkin and Blatty, and on *Sorcerer* Friedkin was the producer *and* director. It was a remake of Henri-Georges Clouzot's 1952 French film *The Wages of Fear*. The story deals with four men trapped in a South American town who agree to drive two trucks full of decaying dynamite through the jungle to the site of an oil-well fire. It should have been perfect material for the director of *The French Connection*.

Unfortunately, the screenplay Friedkin insisted upon does not tell the story as well as Clouzot does. Clouzot's film begins in the squalid little town in South America and by the end of the first twenty minutes we are as desperate as the men to get out. Friedkin's film opens with four sequences that show how each of the men got to the small town. One sequence is set in the Middle East (to show Friedkin can imitate Pontecorvo's brilliant direction of *Battle of Algiers*), and another in New Jersey (to stage a car crash to remind audiences he was the director of *The French Connection*). Friedkin has directed the sequences so badly in terms of identifying the characters that we do not recognize them when they get to the small town.

In Clouzot's film, each episode on the road tells us something about the characters, whom we come to know imtimately throughout the film. In Friedkin's film we get spectacular action sequences, such as the trucks inching across a suspension bridge, that are not particularly involving. The film was one of the more spectacular flops of 1977. The seventies and eighties were littered with scripts and films of a similar nature, such as *1941*, *The Cotton Club*, and *Heaven's Gate*.

Close Encounters vs. *E. T.*

If the auteurists had conspired to create a director for the seventies and eighties, they would have come up with something like Steven Spielberg. He made his first major impact directing Richard Matheson's script for the television movie *Duel*. Spielberg moved into features with the 1974 film *The Sugarland Express*, which shows Spielberg at his best (directing action sequences) and at his worst (directing character sequences: he misses much of the characters' humor from the script). Spielberg made his biggest early impact directing Peter Benchley and Carl Gotlieb's screenplay for *Jaws*.

Paul Schrader worked on Spielberg's next project, a script entitled *Watch the Skies*, and he found Spielberg smarting from the critical reception of *Jaws*. Schrader has been quoted as saying:

> You have to understand how Spielberg felt about *Jaws*. He was furious with Verna (Fields, the studio editor), (producer Richard) Zanuck and Peter Benchley. . . . He felt they had all conspired to take away his credit.[15]

It was not surprising then that Schrader and a number of other writers left the project, which eventually became *Close Encounters of the Third Kind*. The sole screenwriter credited on the film was Steven Spielberg.

Close Encounters is very much a screenplay by and for an auteur director. It is two hours plus of exposition, handled in physically big scenes, such as the discovery of the planes in Mexico in the opening scene, a meeting of scientists in a room ten times the size needed, an unneeded scene in India, and a landing area so large it had to be built in an old airplane hangar in Alabama. What is even worse is that the scenes are not dramatically shaped. When Roy has a mystical sense that he must go someplace, we understand it the first time he builds a model of it in his mashed potatoes, but Spielberg has Roy carry on building larger and larger models. There is one moderately interesting character scene involving a man who claims to have seen Bigfoot, but when Spielberg prepared the rerelease in 1980 he cut that scene and replaced it with yet another action scene set in the Gobi Desert.

The biggest script problem with *Close Encounters* is that the story of flying saucers is more interesting *after* they land than before. Spielberg proved this with his best film *E.T.* in 1982, and for that he was smart enough not to write it himself, but to hire Melissa Mathison, one of the writers on the 1979 film *The Black Stallion*. He told Mathison that he wanted to make a film about an alien stranded on Earth, and eight weeks later Mathison had written the screenplay.[16] The screenplay finds tremendous charm and humor in the interactions of the small alien and the small kids he comes to know, and tells the story in the kinds of characters Spielberg is most comfortable dealing with on screen. There is great variety in the story details, and Mathison provides the moments to truly touch us, which Spielberg's direction does. Sometimes directors are better off with real screenwriters; this time was one of them.

While Spielberg was directing *E.T.*, he also wrote the story, cowrote the screenplay, and produced but did not direct *Poltergeist*. When someone suggested this was perhaps not as much his film as that of the director, Spielberg said, "It derived from *my* imagination and *my* experiences, and it came out of *my* typewriter."[17] I have not been able to find any evidence that he ever made that claim for Matheson on *Duel*, Benchley and Gotlieb on *Jaws*. . . .

25

Alumni

S creenwriters in American film have traditionally come from a great variety of backgrounds, but it was not until the sixties that screenwriters came straight out of film schools. Film schools had been in existence for some time, but it was not until the second round of youth movies that the studios opened up to student filmmakers.

The filmmakers who came through film schools brought several qualities, both good and bad, with them. Film history courses gave them an appreciation of film, which showed itself in different ways. Many film students became hooked on older American films and admired their narrative drive, which led them to make mainstream American films. Too often, however, students had no experience other than old films to use as the subject matter for their films.

On the other hand many students in the sixties were enamored with the European film movements and were more interested in expanding the cinema than entertaining and telling a story. At their best, these graduates made films that went beyond basic moviemaking; at their worst, their films were incoherent.

It was easier for a screenwriter to break into the industry than a director, since all a screenwriter needed was a script, which could be written very cheaply. A generation of film students who, under the influence of the teaching of the auteur theory, wanted to become directors, realized that the quickest way to get to be a director was to write screenplays that sold and then follow the path of Sturges and the others. Los Angeles was, and is, crawling with screenwriting courses at colleges and universities, as well as privately run screenwriting schools. Scenario fever returned. Many would-be directors in screenwriting classes, however, were not interested in writing films so much as creating collections of directorial touches.

Working in a film-school environment, many student filmmakers, including writers, learned about the technology of filmmaking. This not only helped the writers, but also hurt them as well, as in the technical improvements of sound. Sixties' students grew up with high-fidelity stereo sound in their homes and cars, and when they moved into films, the quality and use of sound in films improved. The writer's problem was, and still is, that often the sound technology is used to smother the dialogue. In the old days, the studios insured that dialogue was comprehensible. As the younger filmmakers played around with the range of the new equipment, sound tracks were recorded or mixed so that the dialogue was drowned out by the music and sound effects and was unintelligible to the audiences.

Francis Ford Coppola

The role model for film students was Francis Ford Coppola. Coppola studied theater at Hofstra University, where he not only directed plays, but wrote short stories as well. In 1960 he went west to study film at UCLA.[1] When he saw a notice on the bulletin board that Roger Corman was looking for an assistant he applied.[2]

Coppola went to Europe as the sound man on a Corman production. Corman would never make one movie when he could make two, since he already had the crew there. Coppola wrote the screenplay in three nights for what became *Dementia 13*. He presented it to Corman, who let him make the film.[3] There is very little in the script of *Dementia 13* to suggest Coppola's talent as a screenwriter.

Coppola won the Samuel Goldwyn Screenwriting Contest at UCLA and as a result was hired by Seven Arts. Coppola recalls:

> The day I got my first job as a screenwriter there was a big sign on the bulletin board saying: *"Sell out!"* . . . There was an open resentment. I was making money. And I was sort of *doing* it. . . . But the kids at school are the most narrow-minded of any age group.[4]

Coppola's first screenplay for Seven Arts was an adaptation of Carson McCullers's *Reflections in a Golden Eye*, and it attracted considerable attention in the industry.[5] Coppola said later, "The reaction was such a load of baloney. Everyone read the *Reflections* script and said, 'Fantastic, who's this genius? It must be Dalton Trumbo writing under another name.' They gave me all that junk. Everything is either one hundred percent or nothing."[6] When the film was made later, nothing of Coppola's script was used. Much the same happened with his scripts for such projects as *This Property Is Condemned* and *Is Paris Burning?*

While working as one of ten writers on the latter script, Coppola wrote a script entitled *You're a Big Boy Now* at night "to stay sane."[7] Coppola worked out deals whereby he would direct it, Seven Arts would produce it, and furthermore it would be his master's degree film at UCLA. The 1967 film did well enough for Coppola to keep working.

Coppola formed his own studio, Zoetrope, and to help finance it, Coppola agreed to direct *The Godfather*. Coppola was not at first impressed with the book. He reread it and saw it as a story of a family and the questions of power and succession.[8] The first drafts of the script were written by the author of the novel, Mario Puzo, but he and Coppola worked on subsequent drafts. The flashback material of Vito establishing himself in America was dropped, as was the section about singer Johnny Fontane in Las Vegas. *The Godfather* is a film of extraordinary narrative power, in the classic American narrative film tradition. The power comes both from Puzo's skill as a storyteller and Coppola's willingness to keep to the heart of the matter.

After *The Godfather* Coppola returned to a story he had been working on since 1967–68. Director Irving Kershner mentioned to Coppola that microphones existed that could record conversations in the middle of a crowd. Coppola said later, "I was immediately struck by the idea, which seemed very visual and very cinematic, and I tried to build something around it."[9] Coppola completed a first draft in 1969 that focused more on the people talking than on the people listening. He then began to rewrite to focus on the person listening, who became Harry Caul.

Coppola, unlike many film-school graduates, is not particularly fond of Hitchcock, but realized the best way to tell the story was as a thriller. The two most obvious Hitchcock references in *The Conversation* are to *Rear Window* and *Psycho*. The reference to *Psycho* is in Caul's search of a bathroom, where the blood comes not in the shower as we would expect after *Psycho*, but from the toilet. In *Rear Window* Hitchcock and Hayes play Jeffries's voyeurism for laughs and thriller effects, with only occasional references in the dialogue to the emotional or moral questions, but Coppola focuses strongly on the emotional effect being a professional snoop has on Caul. Coppola gets into the character of Caul in depth, not an easy job, since Caul confides in no one. What Coppola finds is an array of visual details (Caul's keys, the isolation of his workspace in one corner of a warehouse, his silence with others) to express that alienation. *The Conversation* borrows also from Antonioni's cribbing from *Rear Window*, the 1966 film *Blowup*, in using a possible murder to show Caul's alienation from society. Coppola goes deeper into that alienation than Antonioni, and the film elements of the script that make Caul less alienated (lines that suggest he has a sense of humor, a scene with a lawyer who appears to be his friend) have been dropped.[10]

The Conversation, for all its thriller elements, is not a conventional narrative film. We are constantly rehearsing and reseeing the conversation in bits and pieces, and various loose ends are not tied up (at least we do learn there was a murder; in *Blowup* Antonioni, true to form, does not even let us know that much). The film tells its story in a much more complex way than in previous American films. Coppola and his editor/sound supervisor Walter

Murch use the complexity of film, especially cutting and sound, to bring us into the character and the issues of the film. Murch was reorganizing scenes and structure in the film: the "dream sequence" in the film where Caul talks to the woman in the park was in the script the end of an earlier, "real" scene cut from the film.

One reason Walter Murch was so involved in the post-production work on *The Conversation* was that Coppola was writing and directing *The Godfather, Part II*. Coppola once said he would do the sequel only if it were *Abbott and Costello Meet the Godfather*.[11] A screenplay entitled *The Death of Michael Corleone* had been prepared at Paramount, but Coppola did not want Michael either to die or go to jail, "but in a larger sense, I wanted him to be a broken man. And there is no doubt, in the last scene of the film, that Michael, sitting in the chair, victorious but alone, is a living corpse."[12] Coppola did a first draft, which was not acceptable to Al Pacino, and Coppola rewrote the script in three days.[13] Brando and Paramount were not getting along, and Coppola agreed to Robert De Niro as the younger Vito.

Coppola decided to cut back and forth between two stories: one the rise of Vito and the other the decline of Michael. Both stories gain by the juxtaposition, since the narrative drive in each is not strong enough to stand on its own.

The story material on Michael was new. In it one can begin to see Coppola changing from a writer-director into a Director. The Cuban sequence calls for, and receives, a much more elaborate production than needed to make the point. Coppola is beginning here to tumble into the directorial excess that mar his later career. In film after film he gets away from the heart of the material and into "production values." This is most notable on *Apocalypse Now, One from the Heart*, and *The Cotton Club* (which was rumored to have thirty-nine different drafts of its screenplay), but even in *Peggy Sue Got Married*, Coppola the director seems to miss the comic rhythms of the lines while giving us an overproduced high-school reunion and a lodge meeting out of a Spielberg movie.

Other UCLA Screenwriters

After Coppola, there were other screenwriters who came out of the UCLA film school. Nancy Dowd studied both screenwriting and production in the late sixties, then went to work for Jane Fonda. Two scripts she did for Fonda's company were subsequently produced, *Coming Home* (which starred Fonda) and *Swing Shift* (which starred Goldie Hawn). Both scripts were rewritten by other writers. In addition to writing about women in those two films, Dowd also took on male attitudes in *Slap Shot*, a raunchy look at professional hockey players. Its excessively crude language was accurate, but turned off audiences.

One of Barry Sandler's first scripts became *Kansas City Bomber,* and he later wrote the first mainstream American film centered on a homosexual relationship, the rather cautious 1982 picture *Making Love.* Penelope Spheeris's screenplay for her film *Suburbia* is a dark, compelling view of the nastiness of American teens and subteens.

Neil Jimenez wrote *The River's Edge,* a film similar in tone to *Suburbia,* for a class project at UCLA. For his first draft, which his teacher Richard Walter described as having "20 great pages followed by perhaps ninety that were not so great,"[14] Walter told Jimenez that he would get either a C+ for the script as it stood, or Walter would give him an Incomplete and he could rewrite it and improve it. Jimenez did the rewrites and got an A+.[15] It then took six years to get it produced and released.

One of the distinguishing characteristics of the screenwriters who came out of the UCLA film program was their willingness to deal with reality. This is not typical of most film-school scripts. It may come from the school itself. UCLA is a state-supported university, and it was therefore necessary from the beginning to take film seriously as an art form to convince the university officials and the politicians who provided the financial support for the college that film was a legitimate subject for study. The production side of the department deals with film as an expression of an artist's point of view. Each advanced film project is under the control of a single student who makes "his" film.

UCLA's crosstown rival USC looks at the matter differently. John Milius, who went to USC in the late sixties, says, "UCLA trained people for making protests on film. They were concerned with taking drugs and making experimental films." Milius takes a more pleasant view of his own school, "At USC, we were a private school, an elitist school that trained people for Hollywood. We were very much concerned with making the Hollywood film, not to make a lot of money as artists," while Walter Murch, also from USC, does allow that USC did develop a reputation as the "soulless technocrats of film."[16]

USC and George Lucas

The University of Southern California is a private university. Its money comes not from the state, but from private contributions and endowments. Understandably a Los Angeles university like that looks to the movie industry as a source of funds. Industry figures such as Jerry Lewis, Sol Lesser, and Blake Edwards have often taught at USC. The emphasis in the film program has been on Hollywood-type films, and the emphasis in production has been on teamwork, with groups of filmmakers assigned to projects. This teamwork continued as the students moved into the industry, and USC has been enormously influential in the film industry since the early seventies. For better *and* for worse.

If Coppola is the best-known UCLA Film School graduate, George Lucas is the best known from USC. Lucas says of his student films, "My feeling at that time was that scripts were for the birds. I disdained story and character; I didn't want anything to do with them."[17] He was more interested in editing and design and his student films, particularly his best known, *THX-1138:4EB*, show those skills. Dave Johnson, one of his instructors at USC, says,

> He understood very well the use of the camera and sound because he had a sense of structure and visual continuity. His forte was designing and construct-ing film stories, but his attitude was "Let someone else work with the people." Look at his student films—they're all about things and facts. People are just objects.[18]

Lucas's sense of structure is simple. His editing assistant says Lucas's view is "Keep things defined and interesting, with the emphasis on action and dialogue. Keep it moving, keep the pace going."[19] In this Lucas is similar to Thomas Ince, whose main rule was to keep it moving. Ince's sense of narrative complexity was stronger than Lucas's, as was his sense of charac-terization.

After graduating from USC, Lucas connected with Coppola, who helped Lucas arrange for the production of a feature version of *THX-1138*. The speed and visual design of the short film are not enough to carry the feature, and Lucas's weakness in the area of characterization and lack of modulation in the storyline are evident in the feature, which was not a hit, even when released after the success of his later films.

Lucas spent most of his high-school days in Modesto, California, cruising the streets in his car. His father told him that was a worthless activity, and Lucas decided to make *American Graffiti* partially to show his father he was wrong.[20] Lucas wrote the first drafts of the script, which were turned down by the studios. Part of the reason for the turndowns was that Lucas's writing was not very clear. His script consisted of short scenes, with each scene played against a rock song of the late fifties (the film was originally set in 1959). To explain this, he announced in his script that the film was to be a musical. This only baffled the people who read it.

The first script has a great deal of talk about cars, and detailed descriptions of cars, but very little about the characters. The character of the underaged Carol does not appear in this draft. Debbie, the smart-dumb blonde, and

Laurie, Steve's girlfriend, are in the script, but in smaller roles than in the film. George Byron Sage, who read the script for Fox, notes in his comments, "There's nothing to make you feel these characters could be interesting enough to demand such prolonged attention from a general feature audience."[21]

To help him rework the screenplay, Lucas hired a young married couple. Willard Huyck had been at USC with Lucas, while his wife, Gloria Katz, had attended UCLA, and in Los Angeles film-school style they met at a lecture by Roger Corman.[22] Lucas admitted they helped develop the characters. "They were cardboard cutouts in my script, nonpeople. Bill and Gloria made it one hundred percent better with a combination of wit, charm, snappy one-liners, and punched-up characters."[23] In other words, all the things screenwriters are supposed to do. Katz was particularly helpful with the women characters, and she and Huyck were upset that in the title card at the end of the film, the fates of only the four male characters were listed and not the female characters. Lucas insisted it was a movie about the four guys, and even after being justifiably attacked on grounds of male chauvinism, Lucas did not include the women on a title card when the film was rereleased in 1979.

American Graffiti was a low-budget film ($775,000)[24] but a big grossing one ($10,300,000 in its first year of release).[25] That was not enough to convince Universal to make Lucas's next film. The decision cost Universal $250 million.[26]

Star Wars borrows visually from films as diverse as *The Wizard of Oz*, *The Searchers*, *Lawrence of Arabia*, and *Triumph of the Will*. The story line borrows mostly from Akira Kurosawa's 1959 Japanese film *The Hidden Fortress*. Kurosawa's film, set in the middle of a war in feudal Japan, opens with two peasants whom we follow through the film as they get involved in the adventures of more lofty folk. They fall in with a general of the defeated army, played by Toshiro Mifune at his most masculine. Mifune and his army are protecting a sixteen-year-old princess and her family. The film's plot is the journey out of the hidden fortress with the princess and her gold, across enemy and neutral territory, back into friendly territory to establish the family leadership.

The two peasants are obviously forerunners of R2D2 and C3PO, but they are much earthier. They are constantly considering turning over the princess to the other side for the reward, and at two points in the film they clearly lust in their hearts, and elsewhere, for the princess. Mifune's general is an adult, knowledgeable about the world, very aware of his responsibilities. The princess has been brought up like a boy, so she is spunkier than Princess Leia in the *Star Wars* films. It is the princess who insists they buy a prostitute she sees is being mistreated at a bar they stop at. At the end of the film, she thanks the general for letting her see the real world during the trip. The journey into adulthood in the film has been hers.

Lucas's story did not start out so different from *The Hidden Fortress*. The hero was originally an older general, who developed into Obi-Won Kenobi and Darth Vader. Princess Leia was more dominant in the first drafts, but receded as Luke became more prominent. In one draft she was only eleven years old. Although she is sixteen in the film, she still behaves like the bratty kid sister, so much so that it was no surprise to anyone that she turned out in *Return of the Jedi* to be Luke's sister.[27] Kurosawa's film can be enjoyed by people of all ages, whereas *Star Wars* is aimed specifically at the twelve-year-old boy in each of us.

Lucas's writing in the early drafts was as awkward as before. His misspellings were legendary and he seldom spelled a character's name the same way twice.[28] Lucas also showed drafts to his friends, and director Michael Ritchie remembers, "It was very difficult to tell what the man was talking about."[29] The dialogue, as it often is in science-fiction movies, was impossible. Alec Guinness's first reaction to the script was: "I thought the dialogue was pretty terrible and the characters fairly meaningless—but there was a story value. I found I wanted to know what happened next, what was on the next page? In the end I thought: Why not?"[30] William Huyck and Gloria Katz were brought in to help with the dialogue, but Harrison Ford was still often heard to say to Lucas, "You can type this shit, George, but you sure can't say it."[31]

Star Wars moves. It moves quickly. And it moves clearly. The audience always knows where it is. The good guys, or robots, are established quickly; the bad guys are established equally quickly. Lucas believes in not confusing the audience: "If they start getting lost, you're in trouble. Sometimes you have to be crude and just say what's going on, because if you don't, people get puzzled."[32] The speed and clarity of the film are its strengths. Its weaknesses are simplicity of characterization and lack of inventiveness in the plotting. When Luke, Han, and Obi-Won get to the Death Star to rescue Leia and the plans of the Death Star, the film settles into a repetitive series of chases and escapes. The inventiveness in the film has not gone into the story or the characters, but into the visuals.

It used to be said derisively of the Hollywood films of the thirties and forties that they were made for twelve-year-olds. That is not entirely true. The subject matter of those films was often very adult, but the material was presented so it could be understood by audiences of all ages. This made the films seem simpler than they were. With *Star Wars*, the material itself appealed to the mentality of a twelve-year-old, as well as the presentation.

Star Wars opened on May 25, 1977. By the late-afternoon screenings it was clear that there was an audience of phenomenal size for the film, and the only question was whether the crowds would continue. They did. *Star Wars* was such an enormous success that it was quickly seen by the industry as the one true way to turn out a blockbuster.

That true way was to aim at the third youth market: teenagers and subteens. The youth market had developed from a secondary operation making cheap exploitation films to an attempt to upgrade the quality of films to the central force of American filmmaking after 1977. Because the highly volatile teenage market could turn a film into a blockbuster by repeat attendance, the industry lost any sustaining interest in making films for adults. This may be one reason why there have been fewer women screenwriters than ever before in Hollywood's history in theatrical films since 1977. Many of the women screenwriters went to television where films and series for adults found a home.

The USC Film School graduates (nearly all of whom are men, unlike those from UCLA) were equipped to write, produce, direct, and supervise films for the third youth market. One of Lucas's assistants on *Star Wars* notes that Lucas's friends from USC would drop by while they were mixing the film: "It was like a men's club—he would really confide in them and they had great fun. They're all like a bunch of little boys."[33] The virtues of *Star Wars* are the characteristics of American adolescent males: speed, noise, simplicity, and a stunning lack of awareness of the realities of life.

Lucas's adolescent male fantasies are at the heart of the *Star Wars* films just as his nostalgia for his adolescence is at the heart of *American Graffiti*. The second two films in the *Star Wars* series try to deepen the characters and the philosophy, but both resist much deepening. If *Star Wars* is aimed at the twelve-year-old boy in us, *The Empire Strikes Back* is aimed at the fifteen-year-old, and *Return of the Jedi* the seventeen-year-old.

Lucas's two films about Indiana Jones also appeal to kids and teens. Both are fast, simple in story, and relentlessly exciting. It does look in *Raiders of the Lost Ark* that Lucas and his writer Lawrence Kasdan have finally given us an adult woman in Marion Ravenswood, but after a terrific introductory scene, she reverts to being a damsel, albeit a tough one, in distress. One of the weakest moments in *Raiders* is the lack of time the audience is given to mourn when we think Marion is dead, but this is as much a flaw in Spielberg's overbusy direction as the script. The second film, *Indiana Jones and the Temple of Doom*, a rip-off of the 1939 film *Gunga Din*, tries, in the manner of a little boy, to outgross the first film. The woman in the film, singer Willie Scott, is more of a conventional bimbo heroine than Marion was. In the tackiest scene in the film she, Indy, and the young boy are in the jungle and she is afraid of the animals. She screams repeatedly, but Indy and the boy continue playing cards, and Indy comments that the problem with women is that they are so noisy. Coming in a production by George Lucas, who popularized Dolby Stereo, in a scene written[34] and directed by Steven

Spielberg, whose films are as loud as Lucas's, that comment is the height of gall.

Other USC Screenwriters

John Milius affects a macho posture both in life and in his scripts. His early credits include *Jeremiah Johnson* (rewritten by Edward Anhalt because Milius's script was too bloody for the studio)[35] and the second of the *Dirty Harry* films, *Magnum Force*. Milius turned director in the early seventies, and his best film is *The Wind and the Lion*, a charming adventure story told through the eyes of two children. Milius then tried to show that surfers were the equivalent of the Knights of the Round Table in *Big Wednesday*, but the film was as shallow as its characters. It is rumored that in Milius's early drafts for what became *Apocalypse Now* there was a line, intended to be taken seriously, to the effect that the true tragedy of Vietnam was that it killed all the good surfers.[36]

Hal Barwood and Matthew Robbins wrote the screenplays for *The Sugarland Express*, *The Bingo Long Traveling All-Stars and Motor Kings* (about the all-black baseball leagues in the thirties), and *MacArthur* (a script not up to Coppola and Edmund North's script for *Patton*) before *Star Wars* killed off those kinds of films. In the year after *Star Wars* they wrote and Robbins directed *Corvette Summer*, a film in which the leading character spends the entire movie chasing down his stolen Corvette. In 1981 Barwood and Robbins turned in one of the mediocre examples of the sword-and-sorcery films, *Dragonslayer*.

Robert Zemeckis and Bob Gale moved from USC into working for Spielberg, writing (with Zemeckis directing) the 1978 film *I Wanna Hold Your Hand*, which they followed with a dreadful, overblown script for *1941*. Zemeckis and Gale did write, again with Zemeckis directing, a small, nasty, but very funny satire on car dealers, *Used Cars*. Their biggest hit and best film to date has been the brilliantly structured comedy *Back to the Future*.

It would be wrong to assume that the better elements in the screenplays by Willard Huyck and Gloria Katz came from Katz and/or came from Katz because she attended film school at UCLA while Huyck was at USC. After writing *American Graffiti* with Lucas they wrote, and Huyck directed, *French Postcards*. That 1979 film dealt with American college students in their junior year abroad. The film has the same kind of feeling for character that *Graffiti* has, but it does not have the forward drive that Lucas gives his films. Huyck and Katz returned to work with Lucas and wrote *Indiana Jones and the Temple of Doom*, in which their skills were overpowered by Lucas and Spielberg.

In 1986 Huyck and Katz wrote, and Huyck again directed, their most misconceived project, *Howard the Duck*. In the original comic strip, Howard is rude, obnoxious, and has a foul as well as a fowl mouth. The whole point of the Howard the Duck comics is that he is *not nice*. At some point early in the project, a George Lucas presentation, it was decided that Howard would be nice. Huyck and Katz have enough of an ear for dialogue that they could have written a dark, funny film about the real Howard. But it was now not only the age of the blockbuster, but the George Lucas blockbuster, and the film was turned into a bland special-effects extravaganza.

The whole appeal of the first and second youth markets was that they were made up of low-budget films that connected to the audience better than the big-budget Hollywood films. The third youth market became those same empty, big-budget pictures. As the comic-strip character Pogo used to say, "We have met the enemy, and they is us."

26

Comic Independents

In the twenties silent comedians like Chaplin and Keaton were able to control the production of their own films. In the studio system, it was difficult for comic writers to control their own films. Comedies became primarily a group effort, with the exception of writers and writer-stars like Preston Sturges, W. C. Fields, and Mae West. By the late sixties it was once again possible for a comic writer to make films that reflected an individual point of view.

The early comic writers and performers came out of vaudeville, and the later ones came out of electronic vaudeville: television. A program such as *Your Show of Shows*, which ran on NBC from 1950 to 1954, had individual comedy routines and comedy sketches about both everyday life and about a subject that fascinated the writers and performers: movies. Those sketches were created by a large staff of writers working exactly as Sennett's collection of "badly deranged lunatics." Many of the writing staff of *Your Show of Shows* became screenwriters. Two of the three major comedy screenwriting talents of the sixties and later, Mel Brooks and Neil Simon, wrote for the show, and it is wrongly assumed the third did as well.

Woody Allen

Woody Allen did not contribute to *Your Show of Shows*. Allen joined the NBC Writers Development Program at the age of eighteen in 1954, the year *Your Show of Shows* left the air, but Allen was sent to Hollywood. He worked there with Danny Simon, Neil Simon's brother, from whom he learned plot development.[1] In the early sixties, Allen began to perform his own material as a stand-up comic. In his routines, he did not tell jokes, but developed a character (just as Keaton and Chaplin had developed their characters): the anxious neurotic obsessed with, as the title of one of his later films suggests, love and death. The jokes came from character.

Allen wrote some of, and appeared in, two films for producer Charles Feldman, *What's New, Pussycat?* and *Casino Royale*. Allen was appalled at the waste of both his time and talent on the two Feldman films, and he became determined to control the production of his films.[2] His manager,

Charles Joffe, produced the next film, *Take the Money and Run*, which Allen directed from a script he and Mickey Rose wrote. The film tells the story of incompetent bank robber Virgil Starkwell, but tells it in documentary film style. The documentary framework enabled Allen and Rose to throw in as many bank-robbing gags as they could think of without having to develop much of a narrative structure.

The rough cut was a mess. Veteran film editor Ralph Rosenblum saw the cut, then read the script. He said later, "The first thing I discovered when I read the script later that day was that it contained a wealth of jokes, many of them very funny, that I had not seen in the film."[3] Rosenblum agreed to recut the picture, and looked at all the material shot, both from the script and improvised. He discovered that when Allen thought something did not work, he simply got rid of it. As a first-time director, he was unaware how a picture could be helped in the editing room. Rosenblum recut the film, giving it a structure by using the interview material as connecting elements throughout.[4] The film was a success, and Rosenblum continued to work as Allen's editor through *Interiors*.

For his next film, Allen's managers made a deal with United Artists that continues into his current connection with Orion. Within a set budget (increased over the years), Allen is free to make whatever film he wants. He does show the script to the head of UA or Orion, and if the company insists he not make it, he probably would not. However, they never insist. The company also does not look at the rushes and does not discuss the editing or any of the production details with him.[5] Allen still has that deal because his films come in on time, on budget, and generally make money. Even those that do not make money do not lose much money.

His first film for UA was *Bananas*. Allen deliberately overwrote the screenplay so he and Ralph Rosenblum would have enough material to cut together.[6] Allen was determined to have either a chase or a courtroom scene as the climax. Since the budget did not allow for a chase, there is a courtroom scene.[7] There are also echoes of other films and two parodies of ABC-TV's *Wide World of Sports*.

Those echoes and parodies are used in his early films just as gags. In his next three films, *Everything You Always Wanted to Know About Sex (But Were Afraid to Ask)*, *Sleeper*, and *Love and Death*, Allen began to use the material to experiment with the medium. There are seven short films in *Everything*, and each one has a different narrative and cinematic style.

Sleeper gives Allen an opportunity to do slapstick, but he suffers in comparison with Keaton and Chaplin. As Allen himself noted the year before *Sleeper* in an interview,[8] he did not have the physical training that the early silent comedians had. He is better at dialogue, and *Sleeper* includes extended dialogue scenes with Diane Keaton that suggest where Allen's screenwriting was taking him.

Those scenes foreshadowed the complex comic and philosophical discussions Allen and Keaton play at a breakneck pace in *Love and Death*. The dialogue in *Love and Death* is richer, funnier, and more bizarre than anything heard from the American screen since the heyday of Preston Sturges. The film does not seem static and talky because Allen zips through an epic story in eighty-five minutes. The film shows Allen's command of filmmaking. It is one of the few epic comedies (as opposed to merely overproduced) in American films since *The Gold Rush* and *The General*.

Allen was not happy with the size of the production of *Love and Death*.[9] Unlike most directors, he wanted to make smaller films rather than larger ones. He returned to New York City and with his collaborator on *Sleeper*, Marshall Brickman, he wrote the script that became *Annie Hall*. Brickman and Allen discussed it first. Brickman recalls:

> We did everything up to the writing part, and he went off and did the first draft very quickly, in ten days. Then we made a xerox—one only, under guard—so I could take it home and read it, and then we'd start working on the second stage. I'd write a couple of new scenes to be inserted, and so on. . . .
>
> The first script of *Annie Hall* was much more episodic, tangential, and novelistic. . . . It didn't work for us. We started to become interested in the love story between Woody and the Keaton character, which was all over the place. We cut and pasted to make the love story more important, and the structure emerged. The material was telling us what to do.[10]

Much of that original material was shot, which is Allen's pattern in making a film. Rewriting was done after the rough cut was put together. By the time of *Annie Hall* he had written into his contract time and money for retakes.[11] In *Annie Hall* the post-production rewriting brought one of the film's biggest laughs. Later in the film Alvy Singer's leaving for California was established in a scene that was cut. The replacement scene has Alvy with friends, some of whom are dividing a package of cocaine. After saying he is going to California, Alvy sneezes. Into the cocaine.[12] People remember the laugh but structurally the scene's importance is the transition to California.

Three different endings were shot in late 1976, and two different voice-over narrations were written by Allen in a cab on the way to the recording studio on two different days.[13] There are advantages to having the screenwriter around through not only production, but post-production as well.

Annie Hall was the first of four films in which he turned inward. In the earlier films, the fun was the juxtaposition of the "Woody Allen" character with the future and nineteenth-century Russia. *Annie Hall*, by comparison, seemed inbred, although it and its remake, *Manhattan*, both found larger audiences than previous Allen films, primarily because they were about emotion and character as well as gags. After one serious film, *Interiors*, and a grouchy one, *Stardust Memories*, Allen returned to comedy with four small-scale films—not so much small-scale in terms of budget and production value, but in terms of story and substance. *The Purple Rose of Cairo* did provide the best line about screenwriters in the films of the eighties. An actor tells the heroine he created his starring role. Allen has Mia Farrow put on the most innocent expression of her career to ask, "Well, didn't the man who wrote the movie do that?"

In 1986 Allen put together the elements that he had been playing with since *Annie Hall* to write his most well-rounded film yet, *Hannah and Her Sisters*. It is funny, emotionally complex, occasionally sentimental, and probably could not have been written by someone who had not previously written *Annie Hall*, *Interiors*, *Manhattan*, *A Midsummer Night's Sex Comedy*, and *Broadway Danny Rose*. *Radio Days*, which followed a year later, is only slightly less of a film.

The obvious reason for Allen's continued growth and success as a screenwriter is that he makes the system work for him. He has virtually total control over his films, but more importantly, he uses that control responsibly. He does not go over budget and while he experiments he uses that experimentation to deepen his art as a filmmaker. Allen also remains open to the contributions of others. He frequently works with other screenwriters, and with a variety of actors, editors, and cinematographers. He uses those talents effectively to make his films interesting as films, not just as expressions of his own far-reaching intelligence.

Allen has remained a writer in other media as well (plays, short stories), and while he is critically acclaimed in those other media, he is thought of primarily as a filmmaker. Unlike many other directors, he is not thought of as just a stylist, and certainly not just a *visual* stylist. His films are not only written but seen to be written. Because they are written about and shot in New York, Woody Allen's films have finally persuaded the provincial New York cultural establishment, decades after its put-down of screenwriters began, that being a screenwriter might be all right after all. That accomplishment may dwarf the accomplishment of the films themselves.

Mel Brooks

Mel Brooks was one of the writing staff of *Your Show of Shows*. He also contributed a parody of *Death of a Salesman* to the Broadway revue *New Faces of 1952*. When the revue was filmed in 1954, Brooks had his first screenwriting credit. Film parodies became Brooks's screenwriting genre as well.

In the late sixties Brooks finally found a producer for a screenplay he had been working on for years, first as a novel, then as a play. Brooks's script for *The Producers* provides great comic scenes for Zero Mostel and Gene Wilder as well as the parody of a Busby Berkeley musical number, *Springtime for Hitler.* Ralph Rosenblum also edited this film, which Brooks directed, and he discovered that unlike Woody Allen, Brooks tried to keep everything.[14]

A story editor at Warner Brothers sent Brooks a treatment for a comedy western *Tex X*, written by Andrew Bergman. Brooks, Bergman, and two other writers joined Richard Pryor in rewriting the script. Brooks says of the writing of what became *Blazing Saddles:*

> I decided that this would be a surrealistic epic. For nine months we worked together like maniacs. We went all the way—especially Richard Pryor, who was very brave and far-out and catalytic. I figured my career was finished anyway, so I wrote berserk, heartfelt stuff about white corruption and racism and Bible-thumping bigotry. We used dirty language on the screen for the first time, and to me the whole thing was like a big psychoanalytical session. I just got everything out of me—all my furor, my frenzy, my insanity, my love of life and hatred of death.[15]

Warner Brothers refused to let Pryor play the lead, and Cleavon Little gave the character of a black sheriff in the old west an urban sophistication. The film was tasteless and funny enough without Pryor and one can only imagine what it would have been like with him. The picture's success established Brooks as a commercial filmmaker.

The idea and first-draft script of Brooks's next film *Young Frankenstein* came from its star, Gene Wilder. Brooks worked with Wilder on subsequent drafts. Just as the visual and verbal slapstick of *Blazing Saddles* rests on a serious story situation, the basic Frankenstein story provides a strong structure for *Young Frankenstein.* Wilder's quiet sense of character merges with Brooks's sense of parody beautifully in the film. After *Young Frankenstein* Wilder wrote and directed on his own, without the success he had working with Brooks.

Brooks's next parody was *Silent Movie.* The idea, about a movie director who wants a modern studio to let him do a silent film, came from Ron Clark, one of the cowriters on the film. The other two writers were Rudy De Luca and Barry Levinson, both veterans of television's *Carol Burnette Show* that was noted for its movie parodies. (Levinson has since gone on to write such warmer, less slapstick comedies as *Diner* and *Tin Men.*) The writing of *Silent Movie* is uneven: some sequences and gags are brilliant, such as an impromptu video game played on the hospital monitors of a patient, but other sections are bland.

Brooks's next parody subject was Hitchcock, and the film was *High Anxiety.* The film parodies on *Your Show of Shows* rarely ran more than twenty minutes and with good reason: twenty minutes is about the maximum parody by itself can hold an audience's attention. *Blazing Saddles* and *Young Frankenstein* were both based on strong situations. *High Anxiety* gets tiresome very quickly.

Brooks's next film as writer and director was *History of the World-Part 1,* which consisted of five sequences, each in a different film style. Unlike Woody Allen in *Everything You Always Wanted to Know about Sex,* Brooks was not using the different genres for anything other than parody.

By the writing of the 1987 film *Spaceballs,* Brooks learned how to throw out material he thought did not work. He describes the writing process on that film:

> The first draft of *Spaceballs* was 315 pages long. It was terrible. We let 50 people read it. I had them put checks by the stuff they liked, X's by the stuff that didn't work.
>
> Well, the first script was mostly X's. Then we did a 240-page version. It was about 50–50. Next we did an 180-page version. Finally, we got it down to 126 pages. That's the one we shot.
>
> It had a *lot* more checks than X's.[16]

What the readers were checking off were the jokes. The problem is that there is not a lot for the actors to *play* in the script. In comparison, several scenes in *Young Frankenstein* do not read funny, but play very funny. When Freddy is saying good-bye to Elizabeth in the train station in the earlier film, there are no gags in the scene as written.[17] What is in the scene are attitudes for the actors to play: he keeps trying to hold her, but she does not want him to smear her makeup.

Spaceballs only draws blood in its parodying of the Lucas merchandising empire. The irony is that Brooks, who created many of the best interview sketches on *Your Show of Shows,* is an even better promoter of his own films than Lucas. Brooks is the screenwriter as entertaining interviewee.

Neil Simon

Neil Simon and his older brother Danny began writing for radio and moved into television in 1952 to work on *Your Show of Shows.* After Danny left New York for the West Coast, Neil Simon continued writing for Sid Caesar, Garry Moore, and the *Sargeant Bilko* show.[18] Simon thinks the latter was more of a help in his development as a screenwriter than *Your Show of Shows*, since the *Bilko* writers spent four days plotting each episode and only three days on dialogue.[19] While writing for television, Simon wrote the 1961 Broadway play *Come Blow Your Horn*. Since then he has worked primarily, and most successfully, on the stage, but he has done both original screenplays and adaptations of his stage plays for films.

Even on his original screenplays Simon uses techniques he developed in the theater. The original screenplay for the 1977 film *The Goodbye Girl* was written with Richard Dreyfuss and Marsha Mason in mind for the leads. Simon had the actors do a reading of the script three months before rehearsals began for the film. Simon then spent a month rewriting so that when rehearsals started, he needed to do only minor revisions.[20]

Like Allen and Brooks, Simon also writes film parodies. The problem with *Murder by Death* and *The Cheap Detective* is the same problem with Brooks's later parodies: they capture the style without the substance, and the style is interesting for about twenty minutes.

Most of Simon's film work has been in adapting his plays for the screen. As Simon himself pointed out in 1978, his early adaptations were more photographed plays than films.[21]

Simon's later adaptations, such as *California Suite* and *Chapter Two*, are more cinematic. On stage *California Suite* and *Plaza Suite* were structurally similar: a full-length play made up of short plays, each dealing with separate characters who stay in the same hotel room. The film of *Plaza Suite* maintained that structure, as well as the device of having the same leading actor play the leads in each of the stories. In *California Suite* Simon broke up the different stories and cut from one to another throughout the film. The characters were played by different actors, and in one episode, he changed the characters from white to black.

Simon has still not become as cinematic a writer as Woody Allen. Simon's *Brighton Beach Memoirs* is an effective play on stage, where the leading character, talking directly to the audience, is part of theatrical tradition. In the 1986 film, the device seems awkward, and the scenes too long and obviously theatrical for film. Allen's *Radio Days*, covering the same kind of material and released a few months later, is more cinematically inventive. The narrator was never shown, although it was clear which of the characters will grow up to be the narrator.

Simon, unlike Allen, did not become a director. He thought about directing "for about three minutes,"[22] but decided against it. He did become a producer briefly in the early eighties, but with considerable lack of success on *Only When I Laugh*, a weak adaptation of his play *The Gingerbread Lady*. For most of his career as a screenwriter, Simon has worked in connection with producer Ray Stark. Even Stark was unable to protect Simon's original screenplay, *The Slugger's Wife*. The lines we hear in the film do not have Neil Simon's distinctive rhythm, but you can imagine what they probably were in the script. Even a screenwriter with the clout of Simon can still have his work mangled.

Paul Mazursky

Like Allen, Brooks, and Simon, Paul Mazursky grew up in New York and worked in television (he wrote for Danny Kaye in the sixties). Mazursky has a narrower range than Allen, but he is particularly good at films about upper middle-class Americans. Mazursky's first three films, written with his partner Larry Tucker, dealt specifically with the foibles of Californians: *I Love You Alice B. Toklas, Bob and Carol and Ted and Alice* (Mazursky's first film as a director), and *Alex in Wonderland*. Mazursky returned to California later with *Down and Out in Beverly Hills*, a remake of Jean Renoir's *Budou Saved from Drowning*.

Mazursky has also done several films in and about New York. *Moscow on the Hudson* deals with a Russian immigrant's view of America as represented by New York. *Moscow* is a charming film, but it does show Mazursky's limitations, particularly in his writing of the Italian woman the Russian falls in love with. She is charming until she gets her citizenship papers, and then she becomes a typical neurotic New Yorker. A funny point could have been made about this, but it appears to have happened in the script because Mazursky could not think of her behaving any other way.

John Hughes

John Hughes is one of the few comic writers of the independent period who did not begin in television. He wrote the "Vacation" issue of the *National Lampoon* magazine, although he was so worried about his writing ability he wrote it in the guise of a thirteen-year-old writing in the first person.[23] Hughes later wrote the screenplay based on the issue, *National Lampoon's Vacation*. Both were based on his own experiences.

While both *National Lampoon's Vacation* and *Mr. Mom*, his two 1983 film hits, deal primarily with adults, Hughes became quickly known as a writer of movies about teens: *Sixteen Candles, The Breakfast Club, Pretty in Pink, Ferris Beuller's Day Off,* and *Some Kind of Wonderful*. Hughes has a particularly good ear for the way teenagers actually talk, as well as an ability to empathize with their point of view. His empathy with teens is so strong that the films seem to ignore any adult point of view. One would like to hear the reactions of the parents of the kids in *The Breakfast Club*. Hughes creates strong teen characters and his scripts are responsible for making Molly Ringwald, who appeared in three of his films, a star.

Saturday Night Live and its Writers

NBC's *Saturday Night Live* began in 1975 as the brainchild of Lorne Michaels, and while Michaels paid lip service to the idea of quality writing, the writing was the weakest element in the program. The sketches were generally too long and underdeveloped. In an effort to avoid slickness, Michaels and his staff avoided the hard craft of comedy writing as well. Michaels has not had much success outside *Saturday Night Live*. His one coscreenwriting credit was on *Three Amigos*, which was mildly amusing for the first half and then fell apart.

The one writer from the show who has had some success as a screenwriter is Dan Aykroyd. His first screenplay was *The Blues Brothers*, who were fine as a short number on television, but simply not interesting enough as characters to carry a feature. Aykroyd's best screenplay work was on *Ghostbusters*, which brilliantly balanced the comic touches with the special effects.

SCTV and its Writers

A much better and much better written (naturally) satirical show was the Canadian produced *SCTV*. The *SCTV* writers had an advantage in that the show itself provided a structure: the activities and programs on a mediocre television station. This set up terrific satire of television, movies, and the absurdities of public life in general. The *SCTV* writers were much better at developing their ideas and were brilliant at juxtaposing two contrasting elements, such as the time Meryl Streep (in a deadly impression by Catherine O'Hara) appeared on "Farm Film Report" and the two farm types drove her to such tears she "blowed up real good."

The most successful screenwriter to emerge from *SCTV* was one of its creators and its head writer for its first season, Harold Ramis. He was a psychiatric orderly, substitute teacher, and joke editor at *Playboy* before he joined Second City, a theatrical group in Chicago.[24] Ramis also worked for the *National Lampoon*, and when the magazine decided to turn its "High

School Yearbook" issue into a movie, Ramis joined with Doug Kenney to write the screenplay. They quickly decided that the kind of jokes they wanted to do were more appropriate for college than high school, and the script turned into the monster 1978 hit *Animal House*.[25] Ramis was also the writer or cowriter on *Meatballs*, *Stripes*, and *Ghostbusters*.

27

Stars

Howard Hawks best defined star quality when he said, "There are some people the camera loves." But not everybody the camera loves becomes a star. As we have already seen, there have to be writers to write roles that create and maintain stars. From the earliest days stars caused difficulties for writers. Captain Leslie T. Peacocke, a screenwriter, wrote in 1918 that there were at the time actors and actresses who felt "no scenario would be considered any good at all that did not show them in, at least, 75 per cent of the scenes, 45 per cent of which must be closeups of the female stars."[1]

It is commonly thought that when the studio system declined, the importance of stars declined as well. In fact, the opposite happened. Each independent film had to be sold, to theater owners and then to audiences, on its own, usually on the basis of its stars. It is often mistakenly said that stars are "bankable," meaning a bank will give a producer money if he has a star. In fact, banks do not care if he has a star; the banks want to know if the producer can get distribution, since that is how the money will be returned. The star insures that the film will be distributed.[2] The stars therefore became in fact producers: it was their decisions that determined whether a film would get made. The stars' decisions influenced what scripts were written, how they were rewritten, and if they were produced at all.

Burt Lancaster

One of the first stars to form his own production company at the end of the studio period, and one of the most successful at doing so, was Burt Lancaster. Lancaster and Harold Hecht, a literary agent, formed their own company in 1947.[3] Called Norma Productions, it produced such Lancaster films as *The Flame and the Arrow* and *The Crimson Pirate*. Later as Hecht-Lancaster, they signed a deal with United Artists in 1954 providing them with twelve million dollars to make a total of seven movies, five with Lancaster and two without.[4] The films starring Lancaster included *Apache*, *Vera Cruz*, and *Trapeze*, all of them successful commercially.

Hecht-Lancaster also had an eye for interesting, less overtly commercial material. One of its two non-Lancaster films was a film adaptation of a teleplay, "Marty," that won the 1955 Academy Award for Best Picture as well as Best Screenplay. Lancaster himself appeared in offbeat material. In 1957 the company produced *The Sweet Smell of Success*, a tough edgy film in which Lancaster played a marvelous gargoyle of a New York columnist.

As successful as the company was, writers had problems working for it. James Webb recalls:

> I could hardly say I enjoyed working with the Hecht-Hill-Lancaster [James Hill joined the company in 1955] organization. Burt and later Jim Hill were close friends of mine, but Harold Hecht and I never got along well. As a trio they always wanted to talk a story to death, examining every possible situation from every possible angle, to the point where a writer's natural spontaneity tended to go out the window. There were interminable conferences and you were lucky to get home by 7:30 any evening—partly, I think because no one wanted to go home. Despite this, *Apache*, *Vera Cruz*, and *Trapeze* [which Webb wrote] were tremendously successful pictures, but I prophesied that they would never make another real success after I left and the prophesy proved true. I am not claiming that was due to any genius on my part, but they needed somebody who was not afraid of them and would stick to his guns through thick and thin. Without such a balance wheel they flew off in all directions.[5]

John Michael Hayes had the same problems when he worked on the script for their production *Separate Tables*.[6]

Kirk Douglas

In 1955, probably at least in part because of the success of Hecht-Lancaster, several other stars announced the formation of their own production companies: Frank Sinatra, Robert Mitchum, Cornel Wilde, Joan Crawford, Henry Fonda, Rita Hayworth, and Kirk Douglas.[7] Of those, the only one who had any large degree of success was Douglas.

Douglas seemed to thrive on playing unsympathetic parts, which meant he often chose strong scripts, such as *Ace in the Hole*, *The Bad and the Beautiful*, and *Lust for Life*. In one of his company's early productions, *Paths of Glory*, he was afraid that the character was too sympathetic. He later said, "I've made a career, in a sense, of playing sons-of-bitches."[8]

Douglas was also one of the few actor-producers to do strongly political material, such as *Paths of Glory* and *Seven Days in May*. Douglas was also a successful producer of a film he never made. He bought the rights to the novel *One Flew Over the Cuckoo's Nest*, appeared in it on Broadway, and when he was unable to get the film made, he turned over the rights to his son

Michael, who produced the film in 1975. Kirk Douglas made more from his share of that picture than from any he appeared in.[9]

Robert Redford

Robert Redford appeared in his first film in 1962, but it was William Goldman's script for *Butch Cassidy and the Sundance Kid* that made Redford a star in 1969. Since then Redford has shown a talent for the selection of material for himself as a star, a producer, and/or a director.

For his second production, *The Candidate*, Redford hired Jeremy Larner, a former speechwriter for 1968 presidential candidate Eugene McCarthy, to write the script about a California senatorial campaign. Redford worked with Larner and the director, Michael Ritchie, on the script. Ritchie had done television commercials for a candidate for the Senate, John Tunney, and much of the staff of the film had been involved in political campaigns.[10] The film examines in very sharply observed detail the way political campaigns are run in the television age.

The Candidate was released in 1972, and to promote the film Redford made an old-fashioned whistle-stop railroad tour. The tour included political writers and they told Redford the Watergate break-in was business as usual and that they doubted the truth would ever come out.[11] Redford followed the story in the *Washington Post*, and he met Bob Woodward and Carl Bernstein in April 1973. He said he was interested in doing a film about the story, and they told him they were writing a book. It was Redford who suggested they tell it in the form of a detective story: how these two young reporters broke the case.[12]

Woodward remembers that William Goldman was with Redford at their first meeting,[13] but Goldman remembers coming onto the project after Woodward and Bernstein had completed the first draft of their book.[14] Goldman saw major problems in adapting the material, since it was extremely complex, had been covered in great detail by newspapers and television, and could not be rearranged too much for the screen.[15] Goldman decided because of limitations of running time to end the film about halfway through the book, with the rest of the story quickly sketched in.[16]

Goldman turned in his first draft in August 1974 and was horrified to learn a few months later that Carl Bernstein and his girlfriend, essayist Nora Ephron, had written their own draft of the script. Goldman hoped Redford would say rude things to Bernstein and Ephron, but Redford was diplomatic. The only scene from the Bernstein-Ephron version that survived in the film was a totally fictitious scene of Bernstein hustling his way into an office.[17] Rumors began to float around the industry and the media that Goldman's draft was bad, but Redford retained Goldman, who did several more drafts, trying to please Redford, Dustin Hoffman (who had been hired to play Bernstein to Redford's Woodward), and director Alan Pakula, who was unable to make up his mind what he wanted. Eventually other writers were brought in. Goldman wrote later that if he had it to do over again, "I wouldn't have come near *All the President's Men*."[18]

The work of Goldman and the others is an impressive piece of screenwriting work, since it does manage to keep the chronology of the story clear and interesting to the audience—not an easy task. Goldman's decision to end the film at the reporters' mistake is an unusual solution to the problem, but the scenes that are used to tie up the film violate the literalness of the earlier portion of the film, since they suggest connections between Woodward and Bernstein's investigations and later investigations of the CIA that did not literally exist. The scenes also suggest a threat to the reporters that also did not exist.[19] Redford's intelligence and guts in making the film are undercut, if only slightly, by the flaw in the ending.

Redford helps screenwriters and the craft of screenwriting in another way. In 1980 he founded the Sundance Institute, which is designed to develop independent film projects. In 1987 Redford said:

> One of the great functions of the institute is that we're finding writers out there in the bushes and getting them to hook up with filmmakers. There are a number of projects that have come out of here that were born just out of the connections made. They don't come with a project, but a filmmaker comes and a writer comes and they develop an idea.[20]

Screenwriters who have helped as "Resource Screenwriters" for younger writers include Waldo Salt, Ring Lardner, Jr., Frank Pierson, and Jeremy Larner. Films that have been developed out of the Sundance Institute include *Desert Bloom* and *Waiting for the Moon*.

Dustin Hoffman, Elliott Gould, and John Voight

Three stars who came to prominence about the same time Redford did have spottier records at selecting material. Dustin Hoffman smartly followed *The Graduate* with a completely different role two years later in *Midnight Cowboy*. His track record at selecting and shaping material since has been uneven. For every interesting script like *Little Big Man*, there is a *Who Is Harry Kellerman and Why Is He Saying Those Terrible Things About Me?*

An example of both the successes and problems of Hoffman's approach to scripts are found in the making of *Tootsie*, one of his best films. The first script was written by Don McGuire. Producer Charles Evans bought it and hired Robert Kaufman to rewrite it. Kaufman worked on it with director Dick Richards, who eventually showed it to Hoffman, who had Murray Schisgal brought on as a writer. When Columbia came onto the project, Schisgal was replaced by Larry Gelbart. Gelbart worked with Hoffman and the new and final director, Sidney Pollack, whom William Goldman describes as a "writer killer,"[21] a director who asks for so many changes that the first writer gets written out and the director brings on another writer of his own choosing, who is of course more loyal to the director's "vision" of the film.[22]

Gelbart worked on *Tootsie* for two years, finished the script, which was then turned over to Elaine May, one of the legendary script doctors in the business. Pollack was doing rewriting as well ("I can't do a movie without running it through my typewriter myself ";[23] see what Goldman means?), and there were brief contributions from Robert Garland, who had worked with Pollack before, and Valerie Curtin and Barry Levinson. Schisgal came back to do revisions for Hoffman. The decisions as to which revisions were to be kept were hammered out in meetings with Hoffman and Pollack, both of whom were determined to control the project.[24]

The result of all this collaboration was a funny movie. A very funny movie. But an inconsistent one. Hoffman's clout in the production, combined with Pollack's ability to deal with star actors, puts the focus most strongly on the character of Michael Dorsey. At Hoffman's insistence, a large number of scenes were shot of Michael teaching acting classes that in the final film were edited down from forty-five minutes to a minute or two used in the opening sequence.[25] Michael's first girlfriend Sandy seems to change motivation from scene to scene, depending on what is needed in terms of the story. Her best lines, about having read *The Second Sex* and *The Cinderella Complex* and being responsible for her own orgasms, were improvised by Teri Garr,[26] but seem beyond the intelligence of the character as written in the rest of the film. When Michael reveals himself, his *real* girlfriend Julie punches him, and the film never explains why she has so much trouble dealing with him now as a man. The rewriting and improvisations that Pollack and Hoffman and the others went through added enormously to the cost of the film, but did not make it a better film.

Hoffman's costar in *Midnight Cowboy*, John Voight, has been even more uneven in his selection of material. He appeared in *Deliverance* and *Coming Home*, but by the late seventies and early eighties he seemed determined to select the worst material possible. *Table for Five* (1983) was a bland soap opera, and *Lookin' to Get Out* the year before, which Voight cowrote, was one of the worst scripts of the decade. Voight gave an impressive performance in *Runaway Train*, a 1985 film based on a screenplay by Akira Kurosawa, but the film was not a popular hit.

Elliott Gould made his first impact in 1969–70 with *Bob and Carol and Ted and Alice* and *M*A*S*H*, but his follow-up films were weak, such as *Little Murders* and the low point of his career, *Matilda*, a comedy about a boxing kangaroo.

Clint Eastwood

Tom Shales has pointed out that "[Woody] Allen and Clint Eastwood are probably our two most smoothly functioning auteurs."[27] Eastwood formed his own company, Malpaso, in 1968 after being appalled at the waste he saw on productions he appeared in. Eastwood's deal with Warner Brothers (since 1976) is basically similar to Allen's deals with United Artists and Orion, and Eastwood, while not a writer like Allen, has been just as responsible a producer.

Like most other movie stars, Eastwood has a limited range as an actor but also like them he is within that range absolutely compelling and believable on screen. What is remarkable about his career has been his ability to find and select a wide variety of story material that is right for him as an actor. His story editor since the formation of Malpaso has been Sonia Chernus, herself a screenwriter (she did the first drafts for Eastwood's best film *The Outlaw-Josey Wales*), and she says that Eastwood has "a terrific story mind."[28] Chernus reads the material submitted to Malpaso, but Eastwood reads and decides on what will be done.

Unlike Woody Allen, who created his own genre of films, Eastwood has worked with traditional American genres: westerns, thrillers, adventure pictures, and redneck comedies. What his films do is fill out those genres with interesting turns of character and plot. While he works in traditional macho genres, the women characters in his films are so strong that an article in the *Los Angeles Times* went so far as to suggest he might actually be a *feminist* filmmaker.[29]

An indication of the variety of story lines Eastwood uses can be seen in looking at the four "Dirty Harry" films. In *Dirty Harry* he disregards the bureaucrats in the police department to capture a psychotic killer. This film was denounced by several critics as an example of American fascism. In the second film, *Magnum Force*, Harry Callahan goes after a group of *police* fascists. In the third film, *The Enforcer*, Callahan, the macho hero, is teamed with a woman partner. In the fourth film, *Sudden Impact*, he chases a woman who has been killing the men who raped her and her sister, and in the end of the film he lets her go free. In comparison the Charles Bronson *Death Wish* films all tell the same story: a man's friends and/or family are killed and he exacts revenge. This variety of storytelling in Eastwood's films is the reason he has remained one of the top ten box-office stars consistently for the last twenty years, while other stars, such as Bronson, have lost their box-office pull in the United States. Eastwood is in the great American tradition of narrative filmmakers.

Burt Reynolds and Sylvester Stallone

Unlike Eastwood, Burt Reynolds's ability to pick scripts is limited. In the midseventies he appeared in *At Long Last Love, Lucky Lady,* and *Nickelodeon,* all of which flopped, before having a large hit with *Smokey and the Bandit,* a car-chase romp. Although Reynolds did take on semiserious scripts, such as *Semi-Tough* and *Starting Over,* the car-chase films were bigger hits, but the scripts for them got increasingly stale. Reynolds traces his decline as a box-office star from *Stroker Ace* in 1983,[30] but it began earlier with the 1981 commercial hit *The Cannonball Run,* which was successful in spite of its staleness. *Stroker Ace* simply made the decline obvious. It is also a truly terrible script. Whereas Eastwood's women have substance and usually some intelligence, the character written for Loni Anderson in *Stroker Ace* was an embarrassment to all concerned.

Reynolds admits, "In the past, I didn't allow myself to be open to new writers or risky roles. I wanted to do them, but I may have isolated myself too much when I was on top."[31] To do *Stroker Ace,* he turned down the opportunity to do the part of the retired astronaut in *Terms of Endearment.*[32]

Like Woody Allen (with whom he appeared in *Bananas*) Sylvester Stallone writes his own material. He first became a star in *Rocky,* a nice, small script he wrote for himself. Normally scripts actors write for themselves are terrible, but Stallone borrowed from the best of sources for *Rocky*—*On the Waterfront* and *Marty.* Stallone's script shows a beginning talent for character and dialogue.

Stallone contributed to the screenplay for *F.I.S.T.* and wrote *Paradise Alley,* both interesting films, but neither particularly successful. In 1979 Stallone wrote and directed *Rocky II,* and like the Bronson *Death Wish* films, this and the sequels that followed merely repeated the elements of the first film. The pictures, like Reynolds's *Cannonball Run* films, were commercially successful, but increasingly stale. In 1982 Stallone introduced a second popular character, Rambo, in the film *First Blood,* written by a variety of writers. Stallone wrote the sequel, *Rambo: First Blood II,* and the same decline as in the *Rocky* films in quality of the writing began to appear. In 1986 Stallone wrote *Cobra,* clearly intended as his equivalent of Eastwood's Dirty Harry films. *Cobra* did not have the texture of the writing and the variety of plotting that Eastwood insisted upon. It also did not have the wit. Part of Eastwood's appeal is a very dry, understated wit, particularly about his larger-than-life macho characters. The wit keeps Dirty Harry from seeming too preposterous. Without that leavening, *Cobra* simply is ridiculous. *Cobra* was Stallone's *Stroker Ace.*

Jane Fonda

If Redford and Eastwood are the role models of actors of the seventies and eighties who produce their own films, Jane Fonda is the role model for actresses. She established her own production company in 1973, the year after she won an Academy Award for *Klute*. In honor of her antiwar activities, she named it IPC (for the Indochina Peace Campaign), and hired as the producer Bruce Gilbert, whom she had met while he was teaching at her daughter's nursery school.[33] The first film they produced was *Coming Home*.

The first screenplay for what became *Coming Home* was called *Buffalo Ghosts* and was written by Nancy Dowd. It dealt with the relationship between two military wives who met while working in a veterans' hospital. Dowd at first resisted making the hero a paraplegic veteran, then agreed to it, but left the project over disputes in cutting the overlong script.[34] Waldo Salt was brought in and spent a year doing research and developing the characters. He wrote a sixty-five–page treatment that was sent around to the studios, and United Artists expressed interest. Jerome Hellman, an experienced producer, was brought onto the project, and he signed Hal Ashby as director.

Robert C. Jones, a film editor who had done some writing on Ashby's *Bound for Glory*, did further rewriting. In the early drafts, the Marine officer husband, played by Bruce Dern in the film, went on a shooting rampage after returning from Vietnam and discovering his wife's affair with the paraplegic veteran. Dern and the others on the film were not happy with this ending, and Ashby finally had the three actors improvise a confrontation scene between the wife, lover, and husband.[35]

Coming Home's love story is one of the best uses of the freedom that the American movie industry won with the development of the Rating System in the late sixties. The problem with the script as it was developed is that while the characters of the wife and the lover are fresh, rich, and detailed, the character of the officer is still one-dimensional. The problem is not unlike what later happened with the character of Julie in *Tootsie*. The filmmakers, most of them with backgrounds in the antiwar movement, seem to have found it impossible to get into the mind of the officer, who, when he returns at the end of the film becomes the most interesting character in it.

IPC's next film was *The China Syndrome*, and like *Coming Home*, there was an additional producer on it as well. The film began as a screenplay by

Mike Gray, a documentary filmmaker *(The Murder of Fred Hampton)*. Michael Douglas bought the script in 1976. Columbia, which was financing the film, suggested Douglas get together with Fonda. The script was rewritten for her, turning the part of the television reporter into a woman. The film had always had conventional thriller elements in it, and these were emphasized under the new director, James Bridges. The film was nonetheless attacked by the nuclear-power industry, which insisted the story could not happen. Twelve days after the film opened, the disaster at Three Mile Island, which duplicated the film in uncanny ways, happened. Business for the film increased, and Columbia's stock went up.[36] Fonda's brand of American capitalism succeeded again.

Sally Field, Goldie Hawn, and Jessica Lange

Like Fonda, Sally Field has triumphed over her earlier work in lightweight material. After her Oscar for *Norma Rae*, Field's agent and her lawyer both encouraged her to form her own company, which she reluctantly did, having no desire at first to become a producer.[37] She recalled in 1985:

> When I first started my company to develop films about four years ago, I just didn't know how to go about it at all or what I was even looking for. I'm a slow starter. So I went to one actress who really knew how to do it. She met with me, opened up all her offices, she even lent me her script readers. It was incredibly generous. She really gave me a boost. And she's that way with everybody.[38]

The actress of course was Fonda.

What helped Field's company as well is that she has a good sense of material. She has appeared in bombs such as *Beyond the Poseidon Adventure*, but she also did *Places in the Heart*, the best of the three "women-in-the-country" films released in 1984. The first film her company produced was *Murphy's Romance*, which she did after *Places in the Heart*. Her partner, Laura Ziskin, read a novel by Max Schott and Field got Irving Ravetch and Harriet Frank, the husband and wife screenwriting team who wrote *Norma Rae*, to do the adaptation. Fields knows the importance of working with good writers. She says, "I take everything to the Ravetches. About once a week, every Wednesday, I call up and say, 'Hey, guys, I've got something else for you.'"[39] Their screenplay for *Murphy's Romance* is well crafted, warm, and charming, qualities not seen in many recent mainstream screenplays.

Goldie Hawn's ability at picking and developing scripts has been uneven. She had considerable commercial success with *Foul Play* (1978), *Seems Like Old Times* (1981), and especially *Private Benjamin* (1980), but the writing, particularly in *Private Benjamin*, is often sloppy. *Benjamin* seemed unable to focus on a single story line to carry through, and its commercial success was a triumph of marketing (selling the film as "Goldie Joins the Army") rather than screenwriting. The follow-up to *Benjamin*, *Protocol*, or "Goldie Joins the Diplomatic Corps," suffered the same kind of split personality: in some scenes Hawn's character seems smarter than anybody else in the film, in other scenes she is just the old giggling Goldie.

Swing Shift was a script originally written for Jane Fonda by Nancy Dowd and was similar to the same author's original script for *Coming Home*. Even with considerable rewriting up through and after the shooting of the film, the character of the adulterous wife was simply not in Hawn's dramatic range. It remains to be seen whether Hawn can find screenplays that are suitable to her as an adult, but which do not sacrifice her considerable charm.

Jessica Lange had the misfortune to start her career giving such a brilliant comedy performance as a dumb girl in the 1976 film *King Kong* that audiences and the industry alike assumed she was really that dumb. She was not, as later roles proved, particularly in *The Postman Always Rings Twice* and *Frances*. The problem of her later career is she has a tendency to pick material that will give her a great role (as in *Sweet Dreams*), but will not necessarily be a good film. It is a problem that many stars have in the selection of roles: the tendency to go for the vehicle that will make them look good, but often at the expense of the film.

28

Hustlers

W riters usually create alone, but the process of screenwriting is different. Many writers find it difficult to adjust to working in a variety of relationships with other people. To survive, screenwriters have to learn how to use the collaborative process to their best advantage. They have to learn how to hustle. Screenwriters have always had to hustle, but the more the process of screenwriting moves away from the family feeling of silent films or the organized procedures of the studio system, the more the screenwriters have had to learn how to manipulate the system, or, increasingly, the systems of filmmaking. The sections of this chapter will show how five screenwriters have done that, for better and for worse.

Michael Cimino

Michael Cimino attended Michigan State University (but dropped that information from his biography), obtained a master's degree in painting from Yale (but later claimed he was working on a doctorate in architecture there), and made slick television commercials in New York (he later claimed he was noted for making documentaries).[1] With a history like that, it is not surprising he became a director, but he also shows signs of talent as a screenwriter.

Cimino's first screenwriting credits were shared credits on the 1972 film *Silent Running* and the second of the Dirty Harry films, *Magnum Force*. This led to his writing and directing the 1974 Eastwood film *Thunderbolt and Lightfoot*. W. R. Burnett, whose screenwriting credits include *High Sierra* and *This Gun for Hire*, and who wrote the novel *The Asphalt Jungle*, felt that Cimino had ripped off Burnett's 1955 film *Captain Lightfoot* for *Thunderbolt and Lightfoot*.[2] Cimino's script is obviously inspired by Burnett's (and it was perhaps tacky of Cimino not to mention the inspiration), but it also differs substantially. Burnett's screenplay deals with Irish rebels in the 1800s, while Cimino's has some similar adventures in a modern bank-robbery tale set in Montana. Cimino's screenplay is a good caper piece, and he shows the influence of Burnett in another way: the script has the same kind of offbeat characterization as Burnett's *Asphalt Jungle*.

On the success of *Thunderbolt and Lightfoot*, Cimino worked on *The Rose*.

Bill Kerby, who wrote the original script, thought Cimino was hired only to direct. Kerby was surprised to see Cimino's name on the script as cowriter with Bo Goldman when the script was later sent around to other directors. Kerby realized it was mostly his script, and after arbitration by the Guild, the credits listed only Kerby and Bo Goldman as the screenwriters.[3]

Cimino next became involved in *The Deer Hunter*, which he directed and received story credit on along with three other writers. The script is shallow and often unclear, but Cimino's direction pumps the film up with a size and sense of importance the script cannot carry. The power of the film came from the combination of Cimino's epic direction and the significance of its subject matter, the Vietnam War.

One person who saw an early industry screening of *The Deer Hunter* was Stephen Bach, who was impressed with the film, and thought that perhaps he should look at the screenplay of *The Deer Hunter* to see what Cimino had worked from. He never got around to it, to his regret,[4] since Bach found himself involved in Cimino's next film. Bach had recently been named co-head of production for United Artists, which was then trying to recover from the loss of its top executives, who had left the company in early 1978 to form Orion Pictures. The remaining executives at UA were trying to keep the company afloat. This meant obtaining talent, and given the UA tradition, letting them make their films their own way. Which is how United Artists came to make a film from Michael Cimino's screenplay of *Heaven's Gate*.

Cimino had been working on a screenplay about the Johnson County War since the early seventies. His first screenplay, completed in 1971, was the most historically accurate of the scripts, dealing with the fight between the cattle barons of Wyoming and their brutal efforts to stop farmers from settling in the area. The script floated around Hollywood throughout the seventies, with occasional interest from different studios.[5]

It was given to the new management at United Artists in 1978 and their reader was not impressed (as a reader at Fox had not been; one lesson from the *Heaven's Gate* saga is that executives should pay a little more attention to what their readers tell them). He said there were too many characters, with none of them developed very well, and added, "if it is a project we want to do because of Mike Cimino's involvement, we should approach it with the expectations of a major rewrite. If it were not for Cimino, I would pass."[6]

In spite of the reader's criticisms, which Bach agreed with (although he in fact read a different draft),[7] the deal was made. Cimino did a revision of the script, which is dated January 26, 1979, and is the first to have the title *Heaven's Gate*. Bach reports that this script was greeted with more enthusiasm at the company.[8] Cimino's hustle had begun to work, since this draft of *Heaven's Gate* is one of the worst screenplays ever written. The first problem is that there are simply no scenes that make the situation clear or interesting. There are about 30 pages of story material in a script that runs 132 pages.

The second problem is that there is still, as UA's reader noted of the earlier draft, no characterization in terms of either action or dialogue. There is also considerable inconsistency of behavior in the characters.

The third problem, and the one that makes the script so aggravating to read, is that Cimino writes long sections of prose to try, unsuccessfully, to get across his vision, which is just as murky in the screenplay as it is in the film. It is this overwritten prose that helped convince people that there was something important about the script. Bach and the others at UA were not stupid, but they were taken in because they simply did not know how to read a screenplay.

One example from the script and the film demonstrates this. In a 1980 interview before the release of the film, Bach talked about a particular scene in which Champion, the hired gun, comes into Averill's room and tries on his hat. Bach says:

> What could be read [in the script] as a fifteen-second gesture becomes, in the movie, a beautifully attenuated moment where Averill's hat becomes symbolic of everything about him that Champion isn't—background, breeding, that world back East. It becomes a rather lovely, contemplative moment in which you see on [actor Christopher] Walken's face a look into the soul.[9]

In the script the action reads:

> Champion . . . puts on his hat, strikes a pose in the mirror. He smiles, but we feel as we should throughout the film—a striking contrast between this first-generation American and the gentleman Averill.[10]

Cimino had persuaded Bach in this writing that there was more to this scene than Champion just putting on Averill's hat. In the film, however interesting the look on Walken's face, the actor cannot by himself portray those levels of meaning to the gesture. Cimino suggests them in the writing, but the contrast has not been dramatized in the script. Because it has not been dramatized in the script, it is not in the film, and there is no way for the audience to "feel as we should throughout the film."

As bad as Cimino's screenwriting was, his direction was worse. The script runs 132 pages, but Cimino's first cut of the film ran five and a half hours. The additional three hours just padded the script's scenes. Bach's descriptions of the five and a half hour and four and a half hour versions of the film confirm this. As director Cimino also undercut himself as screenwriter by bringing up the ambient sound so loud that the dialogue, which did little enough to provide exposition anyway, was drowned out.[11]

The film went on to become one of the legendary disasters in the history of the motion picture business. Steven Bach has written with great perception of his own involvement in the production. In his comments on the film, he notes that "Characters and story were sacrificed to the filmmaker's love of visual effect and production for their own sakes."[12] If he had read the script right at the beginning, he would have noticed that lack of characterization and story in the script. But like too many people in the industry, he assumed the director would make it right. Bach refers to the experiences of *Heaven's Gate* as taking "the two-year Cimino cure for auteur worship."[13]

Paul Schrader

The one point of similarity between Mel Brooks and Paul Schrader, who writes and directs intense, often violent dramas, is that both men are extremely gifted at using interviews to promote both their films and themselves. For example, Schrader has relentlessly mined his strict Dutch Calvinist upbringing not so much for films as for interview material. The religious background, he says, helped him deal with Hollywood people:

> They just want to change the way you write. You can work and deal and twist and negotiate with *these* people. That's easy in comparison to having been raised by people who want to determine what your private thoughts are.[14]

Schrader broke into screenwriting with the legendary sale of his first screenplay *The Yakuza* to Warner Brothers for $300,000. The sale was managed by Schrader's agent, Robin French. Schrader said later:

> For weeks Robin was going out and doing the complete word-of-mouth routine, going to dinner parties and saying, "There's this fantastic script out." We hit all the right people. It got to the point where people were calling us and asking for scripts. Robin told us to refuse to accept any offers for five or six weeks. Finally, he opened the auction. The day the auction opened there were 16 bids, all in the vicinity of $100,000. It kept going up.[15]

It was a brilliant bit of selling, but a terrible script. The studio brought in script doctor Robert Towne but he could not save it. The script is based on the Japanese *yakuza*, or gangster, films, which have very strict genre rules unknown to western audiences. Schrader let *Film Comment* publish an extract from his script, along with an article by him on the Japanese films.[16] The film was still incomprehensible to Western audiences.

Fortunately Schrader's screenplay of *Taxi Driver* fell into the hands of director Martin Scorsese and actor Robert De Niro. The script[17] has an intensity and drive to it, which Scorsese and De Niro bring out, but the script and the film are marred by the ending. The problem is not Travis Bickle's killing of the pimp (which is partly what made the film a success at the box office, since it appealed to the audience for violent films as well as "serious" films), but after the killing. Travis goes back to driving a cab and he picks up Betsy, the politician's aide. She is now, after he has killed and has apparently been made well by it, attracted to him. When she leaves the cab, she says to him, "Maybe I'll see you again sometime, huh?" He replies, "Sure," but drives away.[18] This is pure wet-dream fantasy on the part of the filmmakers, although given the success they have had making violent films, they may have a point.

In 1977 Schrader began directing from his own scripts. The scripts were interesting ideas for movies, but not well developed. As film critic Peter Rainer writes:

> If there should ever be a Society for the Protection of Great Movie Ideas—and there should be—its first act of office should be to quash Paul Schrader. Without exception, every film he has directed has had a startling premise. He makes movies about subjects that are such "naturals," such grabbers, that the inevitable disappointing results seem doubly disappointing.[19]

Blue Collar, Hardcore, American Gigolo all turn interesting premises into conventional plots.

Schrader is gifted at promoting his films, particularly with the film journals. When *American Gigolo* was released, there was a cover story on it in *Film Comment*, complete with an interview with Schrader. Since Schrader had been a film critic, he knows how to talk to other critics. In the interview, Schrader mentions in reference to *American Gigolo* such foreign films as Claude Lelouch's *A Man and a Woman*, Alain Resnais's *La Guerre Est Finie*, and Robert Bresson's *Pickpocket*. Schrader points out before the interviewer does that the final scene and final line of *American Gigolo* is stolen directly from *Pickpocket*, and says, "I might as well 'fess up, because some day I'm going to get caught."[20]

It was inevitable that Schrader's skills as an interviewee would overcome his skills as a filmmaker, and it happened on a film he directed, but did not write—the 1982 remake of *Cat People*. There were interview-stories in both *Film Comment* (March–April 1982) and *American Film* (April 1982) in which Schrader discussed the feeling and mood he wanted the film to have, but the film itself did not live up to his hype for it. Part of the problem with the film may have been that Schrader was allergic to cats.[21]

In addition to directing, Schrader also continues to write screenplays for other filmmakers. Both actors and directors are attracted to Schrader's scripts because he has the ability to write characters who are obsessed. This quality obviously appeals to directors like Martin Scorsese, Brian DePalma, and Peter Weir, and to actors like De Niro. For Scorsese and De Niro, Schrader wrote several drafts of *Raging Bull*, and the major problem with the scripts and the film is that none of the characters besides Jake La Motta are allowed to breathe. It is not surprising that when De Niro and the other screenwriter on the film, Mardik Martin, talked to La Motta's ex-wife Vicki the question they were most interested in was whether she had been unfaithful to Jake or not.[22] This lack of interest in Vicki as a person and a character harms the film, which is a series of repetitious scenes showing how jealous Jake is.

Oliver Stone

Oliver Stone is not as scholarly in interviews as Paul Schrader (Stone attended New York University, where he studied filmmaking with Scorsese), but he is more entertaining, as are his screenplays. He made his first impact as a screenwriter with his Academy Award–winning screenplay for *Midnight Express* in 1978. Stone wrote the remake of *Scarface* (1983) for director Brian DePalma and worked with Cimino on his comeback picture *Year of the Dragon* (1985), both expansive as well as expensive films. In both films the directors seem more concerned with the logistics of the films than the characters and the stories. Cimino hustled Stone into working on *Dragon* by telling him that if he did, Cimino would arrange to produce a screenplay Stone had written in 1976 about his experiences in Vietnam in 1967. Stone worked on *Dragon*, but the deal to make *Platoon* fell through. Stone felt encouraged to try to revive the project, which had been turned down by the studios in the late seventies, and he and producer Arnold Kopelson took it to Hemdale, a British production company.

Hemdale was already financing another Stone script, *Salvador*.[23] Stone knew journalist Richard Boyle, who had an idea for a film based on his own adventures and got Stone to write it with him. Given Stone's reputation for "cause" scripts and its Latin American subject matter, the studios were not interested. Stone says:

> Certain people hated the script. Mostly, studios would "pass," meaning they don't ever tell you why. But [the script's supposed] anti-Americanism, I heard, was a factor. It took the English (Hemdale) to make it. They had a sense of irony about it. They saw these two scuzzbags (the Richard Boyle and Dr. Rock characters) as funny, almost in Monty Pythonesque terms. I sold it [to Hemdale] as "Laurel and Hardy go to Salvador."[24]

Orion, which bought into both *Salvador* and *Platoon*, wanted Stone to shoot *Platoon* first, but *Salvador* was ready to go earlier. The script Stone directed made a cut that ran two and a half hours. Stone said, "But I couldn't get that version played [distributed], so I cut ruthlessly. So this version is a bit choppy—it's been criticized for being choppy—and they're right."[25] The film is choppy, but that adds to the flavor and intensity of it, and the scenes in the script not in the film would, for the most part, have detracted from the film. There is for example a long talky discussion in which two public-relations types tell Major Max how they can sell him as president.[26] There is also a scene of Boyle going out on patrol with the troops that seems to fit better into *Platoon*.[27]

The script for *Platoon* is not as lively as *Salvador*, but it is more intense and involving. It is one of the few films about Vietnam to capture the horror of that *particular* war (as opposed to war in general). It is more focused and more accurate than the Vietnam films that came before it, particularly *Apocalypse Now* and *The Deer Hunter*. Primarily this is because Stone knows the subject from the inside and is more concerned with getting the sense of the experience across than with showing off his directorial skills.

Those skills are considerable as well, particularly his handling of the actors. Stone is a much better director for his own screenplays than the bigger name directors who had previously directed his scripts. A large part of the impact of both *Salvador* and *Platoon* is Stone's ability, as both writer and director, to make the characters so vivid we cannot but watch them. We can hope in the future that Stone remains a writer and director, instead of becoming a Director.

Alan Rudolph

Alan Rudolph became Robert Altman's assistant in 1972,[28] and cowrote *Buffalo Bill and the Indians* with Altman. In 1977 Altman produced Rudolph's first film as writer and director, *Welcome to LA*. It is Rudolph's equivalent to Altman's *Nashville*, made two years before it. The Rudolph film follows a group of people in Los Angeles as their lives keep connecting or not connecting. Rudolph's film likes and respects all its characters, as strange and bizarre as they sometimes are. Rudolph does not, like Altman, undercut and demean his characters. (Altman also produced Robert Benton's early charmer *The Late Show*; Altman is a better producer than director.)

Rudolph took on the job of directing someone else's script with *Roadie*, a shaggy-dog movie that nearly everybody connected with seems to want to disown. *Roadie* was made for MGM as was Rudolph's next film, *Endangered Species*, which he cowrote. Both films soured Rudolph on working within the studio system. His experience directing *Songwriter*, also not his own script, and the lack of release Tri-Star gave it turned Rudolph to more independent filmmaking.[29]

Fortunately by the early eighties there was a growing group of small producer/distributors who were willing to put up the money for the kind of specialized (non–mass audience) film Rudolph wanted to make. The rise in cable television, the increase in money from syndication of commercial television rights, and most importantly the rise of the videocassette market made it economically feasible for producer-distributors to make films for low budgets. If the budget was low enough, it could be protected by pre-production sales of ancillary rights. It was still necessary to have theatrical distribution, since payments for nontheatrical distribution were often based on theatrical distribution. All of which meant that it was possible to make offbeat material if it could be made for a price.

The company Rudolph turned to was at the time called Island Alive, which subsequently split up into two companies, Island and Alive. His first film for them was the 1984 film *Choose Me*, a return to the kind of story he had dealt with in *Welcome to LA*, but done in a more stylized manner. There was less plot than in the earlier film and fewer characters, but more time spent on the characters. Because of Rudolph's ability to write interesting characters, he was able to get well-known actresses like Leslie Ann Warren and Genevieve Bujold to work for less money. *Choose Me* cost less than one million dollars and brought in five times that at the box office.[30] In 1987 Rudolph was able to get Alive to produce *The Moderns*, a script about the Parisian art world of the twenties that he had been trying for twelve years, through rewrites and over a hundred rejections by the studios, to get made.[31]

Carolyn Pfieffer, the head of Alive Films, says of Rudolph, "I hope he has now earned the right not to have to change scripts to please eight young executives who have never been on a movie set. . . . Alan should be allowed the same kind of career as Woody Allen. If he makes pictures for a good price, he should get autonomy."[32]

John Sayles

John Sayles started writing short stories in a college writing class he took because it was easy: "They graded you on poundage, and I wrote long stories, so I got A's in that, which brought my average up to C for my other courses, which I mostly didn't go to."[33] He had his first short story accepted by the *Atlantic* in 1975, the year he published his first novel, *Pride of the Bimbos*. Upton Brady, his editor at the Atlantic Monthly Press, says, "He comes on like the village idiot, but behind that is one of the great storytellers—and a very, very sensible character."[34]

In 1978 Sayles had his literary agent show around a sample script he had written, and that got him jobs writing films for Roger Corman. The first was *Piranha*, which Sayles claims Spielberg told him was his "favorite ripoff of *Jaws*."[35] Sayles found it easy to work in character detail in exploitation films:

I'm much more interested in character than action so it's been nice sometimes for me to do these hired-gun jobs where they give me a plot or at least a situation because I don't have to think it up. I never would have woken up in the morning and said I had to write a movie about piranhas eating people, but once I was given one, if they agree on what they hand you to begin with, you can make the people whoever you want and they'll never give you a problem.[36]

Sayles is one of the best writers of dialogue among contemporary screenwriters, but he learned early that was not too important in screenwriting:

Most critics figure that the dialogue is the screenplay, but I write shooting scripts, I write images. I always try to do things with as little dialogue as possible. Especially on an action thing, like *Piranha* or *Battle Beyond the Stars*, I think about how I would tell the story if it was a silent movie, so that Japanese people could understand it without subtitles.[37]

Japanese audiences probably had no trouble following *Battle Beyond the Stars*, since Corman had asked Sayles to write *Seven Samurai in Outer Space*.[38]

From his fees on the Corman scripts plus the money he had from a published collection of his short stories, Sayles had forty thousand dollars, which was enough to make his own film to show he could go beyond writing horror films. He wanted to make something the studios would not make, and he knew he could not make it very slick. Instead of a story that would require a lot of camera movement, he could tell the stories of several different people so he could keep the camera stationary and cut between the characters. He knew he could not afford Screen Actors Guild actors, but he had friends who were good actors. They were all getting close to the age of thirty, so he wrote a script that told the story of a reunion of ex-sixties radicals who get together over a weekend at the home of one of the couples in the group.[39] Given the limitations of the production budget, Sayles had to rely on his ear for dialogue, which carried the picture. The film was *The Return of the Secaucus Seven*, and it grossed two million dollars.[40]

Secaucus Seven made that money in spite of its limited release in 1980. There was not yet then the established group of independent producer-distributors. *Secaucus Seven* was not solely responsible for the development of that independent distribution system, but it was a major contributor to it. And it was a writer's film.

Off of *Secaucus Seven* he signed three writing-directing deals with the studios, only one of which resulted in a film. *Baby, It's You* began as a deal at Fox, but distribution was picked up by Paramount. Paramount wanted changes in the film, particularly in the second half, but Sayles rightly says, "It gets interesting and complex in the second half, which is why Paramount doesn't like it."[41] The second half calls into question the Hollywood conventions the first half seems to accept. By the end of his experience on *Baby, It's You*, Sayles was fed up with the major distributors:

> One thing you're almost always dealing with is that most people can't read. They can't tell a good script from a bad script. Some of them have a decent story sense, and they can look for certain elements—and that's the art of writing a selling script, to make those elements come out, so they see right away what is commercial about it. . . .
>
> Development deals just take up too much energy, without a real promise of ever turning into something.[42]

The problem was that Sayles was writing shooting scripts and the people at the studios had been reading selling scripts for so long they did not know how to read a real screenplay. Sayles found he would "hand them in and they [would] say, well, we don't see anything here. Then I [would] have to go back and spell it out in the rewrite without being too condescending."[43]

Sayles continued to write for others, both exploitation scripts and bigger-budget films. He returned to using his fees from studio scripts to finance his own low-budget films. The writing of *Clan of the Cave Bear* helped cover the $340,000 budget of *The Brother from Another Planet*, an adult variation of *E.T.* without the elaborate special effects. Sayles claimed the exterior of the spaceship cost twelve dollars, and outer space was created with black construction paper and a pin.[44] The film grossed four million dollars.[45]

Sayles at the Academy

In December 1986, the Academy of Motion Picture Arts and Sciences held a long overdue tribute to the late Nunnally Johnson. Many of the old Hollywood crowd were there, including Johnson's friends and coworkers like Lauren Bacall, Jerome Hellman, and David Brown. The audience watched a selection of scenes from Johnson's films that showed why he was one of the great screenwriters of all time. The scenes were well crafted, rich in emotional detail, and immensely playable by the first-rate actors who appeared in them.

A month later, on January 12, 1987, John Sayles was in the same auditorium at the Academy to deliver the Marvin Borowsky Lecture on Screenwriting. He told stories, of course, and he answered questions from the audience, including the expected ones about whether he thought Lawrence Kasdan's *The Big Chill* was a big-budget studio rip-off of *The Return of the Secaucus Seven*. He was surprisingly gracious, saying he was struck by the differences between the films, noting that *Secaucus Seven* was lighter and more cheerful, while *The Big Chill* was about people giving up their ideals, "Plus they wear nicer clothes in *The Big Chill*." He added, "If it's a genre, it's a genre of two. Like I'm doing a western and I've got a horse and an Indian and this guy's got a horse and an Indian."

As the evening progressed, the questions from the audience were more and more about the details of his independent productions. While Sayles was dressed out of *Secaucus Seven*, most of the people in the audience were dressed out of *The Big Chill*. There were two questions that were unasked. The first is whether what remains of the major distributors can possibly adjust to Sayles, or whether he is better off on his own. The second is whether the people in the audience, the younger executives, sensed the decline of the Hollywood systems of making films and whether Sayles, who is first of all a writer, was showing the way of the future.

Notes

Chapter 1: Starting Up

1. Terry Ramsaye, *A Million and One Nights* (New York: Simon and Schuster, 1926), p. 83.

2. Gordon Hendricks, "A Collection of Edison Films," in Marshall Deutelbaum, ed., *Image on the Art and Evolution of Films* (New York: Dover, 1979), pp. 9–19.

3. Ramsaye, p. 288.

4. Ibid., p. 367.

5. Ibid., p. 368.

6. Ibid., p. 370.

7. Ibid., p. 371.

8. Edward Azlant, "The Theory, History, and Practice of Screenwriting, 1897–1920," unpublished doctoral dissertation, University of Wisconsin, 1980, p. 64.

9. Epes Winthrop Sargent, "The Literary Side of Pictures," *Motion Picture World*, July 11, 1914, p. 199.

10. Benjamin Hampton, *History of the American Film Industry* (New York: Dover, 1970), p. 30. This is a reprint of Hampton's 1931 book *A History of the Movies*. Hampton says McCardell went to work for Biograph in 1900, but Sargent says 1898.

11. Charles Musser's 1983 film on Porter, *Before the Nickelodeon*, includes *Jack and the Beanstalk*.

12. Ramsaye, p. 416.

13. Nicholas Vardac, *From the Stage to the Screen* (Cambridge: Harvard University Press, 1949), p. 63.

14. Ramsaye, p. 416.

Chapter 2: Early Writing

1. Gene Gauntier, "Blazing the Trail," unpublished manuscript in the film collection of the Museum of Modern Art (MOMA), p. 3. There was a version of this published in *Woman's Home Companion* in 1928–29, but I am referring here to the original MS. A number of film historians have tended to dismiss Gauntier's memoirs, when they pay attention to them at all. The stated reason for their disdain is that she is inaccurate about one or two general historical details not relating specifically to her experiences. I suspect the true reason film historians do not like her is that (1) she is a woman and (2) she is a screenwriter. Her memoirs are based in large part on her diaries, and my estimation is that in matters referring to her and her activities they are more accurate than most directors' memoirs. I realize that may not be saying much. . . .

2. Ibid., p. 12.

3. Ibid., p. 13.

4. Ibid., p. 21.
5. Ibid., p. 27.
6. Ibid., p. 54.
7. Ibid., p. 58.
8. Ibid., pp. 71–72.
9. Ibid., p. 79.
10. Ibid., p. 164.
11. Ibid., pp. 186–87.
12. Ibid., pp. 212–13.
13. The logbook of the Biograph Story Department is in the film collection at MOMA.
14. Louella Parsons, *The Gay Illiterate* (Garden City, N.Y.: Doubleday Doran, 1944), p. 21.
15. Ibid.
16. Budd Schulberg, *Moving Pictures* (Briarcliff Manor, N.Y.: Stein and Day, 1981), p. 15.
17. Ibid., pp. 16–17.
18. William de Mille, *Hollywood Saga* (New York: E. P. Dutton, 1939), pp. 14–16.
19. Ibid., p. 18.
20. Ibid., pp. 78–79.
21. Agnes de Mille, *Dance to the Piper* (Boston: Atlantic, Little, Brown, 1951), p. 12.
22. William de Mille, p. 126.
23. Pamphlet in the Screenwriting file at the Margaret Herrick Library of the Academy of Motion Picture Arts and Sciences, (Academy Library).
24. Epes Winthrop Sargent, *Technique of the Photoplay* (New York: Chalmers, 1920), p. 14.
25. Ibid., p. 302.
26. Schulberg, p. 17.
27. See note 23.

Chapter 3: Griffith and Woods

1. Richard Schickel, *D. W. Griffith: An American Life* (New York: Simon and Schuster, 1984), p. 74.
2. Mrs. D. W. Griffith, *When the Movies Were Young* (New York: Dover, 1969), p. 40. This is a republication of the book, which was originally published in 1925 by E. P. Dutton.
3. Ibid., p. 36.
4. Ibid., p. 40.
5. Ibid.
6. Ibid., p. 41; Schickel, p. 106–7. Ramsaye, p. 457.
7. Mrs. Griffith, p. 48.
8. Gauntier, p. 41.
9. Ibid.
10. Mrs. Griffith, p. 50.

11. Robert Henderson, *D. W. Griffith: The Years at Biograph* (New York: Farrar, Straus & Giroux, 1970), pp. 237–43.

12. Quoted ibid., p. 91.

13. Letter to the author, January 11, 1983.

14. Mrs. Griffith, pp. 62–63.

15. Some of Woods's reviews are reprinted in George Pratt, *Spellbound in Darkness* (Greenwich, Conn.: New York Graphic Society, 1973), pp. 56–57, 59–68, 83–88.

16. Schickel, p. 140.

17. Henderson, pp. 151–52.

18. Frank Woods, "Growth and Development," *Introduction to the Photoplay*, unpublished collection of the 1929 series of USC lectures, Academy Library, p. 24.

19. Ibid.

20. Russell Merritt, "Dixon, Griffith and the Southern Legend: A Cultural Analysis of *The Birth of a Nation*," reprinted in Richard Dyer MacCann and Jack Ellis, eds., *Cinema Expanded* (New York: Dutton, 1982), p. 178. Merritt does not give a source in the article for this information, and it does not appear in the article he wrote to me he thought it was in.

21. Woods lecture, p. 25.

22. Schickel, p. 236.

23. Lillian Gish, *The Movies, Mr. Griffith, and Me* (New York: Avon, 1969), p. 122.

24. Karl Brown, *Adventures with D. W. Griffith* (New York: Farrar, Straus & Giroux, 1973), p. 42.

25. Ibid., p. 86.

26. Anita Loos, *A Girl Like I* (New York: Viking, 1966), p. 93.

27. Gish, p. 167.

28. Woods lecture, p. 28.

29. Frank Woods, "Features and Short Subjects," pamphlet in the *Improvement of Screen Entertainment* series, August 1931, p. 8.

30. Loos, p. 103

31. Quoted in Kevin Brownlow, *The Parade's Gone By* (New York: Knopf, 1968), p. 63.

32. Schickel, p. 317.

33. Brown, p. 163.

34. Kalton Lahue, *Dreams for Sale: The Rise and Fall of the Triangle Film Corporation* (South Brunswick, N.J.: A. S. Barnes, 1971), p. 148.

35. Ibid., p. 20. Another scholar of the period, Anthony Slide, feels that the production values and the acting and directing of the films were better than the scripts (Slide, notes to the author on the early draft of this book).

36. Letter to the author, May 11, 1984.

Chapter 4: Silent Comedy

1. Ramsaye, p. 83.

2. This film is part of the *Before Hollywood* program of films, organized by the American Federation of Arts. Information on this film can be found in *Before*

Hollywood: Turn-of-the-century American Film (New York: Hudson Hills Press), 1987, p. 107.

3. Musser, *Before the Nickelodeon.*

4. Gene Fowler, *Father Goose* (New York: Avon, 1974), pp. 211, 53.

5. For a more extended version of this section on Sennett, see my article, "The Sennett Screenplays," *Sight and Sound*, winter 1985–86, pp. 58–60.

6. Clarence Badger, "Reminiscences of the Early Days of Movie Comedies," in Deutelbaum, p. 99.

7. Fowler, pp. 190–212.

8. Mack Sennett, as told to Cameron Shipp, *The King of Comedy* (Garden City, N.Y.: Doubleday, 1954), p. 126.

9. Lahue, *Dreams for Sale*, pp. 156–157.

10. The information on each film discussed comes from the file for that particular film in the Sennett Collection at the Academy Library.

11. Aljean Harmetz, "The Prince of Silent Comedy," *Los Angeles Herald Examiner*, March 13, 1984, p. C-7.

12. Fowler, p. 190.

13. Ibid., pp. 192 (Del Ruth), 202 (Griffith).

14. Frank Capra, *The Name above the Title* (New York: Macmillan, 1971), p. 51.

15. Brownlow, pp. 464–65.

16. Buster Keaton and Charles Samuels, *My Wonderful World of Slapstick* (New York: Da Capo, 1982), p. 129.

17. Ibid., p.208.

18. David Robinson, *Chaplin: His Life and Art* (New York: McGraw Hill, 1985), p. 98.

19. Ibid., p. 131.

20. Brownlow, p. 499.

21. Quoted in Anthony Slide, *Early American Cinema* (New York: A. S. Barnes, 1970), p. 73.

22. Robinson, p. 296.

23. Brownlow and Gill have made three films out of the Chaplin film material under the general title *The Unknown Chaplin*, broadcast by PBS in 1986.

24. Robinson, pp. 499–500.

Chapter 5: Titles

1. Kemp Niver, *The First Twenty Years* (Los Angeles: Artisan Press, 1968), pp. 34, 80, 91, 98, 101.

2. J. Stuart Blackton, "Hollywood with Its Hair Down," unpublished manuscript in the Academy Library, p. 100.

3. Ramsaye, p. 514.

4. Mrs. Griffith, pp. 248–49.

5. Brown, p. 85.

6. Loos, p. 98.

7. Richard Schickel, *His Picture in the Papers* (New York: Charterhouse, 1973), p. 39.

8. Frank Woods, "Functions of the Editorial Department," *Opportunities in the Motion Picture Industry*, volume 2 (Los Angeles: Photoplay Research Society, 1922), p. 23.

9. Katharine Hilliker, "Writing the Titles," in *Opportunities*, p. 51.

10. David Bordwell, Janet Staiger, and Kristin Thompson, *The Classical Hollywood Cinema* (New York: Columbia University Press, 1985), p. 184. There is an excellent section in this book on early titling, pp. 183–89.

11. "2nd Run Titles," "Title Sheet," A *Finished Product* file, Sennett Collection, Academy Library.

12. *Picture Play Magazine*, August 1922, p. 22, quoted in Brownlow, p. 299.

13. Elmer Rice, *Minority Report: An Autobiography* (New York: Simon and Schuster, 1963), pp. 174–75.

14. *Variety*, September 24, 1922. The picture was released under the title *Help Yourself.*

15. Brownlow, p. 310.

16. Clara Beranger, "The Story," lecture, in *Introduction to the Photoplay*, p. 75.

17. Brownlow, pp. 296–97.

18. Anita Loos and John Emerson, *How to Write Photoplays* (New York: James A. McCann Company, 1920), pp. 79–81.

Chapter 6: Ince and Sullivan

1. The most detailed analysis of Ince's system, as a system, can be found in Janet Staiger, "Dividing Labor for Production Control: Thomas Ince and the Rise of the Studio System," in *Cinema Expanded*, pp. 144–53.

2. The entire script is reprinted in Pratt, pp. 147–73. This scene is on p. 149.

3. C. Gardner Sullivan, *The Dividend*, screenplay at the Academy Library. This is scene 99.

4. "C. Gardner Sullivan," obituary, *Daily Variety*, September 7, 1965.

5. Both script and film are in the Motion Picture Division of the Library of Congress in Washington, D.C.

6. C. Gardner Sullivan, *Sex*, scenes 37, 38.

7. Ibid., scene 57.

8. The legendary Rubber Stamp of Thomas Ince is one of the mysteries of film historiography. It first appears in Lewis Jacobs's 1939 book *The Rise of the American Film* (reprinted by Teachers College Press, New York, 1968, p. 204) as just a "stamped order," but none of the sources Jacobs lists for Ince make any mention of it. By Arthur Knight's *The Liveliest Art* in 1957 (New York: Mentor, p. 38) it has become a rubber stamp, which it has remained in nearly all the current film-history books. I have had friends and associates around the world trying for five years to find earlier sources, but so far no one has.

9. Azlant, p. 169.

10. Ibid., p. 171.

11. See note 5 above. The rest of the films and scripts discussed in this chapter are also at the Library of Congress.

Chapter 7: Silent Studios

1. Hampton, p. 193.
2. Arthur Marx, *Goldwyn: A Biography of the Man Behind the Myth* (New York: W. W. Norton, 1976), p. 97–98.
3. Ibid., pp. 100–101.
4. Rice, p. 172.
5. Marx, pp. 102–6.
6. From Goldwyn's 1923 ghostwritten autobiography, *Behind the Screen*, quoted in Marx, p. 102.
7. Mary Roberts Rinehart, *My Story: A New Edition and Seventeen New Years* (New York: Rinehart & Co., 1948), p. 292. This was a new edition, the first having been published in 1931.
8. Rice, p. 173.
9. Ibid., p. 179.
10. Ibid.
11. Bosley Crowther, *The Lion's Share* (New York: Dutton, 1957), pp. 54–55.
12. Ibid., p. 88.
13. Ibid., pp. 93–96.
14. There is a vivid account of the making of the film in Brownlow, pp. 385–414.
15. De Mille, pp. 157–58.
16. Ibid., p. 159.
17. Ibid., p. 163.
18. Ibid., p. 165.
19. Ibid., p. 119.

Chapter 8: Sound

1. For details about the first Vitaphone programs, see Harry Geduld, *The Birth of the Talkies* (Bloomington: Indiana University Press, 1975), pp. 123–36, 147–50, 151.
2. This change in the Vitaphone shorts and the reasons for it have been discovered by Douglas Gomery during his study of the transition to sound: Gomery's discussion with author on first draft.
3. *The Jazz Singer* screenplay has been published by the University of Wisconsin Press as part of its Wisconsin/Warner Brothers Screenplay Series.
4. An interesting view of the *ease* with which the industry made the transition is found in David Bordwell, "The Introduction of Sound," in Bordwell, Staiger, and Thompson, pp. 298–308.
5. Alexander Walker, *The Shattered Silents* (New York: Morrow, 1979), p. 104.
6. "Writers in Hollywood Give Varied Views on 'Talkies'; Title Writing Very Important," *Variety*, May 9, 1928, p. 9.
7. Ibid.
8. The *Queen Kelly* script materials are in the Benjamin Glazer Collection in the Special Collections of the Graduate Research Library at UCLA.
9. Frances Marion, *Off with Their Heads!* (New York: MacMillan, 1972), p. 14.
10. Robinson, p. 166.

11. The May 29, 1929, script of *His Glorious Night* is in the Louis B. Mayer Library of the American Film Institute (AFI) in Hollywood.

12. Marion, p. 190.

13. Ibid., p. 185.

Chapter 9: Visitors from the East

1. The most thorough examinations of the migration of eastern writers to Hollywood can be found in Richard Fine. *Hollywood and the Profession of Authorship* (Ann Arbor, Mich.: UMI Research Press, 1985), and John Schultheiss's dissertation "A Study of the 'Eastern' Writer in Hollywood in the 1930's" (USC, 1973). A preliminary version of this was published as an article entitled "The 'Eastern' Writer in Hollywood" in *Cinema Journal* in 1971, reprinted in *Cinema Examined*. The additional references to Schultheiss's work are to the article as published in *Cinema Examined*.

2. Walker, p. 112.

3. Ben Hecht, *A Child of the Century* (New York: Signet, 1954), p. 435.

4. Creelman, Eileen, "Picture Plays and Players," *New York Sun*, November 9, 1934.

5. Schultheiss, pp. 65–66.

6. Ibid., p. 66.

7. Ibid., p. 57.

8. John Updike, *Bech: A Book* (New York: Knopf, 1970), p. 18.

9. Tom Dardis, *Some Time in the Sun* (New York: Scribner's, 1976), pp. 139–40.

10. Schultheiss, pp. 64–65.

11. Dardis, p. 181.

12. Ibid., p. 24.

13. Ibid., p. 22.

14. See both Dardis and Aaron Latham, *Crazy Sundays* (New York: Viking, 1971), for many examples.

15. Latham and Wheeler Winston Dixon, *The Cinematic Vision of F. Scott Fitzgerald* (Ann Arbor, Mich.: UMI Research Press, 1986).

16. The scripts by both writers are in the Twentieth Century-Fox story files.

17. Dardis, pp. 29–30.

18. Ibid., pp. 2–4, 26–27.

19. Edmund Wilson, "The Boys in the Back Room," reprinted in *Classics and Commercials* (New York: Noonday Press, 1967), p. 21.

20. Ibid., pp. 47–48.

21. Hortense Powdermaker, *Hollywood: The Dream Factory* (Boston: Little, Brown & Co., 1950), pp. 134, 135.

22. Hortense Powdermaker, *Stranger and Friend, The Way of the Anthropologist* (New York: Norton, 1966), p. 229.

23. Ibid., p. 211.

24. Ibid., p. 228.

Chapter 10: Metro-Goldwyn-Mayer

1. George Oppenheimer, *The View from the Sixties* (New York: David McKay Company, 1966), p. 162.
2. Samuel Marx, *Mayer and Thalberg: The Make-believe Saints* (New York: Random House, 1975), p. 79.
3. Donald Ogden Stewart, *By a Stroke of Luck: An Autobiography* (New York: Paddington Press, 1975), p. 197.
4. Marx, p. 79.
5. David Chierichetti, "Oral History of George Seaton," unpublished, AFI, 1974, pp. 37–38.
6. Aljean Harmetz, *The Making of the Wizard of Oz* (New York: Limelight Edition, 1984), p. 26.
7. Joe Adamson, *Groucho, Harpo, Chico, and Sometimes Zeppo* (New York: Simon and Schuster, 1973), pp. 437–39.
8. William Ludwig, quoted in Lee Server, *Screenwriter: Words Become Pictures* (Pittstown, N.J.: Main Street Press, 1987), pp. 118–19.
9. Stewart, pp. 197–98.
10. The most detailed study of Freed's career and the Freed unit at MGM is in Hugh Fordin, *The World of Entertainment* (New York: Equinox/Avon, 1975). The material here on Freed's earliest days at MGM are from pp. 1–28.
11. Fordin, pp. 91–93.
12. Ibid., p. 79.
13. Ibid., pp. 93–94.
14. Ibid., p. 94.
15. Ibid., p. 95.
16. Ibid.
17. Nat Perrin, quoted in Server, p. 141; Lenore Coffee, *Storyline: Recollections of a Hollywood Screenwriter* (London: Cassell, 1973), p. 97.
18. Coffee, p. 124.
19. Marion, p. 179.
20. Todd McCarthy and Joseph McBride, "Bombshell Days in the Golden Age," *Film Comment*, March–April 1980, p. 62.
21. Ibid., p. 62.
22. Crowther, *Lion's Share*, p. 212.
23. Stewart, p. 207.
24. Draft screenplay dated 3 December 1937, in the Mayer Library at the AFI.
25. Thalberg died in 1936 and the production was taken over by Hunt Stromberg. Franklin was replaced as director by W. S. ("One-take") Van Dyke.

Chapter 11: Twentieth Century-Fox

1. Tom Stempel, "Oral History of Nunnally Johnson," unpublished, UCLA, 1968–69, p. 31.
2. *Wabash Avenue* (1950) is an unofficial remake of *Coney Island* (1943), with Betty Grable starring in both as the female side of the love triangle. The legend that the

same scripts were used, with new names penciled in for the characters, appears to be untrue.

3. Stempel, "Johnson Oral History," p. 33.

4. Tom Stempel, "Oral History of Philip Dunne," unpublished, AFI, 1970–71, pp. 65–66.

5. In *Jesse James*, for example, the entire parade at the beginning of the script welcoming the railroad to Missouri was shot and cut from the film. In *The Grapes of Wrath*, the scene that shows why cousin Noah left the Joads' trek was cut, and Noah just disappears in the middle of the film.

6. Maynard Smith, "Lamar Trotti," *Films in Review*, August–September 1958, p. 380.

7. Dudley Nichols, letter in *Films in Review*, October 1958, p. 474.

8. Dan Ford, *Pappy: The Life of John Ford*, (Englewood Cliffs, N.J.: Prentice Hall, 1979), p. 137.

9. Stempel, "Dunne Oral History," p. 123.

10. Tom Stempel, "Oral History of Henry King," unpublished, AFI, 1970–71, p. 156.

11. Nichols, pp. 474–75.

12. Stempel, "Dunne Oral History," p. 67.

13. Ibid., p. 16.

14. Ibid.

15. Tom Stempel, *Screenwriter: The Life and Times of Nunnally Johnson* (San Diego, CA.: A. S. Barnes, 1980), p. 145.

16. Stempel, "Dunne Oral History," p. 42.

17. Ibid., p. 28.

18. Ibid., p. 42.

19. Ibid., p. 132.

20. Mel Gussow, *Don't Say Yes Until I Finish Talking* (Garden City, N.Y.: Doubleday, 1971), p. 87.

21. Latham, pp. 172–73.

22. Quoted by Dorris Bowden Johnson to the author.

23. Gussow, pp. 92–93.

24. See my *Screenwriter*, pp. 83–84, 196. I am *truly* surprised people who should know better are still repeating Zanuck's claim as if it were the truth.

25. George Seaton, "Nunnally Johnson," *WGAw News*, May 1977, p. 7.

26. Stempel, "King Oral History," p. 100.

Chapter 12: Warner Brothers

1. This quote appears in many places, but to name one: James Silke, *Here's Looking at You, Kid* (Boston: Little, Brown, 1967), p. 62.

2. Jack L. Warner, with Dean Jennings, *My First Hundred Years* (New York: Random House, 1965), p. 130.

3. Gussow, p. 40.

4. Gerald Perry, introduction to the published screenplay of *Little Caesar* (Madison: University of Wisconsin Press, 1981), pp. 14–16.

5. Henry Cohen, introduction to the published screenplay of *Public Enemy* (Madison: University of Wisconsin Press, 1981), p. 18.

6. John O'Conner, introduction to the published screenplay of *I Am a Fugitive from a Chain Gang* (Madison: University of Wisconsin Press, 1981), pp. 11–12.

7. Mervyn LeRoy as told to Dick Kleiner, *Mervyn LeRoy: Take One* (New York: Hawthorn, 1974), p. 110.

8. O'Conner, p. 22.

9. LeRoy, p. 110.

10. O'Conner, p. 36.

11. John Huston, *An Open Book* (New York: Ballantine Books, 1980), p. 82.

12. Ibid., p. 83.

13. Quoted in Silke, p. 63.

14. "Profile on Casey Robinson," *WGAw Newsletter*, November 1970, p. 8.

15. Casey Robinson, "Elizabethan Awakening in Store for Cinema Art," *Los Angeles Times Calendar*, April 7, 1968, p. 16.

16. Ibid. A more detailed version appears in Bernard F. Dick's introduction to the published screenplay *Dark Victory* (Madison: University of Wisconsin Press, 1981), pp. 9–16.

17. Robinson, pp. 16 and 20.

18. Hal Wallis and Charles Higham. *Starmaker: The Autobiography of Hal Wallis* (New York: MacMillan, 1980), p. 100.

19. Ibid.

20. Charles Francisco, *You Must Remember This . . . The Filming of Casablanca* (Englewood Cliffs, N.J.: Prentice-Hall, 1980), p. 32. There are many accounts of the writing and making of *Casablanca*. Francisco's is the most detailed and most accurate I have found. It is also the most objective and based on the greatest variety of sources.

21. Ibid., p. 38.

22. Robert Buckner, memo to Wallis, January 6, 1942, printed in Rudy Behlmer, *Inside Warner Brothers (1935–1951)* (New York: Viking, 1985), p. 198.

23. Quoted in Francisco, p. 42.

24. Francisco, p. 33.

25. Jerry Wald memo December 23, 1941, in Behlmer, p. 196.

26. Although how much Wald actually contributed to the scripts is open to question. See Howard Koch, *As Time Goes By* (New York: Harcourt Brace Jovanovich, 1979), p. 92.

27. Julius J. Epstein, quoted in Koch, p. 78.

28. Francisco, p. 106. I know Koch is quoting Epstein directly, but why do you think people thought the Epsteins were such great storytellers?

29. Francisco, p. 44.

30. Ibid., p. 140.

31. Ibid., p. 152.

32. Ibid., p. 163.

33. Ibid., p. 162.

34. Ibid., pp. 154, 165–66.

35. Ibid., p. 177.

36. Ibid., p. 178.

Chapter 13: Paramount

1. Philip French, *The Movie Monguls* (London: Weidenfeld and Nicholson, 1969), p. 149. For a longer and more detailed account of Schulberg's career, see his son Budd's *Moving Pictures*.

2. Both quoted in Richard Meryman, *Mank: The Wit, World, and Life of Herman J. Mankiewicz* (New York: Morrow, 1978), p. 95.

3. Ibid., 131.

4. Ibid., p. 130.

5. Adamson, pp. 59, 120–125.

6. Ibid., pp. 125–35.

7. Ibid., p. 166.

8. Meryman, p. 147.

9. James Moore, "Waldemar Young," *Dictionary of Literary Biography*, volume 26, *American Screenwriters* (Detroit: Gale, 1984), pp. 341–45.

10. Cecil B. De Mille, *Autobiography* (Englewood Cliffs, N.J.: Prentice-Hall, 1959), p. 113.

11. Phil Koury, *Yes, Mr. De Mille* (New York: Putnam's, 1959), p. 80.

12. De Mille, pp. 247–48.

13. Koury, p. 81.

14. Quoted in Charles Higham, *Cecil B. De Mille* (New York: Scribner's, 1973), p. 109.

15. Ibid., p. 110.

16. De Mille, p. 342.

17. Harry Brand, *Twentieth Century-Fox Studio Biography of LeBaron*, 1941.

18. Ibid.

19. James Ursini, *Preston Sturges: An American Dreamer* (New York: Curtis, 1973), p. 37.

20. Details of the dispute, including Sturges's comments on it, can be found in James Curtis, *Between Flops* (New York: Harcourt Brace Jovanovich, 1982), pp. 82–86.

21. Ibid., p. 108.

22. Ibid., p. 113.

23. Ibid., pp. 127–28.

24. H. Allen Smith, *Lost in the Horse Latitudes* (Garden City, N.Y.: Doubleday, 1944), p. 69.

25. Ibid., p. 70.

26. Maurice Zolotow, *Billy Wilder in Hollywood* (New York: Putnam, 1977), p. 127.

Chapter 14: Columbia

1. Quoted in Bob Thomas, *King Cohn* (New York: Bantam Books, 1967), p. 44. Thomas notes that these are probably not direct quotes from Cohn, but his philosophy as worked over by the press people at the studio.

2. Ibid., p. 74.

3. Ibid., pp. 75–76.

4. Ibid., p. xii. ·

5. Ibid., p. 127–28.

6. Interview with Sam Frank, who has studied the scripts and production materials of the film.

7. Capra, p. 256.

8. Ibid., p. 260.

9. Thomas, p. 134. The information here seems to have come from Buchman himself.

10. Ibid., pp. 204–5.

11. Sam Frank, "Robert Riskin," *Dictionary of Literary Biography*, volume 26, *American Screenwriters*, p. 250.

12. The story has been reprinted in *Stories into Film* (New York: Harper and Row, 1979), pp. 32–91.

13. Conversation with Philip Dunne, September 1987.

14. Frank Capra, " 'One Man, One Film'—the Capra Contention," *Los Angeles Times Calendar*, June 26, 1977, p. 12.

Chapter 15: Other Studios, Other Writing

1. I. G. Edmonds, *Big U: Universal in the Silent Days* (New York: A. S. Barnes, 1977), pp. 43–45.

2. Higham, *Cecil B. De Mille*, p. 38.

3. Curtis, pp. 76–77, 98–100.

4. James Moore, "John Balderston," *Dictionary of Literary Biography*, volume 26, *American Screenwriters*, p. 26.

5. Ibid., p. 27.

6. Ron Haver, "The Mighty Show Machine, Part One," *American Film*, November 1977, p. 57.

7. Betty Lasky, *RKO: The Biggest Little Major of Them All* (Englewood Cliffs, N.J.: Prentice Hall, 1984), p. 44.

8. Ibid., p. 55.

9. Dore Schary, *Heyday* (New York: Berkley, 1981), p. 158.

10. John Paxton, interviewed in J. D. Marshall, *Blueprint on Babylon* (Tempe, Arizona: Phoenix House, 1978), pp. 263–64.

11. Irving Bernstein, "The Position of the Story Analyst in the Motion Picture Industry," pamphlet done for the Story Analysts Guild, October 15, 1958, pp. 8–10.

12. William Dozier, "Story Information," pamphlets prepared for studio use, forewords to 1942 and 1943 editions.

13. The George Byron Sage Collection at the AFI's Louis B. Mayer Library in Hollywood. An analysis of some of the material in the Sage Collection can be found in Tom Stempel, "George Byron Who?" *Sight and Sound*, summer 1985, pp. 211–13.

14. Charles Palmer, *The Case History of a Movie* (New York: Random House, 1950), pp. 7–8.

15. Capra, p. 254.

16. Stempel, "Johnson Oral History," pp. 360–61.

17. Silke, p. 119.

18. Ibid., p. 120.

19. Schary, p. 124.

20. Chierichetti, "Seaton Oral History," p. 33.

21. Ibid., p. 32.

22. Ibid., p. 33.

23. Ibid., p. 35.

24. Quoted ibid., p. 35.

25. Marshall, p. 77.

26. Schary, p. 73.

27. Quoted in Christopher Finch, *The Art of Walt Disney: From Mickey Mouse to the Magic Kingdom* (New York: Harry Abrams, 1973), p. 35.

28. A page of the *Steamboat Willie* script can be seen in Finch, p. 51.

29. Richard Schickel, *The Disney Version* (New York: Avon, 1968), p. 121.

30. Ibid., p. 122–23.

31. Finch, p. 59.

32. Schickel, *Disney Version* p. 145. Transcripts of two story conferences on a scene in *Snow White and the Seven Dwarfs* can be found in Frank Thomas and Ollie Johnston, *Disney Animation: The Illusion of Life* (New York: Abbeville, 1981), pp. 384–85.

33. Finch, p. 182.

34. Joe Adamson, *Tex Avery: King of Cartoons* (Teaneck, N.J.: Popular Library, 1975), p. 125.

35. Ibid., p. 130.

36. Ibid., pp. 171–72.

37. Quoted ibid., p. 176.

Chapter 16: Independent Screenwriters

1. Hecht, A *Child of the Century*, p. 447.

2. Quoted in Josef Von Sternberg, *Fun in a Chinese Laundry* (New York: Mac-Millan, 1965), p. 215.

3. Doug Fetherling, *The Five Lives of Ben Hecht* (Toronto: Lester and Orpen, 1977), p. 99.

4. Quoted by Hecht in *Child of the Century*, p. 449.

5. Conversation with the author.

6. Hecht, pp. 455–57.

7. Ibid., p. 456.

8. Richard Harwell, introduction to *GWTW: The Screenplay* (New York: Collier Books, 1980), p. 30.

9. Ibid., p. 28.

10. Pauline Kael, *Kiss Kiss Bang Bang* (Boston: Atlantic, Little, Brown, 1968), p. 59.

11. Renee D. Pennington, "Jules Furthman," *Dictionary of Literary Biography*, volume 26, *American Screenwriters*, p. 121.

12. Richard Koszarski, "Jules Furthman," *Film Comment*, winter 1970–71, p. 29.

13. Paul Jensen, "The Career of Dudley Nichols," *Film Comment*, winter 1970–71, p. 56.

14. Stephen Lesser, "Dudley Nichols," *Dictionary of Literary Biography*, volume 26, *American Screenwriters*, p. 229.

15. The short story and the screenplay of *Stagecoach* are in the volume of the same name published as part of the Classic Film Scripts series by Simon and Schuster, 1971.

16. Robert Carringer, *The Making of Citizen Kane* (Berkeley: University of California Press, 1985), p. 17. Carringer lists all the claimants and their versions. Carringer's is the most detailed and scholarly examination yet written of the making of *Kane*. It is also the fairest, which alone makes it a considerable achievement in the field of writing about that particular film.

17. Ibid., pp. 29–31.

18. Ibid., pp. 33–34.

19. Ibid., p. 123.

20. These comments are based on a reading of the August 15, 1941, draft, with corrections up through October 2, which Carringer identifies as the first draft of the script on p. 161 of his book.

Chapter 17: Writer-Producers

1. Schary, p. 118.

2. Both Mayer and Mankiewicz quoted in Kenneth L. Geist, *Pictures Will Talk* (New York: Scribners, 1978), pp. 73–74.

3. Ibid., p. 23.

4. Ibid., pp. 79–80.

5. Quoted ibid., pp. 89–90, from "People Will Talk," *The Movies*, BBC-TV, March 13, 1967.

6. The letter is published in *The Letters of F. Scott Fitzgerald*, Andrew Turnbull, ed., (New York: Dell, 1966), pp. 585–87.

7. Quoted in Aaron Latham, *Crazy Sundays*, pp. 123–24.

8. Both quoted ibid., p. 121.

9. Quoted in Geist, p. 112.

10. Stempel, "Dunne Oral History," p. 133.

11. Ibid., p. 135.

12. Ibid., pp. 140–41.

13. Virginia Wright, column in Los Angeles *Daily News*, December 18, 1946.

14. Stempel, "Johnson Oral History," pp. 49–50.

15. Ibid., pp. 47–48.

16. The problems of dealing with Cohan are described in the memos from the production found in Behlmer, pp. 178–84.

17. Koch, *As Time Goes By*, pp. 92–93.

18. Behlmer, pp. 256–61.

19. Stempel, "Dunne Oral History," pp. 188–89.

20. Lincoln Barnett, "The Happiest Couple in Hollywood," *Life*, December 11, 1944, pp. 98–112.
21. Thomas, *King Cohn*, p. 254.
22. Ibid., pp. 201–2.

Chapter 18: Writer-Directors

1. Charles Hopkins, program notes on *Blood Money*, 1977 Los Angeles Film Exposition Catalog, p. 64.
2. Stempel, "Dunne Oral History," p. 49.
3. Ibid., pp. 49, 51.
4. Geoff Brown, "Better Than Metro Isn't Good Enough!" *Sight and Sound*, summer 1975, p. 155.
5. Capra, p. 244.
6. For a more detailed and more sympathetic look at Leisen's career, see David Chierichetti, *Hollywood Director* (New York: Curtis Books, 1973).
7. Zolotow, *Billy Wilder in Hollywood*, p. 67.
8. Curtis, pp. 125 and 127.
9. Huston, p. 88.
10. Ibid., pp. 89–90.
11. Comparison of the final script dated May 26, 1941, to the film.
12. Zolotow, p. 69.
13. Ibid., p. 104.
14. Ibid., p. 105.
15. Ibid., p. 106.
16. Ibid.
17. Ibid.
18. Chierichetti, "Seaton Oral History," p. 101.
19. Ibid., p. 102.
20. Ibid., p. 103.
21. Geist, pp. 114–22.
22. Stempel, "Dunne Oral History," p. 238.

Chapter 19: The Guild

1. Azlant, pp. 149–52.
2. Alfred Hustwick, "The Screen Writers' Guild and Its Club 'The Writers,'" *Opportunities in the Motion Picture Industry*, volume 2, (Photoplay Research Society, 1922), p. 67.
3. Quoted in Nancy Lynn Schwartz, *The Hollywood Writers' Wars*, (New York: Knopf, 1982), p. 13.
4. Lester Cole, *Hollywood Red* (Palo Alto, CA.: Ramparts Press, 1981), p. 120.
5. Ibid., pp. 121–24. Cole gives the most detailed account of the first meeting, and he quotes in detail from the four-page proposal, but he mentions that his copy is missing page three, which he recalls included the demands for control of material.
6. Ibid., p. 124.

7. Larry Ceplair and Steven Englund, *The Inquisition in Hollywood: Politics in the Film Community 1930–1960* (Garden City, N.Y.: Anchor Press/Doubleday, 1980), p. 24. Their account of the formation of the Screen Writers' Guild is the most objective and accurate in print, although Schwartz's (see above) is the more detailed and vivid.

8. Cole, p. 124; Ceplair and Englund, p. 18.

9. "Writers Guild Files Official Dissolve Ms," *Variety*, March 3, 1937.

10. Ceplair and Englund, pp. 27, 28.

11. Ibid., pp. 28–30.

12. Bob Thomas, *Thalberg: Life and Legend* (Garden City, N.Y.: Doubleday, 1969), p. 267.

13. Oppenheimer, p. 150.

14. A description of the meeting is found in Thomas, *Thalberg*, pp. 267–68, as well as in Marion, p. 240.

15. Ceplair and Englund, p. 37.

16. Ibid., p. 33.

17. Ibid., p. 40.

18. McCarthy and McBride, pp. 65–66.

19. Estelle Changas, "An Oral History of John Lee Mahin," unpublished, Oral History of the Motion Pictures Project, UCLA, 1968. The transcript of the interview is in the UCLA Special Collections section of the Graduate Research Library. The section on the Screen Playwrights is on page 20.

20. Ceplair and Englund, p. 38.

21. Ibid., pp. 44–45.

22. Stempel, "Dunne Oral History," pp. 99–100.

23. William Pomerance, quoted in Ceplair and Englund, p. 46.

24. "Writers Guild Sez 90% of Pic Scribs Are Members," *Daily Variety*, September 20, 1944.

25. Thomas Brady, "Hollywood Jottings," *New York Times*, February 16, 1948. Mahin in the McCarthy-McBride interview says he rejoined in 1945.

26. Stempel, "Dunne Oral History," pp. 97–98.

27. "How Hollywood Writers Arbitrate," weekly *Variety*, July 7, 1965; Fay Kanin, quoted in William Froug, *The Screenwriter Looks at the Screenwriter* (New York: Macmillan, 1972), pp. 335–36; Kirk Honeycutt, "Whose Film Is It Anyway?" *American Film*, May 1981, pp. 34–38, 70.

28. Philip K. Scheuer, "Guild Man Defends Ruling Against Fry," *Los Angeles Times*, November 2, 1959.

29. "Writers Set 1-Union Merger for August 25," *Daily Variety*, August 9, 1954.

30. "Writers 1980 Resids Should Top $22 Mil," *Daily Variety*, December 31, 1980. The other $17+ million was from residuals from television programs.

31. John Horn, "Gunfight at the Writers Guild Corral," *Los Angeles Times Calendar Magazine*, September 1, 1985, p. 14.

32. Michael Kurcfeld, "Such a Deal," *L.A. Weekly*, March 22–28, 1985, p. 9.

Chapter 20: The Party

1. Ceplair and Englund, p. 33.

2. Abraham Polonsky, quoted in David Talbot and Barbara Zheutlin, *Creative Differences: Profiles of Hollywood Dissidents* (Boston: South End Press, 1978), p. 66.

3. Cole, pp. 137–38.

4. Bruce Cook, *Dalton Trumbo* (New York: Scribners, 1977), p. 147.

5. McCarthy and McBride, p. 65.

6. Victor Navasky, *Naming Names* (New York: Penguin Books, 1981), p. 296.

7. Ceplair and Englund, p. 59.

8. Dorothy B. Jones, "Communism and the Movies: A Study of Film Content," printed in John Cogley, *Report on Blacklisting*, volume 1, *The Movies* (N.P.: Fund for the Republic, 1956), p. 222.

9. Ibid., pp. 224–25.

10. Ibid., p. 225.

11. Ceplair and Englund, pp. 314–15; Navasky, pp. 236–37.

12. Ceplair and Englund, pp. 181–82.

13. This description of the early investigations is from Ceplair and Englund, pp. 155–57.

14. Philip Dunne, *Take Two: a Life in Movies and Politics* (New York: McGraw-Hill, 1980), p. 131.

15. Ceplair and Englund, pp. 157–58.

16. Ibid., p. 161.

17. Both Schwartz and Ceplair and Englund make this point one of the themes of their respective books.

18. Schwartz, pp. 160–70; Navasky, pp. 239–40. Schwartz suggests the "anti-Semitism" element in the novel was what offended the Party.

19. Ceplair and Englund, pp. 209–11.

20. Ibid., pp. 211–12.

21. Howard Suber, "The Anti-Communist Blacklist in the Hollywood Motion Picture Industry," unpublished doctoral dissertation, UCLA, 1968, p. 20.

22. Ceplair and Englund, p. 259.

23. Ceplair and Englund, pp. 259–60; Suber, p. 23.

24. Ceplair and Englund, p. 261; pp. 439–40 for the list of those called.

25. Ibid., p. 263.

26. Schwartz, pp. 266–67.

27. Ceplair and Englund, pp. 277–79.

28. Dunne, p. 193.

29. Ibid., p. 200.

30. Ceplair and Englund, pp. 328–29; Suber, pp. 30–32.

31. The complete text of the statement appears in Ceplair and Englund, p. 445.

Chapter 21: Decline of the Studios

1. Lewis Milestone, quoted in Charles Higham and Joel Greenberg, *The Celluloid Muse* (London: Agnus and Robertson, 1969), pp. 166–67. On the other hand, Charles G. Clarke, the cinematographer on the film, claimed in my "Oral History" with him (AFI, 1970–71, pp. 52–53) that Milestone had told him he intended to stretch the filming out over two calendar years so that Milestone could get a tax break.

2. Navasky, pp. 41–42.

3. McCarthy and McBride, p. 66.

4. Donald Knox, *The Magic Factory* (New York: Praeger, 1973), p. 56.

5. Fordin, pp. 456, 459.

6. Ibid., pp. 489–93.

7. Details of the production from Fordin, pp. 496–503.

8. John Houseman, *Front and Center* (New York: Touchstone, 1979), p. 359.

9. Ibid., pp. 372–76.

10. Ibid., pp. 454–55.

11. Budd Schulberg, afterword to the published screenplay *On the Waterfront* (Carbondale, IL.: Southern Illinois University Press, 1980), pp. 146–47.

12. Stempel, "Johnson Oral History," p. 431.

13. Dunne, p. 284.

14. Ibid., p. 289.

15. Tino Balio, *United Artists* (Madison: University of Wisconsin Press, 1976), p. 235.

16. Huston, p. 213.

17. Ibid., p. 215.

18. Ibid., pp. 275–77.

19. Zolotow, p. 202.

20. Geist, p. 240.

21. B-picture credits from Larry Langman, *A Guide to American Screenwriters, volume 1, Screenwriters* (New York: Garland, 1984); television credits from Vincent Terrace, ed., *Encyclopedia of Television Series, Pilots, and Specials* (New York: New York Zoetrope, 1986).

22. The history of AIP can be found in Mark Thomas McGee, *Fast and Furious: The Story of American International Pictures* (Jefferson, North Carolina: McFarland, 1984). The social change that created the teenage market is examined in Michael Pye and Linda Myles, *The Movie Brats: How the Film Generation Took Over Hollywood* (New York: Holt Rinehart Winston, 1979).

23. Quoted in McGee, p. 18.

24. Ibid., p. 35.

25. David Colker, "Off-Broadway Play Stems from 1960's Cult-Horror Film," *Los Angeles Herald-Examiner,* April 19, 1983, p. B-2.

26. McGee, p. 95.

27. Ibid., p. 97.

Chapter 22: The Black Market

1. Ceplair and Englund, pp. 349, 367.

2. Navasky, pp. 314–17.

3. Ibid., p. 248.

4. Ibid., p. 255.

5. Ibid., p. 303.

6. Ibid., p. 268.

7. Ibid., p. 140.

8. Ibid., p. 141. Cohen also discussed potential witnesses with HUAC investigator William Wheeler.

9. A copy of "The Golden Warriors," with no date on it, is in the Theatre Arts Reading Room of the Graduate Research Library, UCLA.

10. Published by Southern Illinois University Press, Carbondale, 1980.

11. *Golden Warriors*, pp. 110–15.

12. Ibid., p. 106.

13. Koch, p. 169.

14. Ibid., pp. 179–80.

15. Suber, p. 113.

16. Pat McGilligan, *Backstory* (Berkeley: University of California Press, 1986), p. 348.

17. Stewart, p. 299.

18. Burt A. Folkart, " 'High Noon' Writer Carl Foreman, Ex-film Exile, Dies," *Los Angeles Times*, June 27, 1984, part 2, p. 3. The quote is from a 1968 interview with Foreman.

19. Foreman, Marvin Borowsky lecture at the Academy of Motion Picture Arts and Sciences, November 17, 1980.

20. When Kramer pushed Foreman out of the company, Cooper offered to help finance a company of Foreman's, at least until the other right-wing studio heads heard about it and put pressure on Cooper not to. Peter Brown, "Blacklist: The Black Tale of Turmoil in Filmland," *Los Angeles Times Sunday Calendar*, February 1, 1981, p. 5.

21. I was living in Indiana when *High Noon* was released and remember people talking about the film in those terms.

22. Navasky, pp. 156–60.

23. Ibid., p. 163–64.

24. Ceplair and Englund, p. 399.

25. Seaton, p. 7.

26. Chierichetti, "Seaton Oral History," p. 337–38.

27. A detailed description of Gang's techniques appear in Navasky, p. 98ff.

28. Ibid., p. 354; Cogley, pp. 104–5.

29. Private source.

30. Will Tusher, "Kanin Reveals 'Gray List' as WIF Honors Her, Burnett, Nolan," weekly *Variety*, June 9, 1980.

31. Ceplair and Englund, p. 369.

32. Ibid., p. 411.

33. "SWG OK's Removal of Commies' Credit," *Hollywood Reporter*, April 23, 1955.

34. Cogley, p. 155.

35. Cook, p. 191.

36. Ibid., p. 192.

37. Helen Manfull, ed., *Additional Dialogue* (New York: Bantam Books, 1972), pp. 64, 88.

38. Suber, p. 82.

39. Cook, p. 193.

40. Suber, pp. 94–95.
41. Cook, p. 296.
42. Suber, pp. 94–95.
43. Ibid., pp. 105.
44. Langman, pp. 248, 104.
45. Cook, p. 206.
46. Foreman, Borowsky lecture.
47. Ring Lardner, quoted in Froug, pp. 133–34.
48. Navasky, p. 174.
49. Ibid., pp. 344, 356.
50. Manfull, pp. 560, 428.
51. Ibid., p. 564.
52. Navasky, p. 185; Capra, pp. 403–4, 424; Axel Madsen, *William Wyler* (New York: Crowell, 1973), pp. 325–26.
53. Suber, p. 81.
54. Manfull, p. 283.
55. Cook, p. 260.
56. Navasky, p. 160.
57. Manfull, pp. 495–96.
58. Suber, pp. 128–30.
59. Manfull, pp. 495–517 for letters that show Trumbo's involvement in the activities surrounding *The Defiant Ones*.
60. Ibid., p. 498.
61. Quoted in Manfull, p. 497.
62. Ibid., p. 508.
63. Suber, p. 69.
64. Ibid., p. 115.
65. Cook, pp. 273–75.
66. Suber, pp. 137, 152, and 150.
67. Cook, p. 277.
68. Cole, pp. 390–92.

Chapter 23: Projects

1. Abel Green, "Darryl Zanuck Might Resume Despite Man Breaker Situation in Agent-bossed Hollywood," *Variety,* June 13, 1956.
2. Marshall, pp. 213–16.
3. Ibid., p. 224.
4. Carroll Baker, *Baby Doll* (New York: Dell, 1983). The section on *Harlow* is on pp. 257–79.
5. John Brady, *The Craft of the Screenwriter* (New York: Simon and Schuster, 1981). The material on Lehman's early life, pp. 177–78; material on *Sweet Smell of Success*, pp. 192–93.
6. Ibid., pp. 194–95; also see Zolotow, pp. 181–87.
7. Brady, pp. 198–99.
8. Ibid., p. 197.

9. Ibid., pp. 212–13.
10. "Can Great Books Make Good Movies? Seven Writers Just Say No!" *American Film*, July–August 1987, p. 38.
11. Brady, p. 209.
12. Ibid., p. 185.
13. Froug, p. 255.
14. Ibid., p. 265.
15. Ibid., p. 273.
16. Ibid., p. 256. Actually, Anhalt's credits only show one Elvis Presley film, but why spoil a good line? Besides, he may have written one that was not made.
17. Brady, p. 85.
18. William Goldman, *Adventures in the Screen Trade* (New York: Warner Books, 1983), p. 179.
19. Ibid., p. 123.
20. Sage Collection, AFI. These notes are dated January 23, 1967.
21. Ibid., notes dated October 23, 1967, on different draft.
22. Brady, p. 79.
23. Ibid.
24. Ibid., p. 36.
25. Ibid., p. 37.
26. Michael Sragow, "A Yates/Tesich Film," *Los Angeles Herald-Examiner*, July 15, 1979, p. E-10.
27. John Gregory Dunne, *The Studio* (New York: Farrar Straus Giroux, 1968), p. 100.
28. A former student of mine who prefers not to be named.
29. Brady, pp. 169–70.
30. Dale Pollock, "John Huston: Direct Hit on Award of a Lifetime," *Los Angeles Times*, March 3, 1983, p. vi-2.
31. Beverly Walker, "The Majors:Limbo Land," *Film Comment*, February 1987, p. 34.
32. David T. Friendly, "Development Game: All's Fair," *Los Angeles Times*, September 25, 1986, p. vi-1.
33. Walker, p. 35.
34. Conversation with author, July 1986.
35. Peter Bart, "Oh, for the Days When the 'Bests' Were *Great*," *Los Angeles Times Sunday Calendar Magazine*, January 25, 1987, pp. 26–27.

Chapter 24: European Influences

1. David Newman and Robert Benton, "Lightning in a Bottle," *Bonnie and Clyde* (New York: Lorrimer, 1972), pp. 13–14. The remaining description of the writing of the script of *Bonnie and Clyde* is from this source, unless otherwise noted.
2. Ibid., p. 23.
3. Cast list ibid., p. 34.
4. Joseph Gelmis, *The Film Director as Superstar* (Garden City, N.Y.: Doubleday, 1970), pp. 223–24; Brady, pp. 395–96. Penn claims he thought of the change, Towne

claims he did. Take your pick, although I tend to side with the writer's version in matters like this.

5. Newman and Benton, p. 19.
6. Gelmis, p. 284.
7. Ibid., p. 281.
8. Ibid., p. 284.
9. Dennis Schaefer and Larry Salvato, *Masters of Light* (Berkeley: University of California Press, 1984), p. 181.
10. Estelle Changas, " 'Easy' Author on Cutting Edge of Lib in Films," *Los Angeles Times Sunday Calendar Magazine*, May 2, 1971, pp. 1, 22.
11. Sage Collection, AFI, 1969 boxes.
12. "Big Rental Films of 1970," *Variety*, January 6, 1971, p. 11; "Big Rental Films of 1971," *Variety*, January 5, 1972, p. 9.
13. Andrew Sarris, *The American Cinema* (New York: Dutton, 1968), pp. 155–171.
14. Donald Spoto, *The Dark Side of Genius* (Boston: Little, Brown, 1982), pp. 345–46. Spoto went to great lengths to interview the writers who worked with Hitchcock for this book, and the book gives excellent detailed accounts of the writing of his films.
15. Interview with Schrader in *Cinefantastique Magazine*, quoted in Pat Broeske, "The Little Magazine That Could," *Los Angeles Times Sunday Calendar*, March 16, 1986, pp. 23, 42.
16. Deborah Caulfield, "E.T. Author Mathison on E.T.," *Los Angeles Times Calendar*, March 23, 1983, p. 4.
17. Dale Pollock, "*Poltergeist*: Whose Film Is It," *Los Angeles Times Calendar*, May 24, 1982, p. 1.

Chapter 25: Alumni

1. Jean-Paul Chaillet and Elizabeth Vincent, *Francis Ford Coppola* (New York: St. Martin's Press, 1984), pp. 1–2.
2. Ibid., pp. 3–5.
3. Gelmis, p. 180.
4. Ibid., p. 186.
5. For an example of industry reaction see Stempel, "George Byron Who?" p. 213.
6. Gelmis, p. 181.
7. Ibid., p. 181.
8. Chaillet and Vincent, p. 33.
9. Ibid., p. 43.
10. Comparison of November 13, 1972, draft of *The Conversation* to the film.
11. Chaillet and Vincent, p. 49.
12. Ibid.
13. According to Maureen Orth, quoted ibid., p. 49.
14. Richard Walter, letter to *Los Angeles Times*, July 25, 1987, p. vi-2.
15. Ibid.
16. Quotes from both Milius and Murch, Pye and Myles, p. 55.

17. Dale Pollock, *Skywalking: The Life and Films of George Lucas* (New York: Harmony Books, 1983), pp. 54–55.

18. Ibid., p. 53.

19. Duwayne Dunham, quoted ibid., p. 53.

20. Ibid., p. 104. Pollock writes that Lucas was "half-joking" when he claimed this.

21. Sage comments, February 16, 1972, Sage Collection, AFI.

22. Pye and Myles, p. 120.

23. Pollock, p. 105.

24. Ibid., p. 280.

25. "Big Rental Films of 1973," weekly *Variety*, January 9, 1974, p. 19.

26. Pollock, p. 136.

27. Descriptions of the early drafts of *Star Wars* from Pollock, pp. 144–46. It is curious that there is no mention of Kurosawa's film by Pollock or Lucas in this book, although it has been freely mentioned as a source elsewhere.

28. Ibid., p. 148.

29. Ibid., p. 147.

30. William Hall, "A Draught of Guinness at the Connaught," *Los Angeles Times Sunday Calendar Magazine*, March 20, 1983, p. 3.

31. Pollock, p. 164.

32. Ibid., p. 209.

33. Miki Herman, quoted ibid., p. 50.

34. The screenplay was by Huyck and Katz, but that scene was written by Spielberg: Roderick Mann, "Capshaw: Her Career Is Not Constricting," *Los Angeles Times Sunday Calendar Magazine*, June 10, 1984, p. 5.

35. Froug, p. 283.

36. I have not seen this line in print, but it was told to me by someone who had seen the script.

Chapter 26: Comic Independents

1. Eric Lax, *On Being Funny: Woody Allen and Comedy* (New York: Charterhouse Press, 1975), pp. 183–84.

2. Robert Mundy and Stephen Mamber, "Woody Allen Interview," *Cinema*, winter 1972–73, pp. 14–15.

3. Ralph Rosenblum and Robert Karen, *When the Shooting Stops* (New York: Viking, 1979), p. 245.

4. Ibid., pp. 246–47.

5. Mundy and Mamber, p. 18; Stephen Bach, *Final Cut* (New York: Morrow, 1985), pp. 109–10.

6. Rosenblum and Karen, pp. 258–59.

7. Mundy and Mamber, p. 14.

8. Ibid., pp. 19–20.

9. Rosenblum and Karen, p. 267.

10. Dan Yakir, "Allen's Alley," *Film Comment*, June 1986, p. 24.

11. The recutting of *Annie Hall* is discussed in detail in Rosenblum and Karen, pp.

273–90. The change in contract to include retakes is mentioned in Rosenblum and Karen, p. 262.

12. Ibid., p. 284.

13. Ibid., pp. 286–87.

14. Ibid., p. 205.

15. Kenneth Tynan, "Profiles: Frolics and Detours of a Short Hebrew Man," *New Yorker*, October 30, 1978, p. 120.

16. Patrick Goldstein, "Mel Brooks: Back on the Launch Pad," *Los Angeles Times Sunday Calendar Magazine*, March 8, 1987, p. 23.

17. Mel Brooks and Gene Wilder, *Young Frankenstein*, 3rd draft dated December 17, 1977, pp. 21–22.

18. Brady, p. 314.

19. "Dialogue on Film: Neil Simon," *American Film*, March 1978, p. 40.

20. Brady, pp. 350–51; "Dialogue," pp. 42–43.

21. "Dialogue," p. 36.

22. Ibid., p. 43.

23. Sean Mitchell, "John Hughes *Likes* Making Teen Movies," *Los Angeles Herald Examiner*, June 22, 1986, p. E-11; Michael London, "'Mr. Mom' Author Defies Tinsel Typewriter Image," *Los Angeles Times*, November 23, 1983, p. vi-1.

24. Donna McCrohan, *The Second City* (New York: Perigee, 1987), p. 72.

25. Myron Meisel, "Welcome to the Last Chance, Lampoon," *Film Comment*, November–December 1982, pp. 57–58.

Chapter 27: Stars

1. Captain Leslie T. Peacocke, "Ten Million Scenario Writers—Listen," *Los Angeles Times Illustrated Magazine*, June 9, 1918, p. 7.

2. For a discussion of "bankability," including quotes from bankers on the subject, see Paul Kerr, "Stars and Stardom," in David Pirie, *Anatomy of the Movies* (London: Windward, 1981), pp. 104–15.

3. Bill Edwards, "Producer Harold Hecht, Seventy-seven, Dies; Ushered in New Hollywood Era," *Variety*, May 29, 1985, pp. 4, 41.

4. "Twelve-Million-Dollar Movie Deal," *New York Times*, February 8, 1954.

5. Marshall, pp. 202–3.

6. Ibid., p. 233.

7. Stephen Farber and Marc Green, *Hollywood Dynasties* (New York: Delilah, 1984), p. 211.

8. Ibid., p. 208.

9. Ibid., pp. 204–5.

10. James Monaco, "Realist Irony: The Films of Michael Ritchie," *Sight and Sound*, summer 1975, p. 145.

11. Jack Hirshberg, *A Portrait of All the President's Men* (New York: Warner Books, 1976), p. 24.

12. Ibid., pp. 30–31.

13. Ibid., p. 31.

14. Goldman, *Adventures*, p. 232.

15. Ibid., p. 233.
16. Ibid., p. 235.
17. Ibid., pp. 238–40.
18. Ibid., p. 244.
19. A discussion of this last section of the film appeared in my letter to *Los Angeles Times Sunday Calendar,* June 6, 1966, p. 2.
20. Duane Byrge, "Redford: 'MBA Mentality' Pervades the Movie Industry," *Hollywood Reporter,* January 20, 1987, p. 8.
21. Goldman, *Adventures,* pp. 212–13.
22. Susan Dworkin, *Making Tootsie* (New York: Newmarket Press, 1983), pp. 7–10.
23. Ibid., p. 17.
24. Ibid., pp. 16–17.
25. Ibid., pp. 68–71.
26. Ibid., p. 94.
27. Tom Shales, "Woody: The First Fifty Years," *Esquire,* April 1987, p. 93.
28. Interview with the author, August 1984.
29. Tom Stempel, "Let's Hear It for Eastwood's 'Strong' Women," *Los Angeles Times Sunday Calendar Magazine,* March 11, 1984, p. 5.
30. Craig Modderno, "Burt Reynolds Is the Comeback Kid," *Los Angeles Times Sunday Calendar Magazine,* January 4, 1987, p. 6.
31. Ibid., p. 34.
32. Ibid., p. 6.
33. Farber and Green, p. 161.
34. Ibid.; Kirk Honeycutt, "The Five-Year Struggle to Make *Coming Home, New York Times,* February 19, 1978.
35. Honeycutt.
36. Arelo Sederberg, "Accident No 'Boom' for Industry," *Los Angeles Herald Examiner,* March 31, 1979, p. A-5.
37. Michael London, "Field's Newest Role Is Actress-Producer," *Los Angeles Times,* May 9,1984, p. vi-1.
38. Liz Smith Column, *Los Angeles Herald Examiner,* December 26, 1985.
39. Sean Mitchell, "No More Apologies for Sally Field," *Los Angeles Herald Examiner,* December 24, 1985, p. D-1.

Chapter 28: Hustlers

1. Bach, pp. 168–71.
2. McGilligan, p. 78.
3. Dan Yakir, "Bill Kerby Interviewed by Dan Yakir," *Film Comment,* January–February 1980, pp. 51–52.
4. Bach, pp. 99–101.
5. Rex McGee, "Michael Cimino's Way West," *American Film,* October 1980, pp. 37–38. Bach covers the history of the script as well, pp. 139–42. Bach's version is more detailed and seems to be more accurate about dates, but McGee's has some interesting comments from people about the script.
6. Memo from Steve Bussard, quoted in Bach, p. 122.

7. Ibid., p. 124.

8. Ibid., p.176.

9. Rex McGee, p. 40.

10. Michael Cimino, *Heaven's Gate*, January 26, 1979, draft, p. 57.

11. Bach, pp. 338–40.

12. Ibid., p. 416.

13. Ibid., p. 365.

14. Brady, pp. 265–66.

15. Stephen Farber, "Where Are the Hemingways, Fitzgeralds, Benchleys, and Parkers of Yesteryear," *New Times*, September 19, 1975, p. 58.

16. Paul Schrader, "*Yakuza-Eiga*: A Primer," *Film Comment*, January–February 1974, pp. 9–17.

17. Comments based on April 29, 1975, "Final Shooting" draft, UCLA Theatre Arts Reading Room.

18. Ibid., p. 105.

19. Peter Rainer, "Mishmash of a Movie on the Life of Mishima," *Los Angeles Herald Examiner*, October 4, 1985, Style Section, p. 9.

20. Mitch Tuchman, "Gigolos: Paul Schrader Interviewed by Mitch Tuchman," *Film Comment*, March–April 1980, p. 51.

21. David Thompson, "Cats: Paul Schrader Interviewed by David Thompson," *Film Comment*, March–April 1982, p. 52.

22. Jean Vallely, "Raging Beauty," *Playboy*, November 1981, p. 122.

23. Pat McGilligan, "Point Man: Oliver Stone Interviewed by Pat McGilligan," *Film Comment*, January–February 1987, p. 18–19. Arnold Kopelson, one of the producers of *Platoon*, tells a slightly different version (in Jack Mathews, "*Platoon*-Hollywood Steps on a Gold Mine," *Los Angeles Times Sunday Calendar Magazine*, January 25, 1987, (p. 7) in which he seems to suggest that Kopelson brought Stone and Hemdale together *after* Stone had started *Salvador*. Stone's version seems more precise and therefore more accurate. Besides, if it's a choice between a producer's version and a writer's. . . .

24. McGilligan, "Point Man," p. 19.

25. Ibid.

26. Oliver Stone and Richard Boyle, *Salvador*, April 1985 draft, pp. 58–61, Academy Library.

27. Ibid., pp. 48A–D.

28. David Rensin, "The Man Who Would Be Different," *American Film*, March 1986, p. 54.

29. Ibid., p. 53.

30. Richard Natale, "Hollywood Claims its Independents," *Los Angeles Herald Examiner*, November 12, 1986, p. B-1.

31. Jack Mathews, "'Moderns' Finds its Time, Place," *Los Angeles Times Sunday Calendar Magazine*, May 31, 1987, p. 22.

32. Rensin, p. 54.

33. David Chute, "John Sayles: Designated Writer," *Film Comment*, May–June 1981, p. 57.

34. David Osborne, "John Sayles: From Hoboken to Hollywood—and Back," *American Film*, October 1982, p. 32.

35. John Sayles, Marvin Borowsky Lecture at the Academy of Motion Picture Arts and Sciences, January 12, 1987.

36. Tom Schlesinger, "Putting People Together," *Film Quarterly*, summer 1981, p. 5.

37. Chute, p. 59.

38. "Mill Valley Grist," weekly *Variety*, October 10, 1984, p. 22.

39. Chute, pp. 54–55; Sayles, Borowsky Lecture; Schlesinger, p. 6.

40. Osborne, p. 32.

41. Ibid., p. 36.

42. Ibid.

43. Schlesinger, p. 4.

44. Dale Pollock, " 'Brother' Director Is an Alien to Hollywood," *Los Angeles Times*, October 20, 1984, p. IV-1.

45. Clarke Taylor, "Union Label," *Los Angeles Times Sunday Calendar Magazine*, August 16, 1986, p. 34.

Index